Black Man in a White Coat

Black Man in

A DOCTOR'S REFLECTIONS

ON RACE AND MEDICINE

a White Coat

Damon Tweedy, M.D.

PICADOR

New York

The names and identifying features of patients and their family members have been changed to preserve their confidentiality. I have also changed the names and identifying details of medical students, nurses, and doctors to protect their privacy, with the exception of those doctors whom I identify by their full name. Some dialogue has been reconstructed to the best of my recollection.

Contents

Introduction

On a spring morning in 1997, Jim Harper, a young man from Durham, North Carolina, woke up in his two-bedroom apartment with no clue that he would soon become gravely ill.

The first signs of trouble seemed innocent enough: some numbness on the right side of his face and in his right arm and hand, easily chalked up to having slept on that side of his body. He stumbled as he got out of bed, but figured he was simply tired from the previous day's shift managing angry teens at a group home. His fiancée, Regina, asked if he needed to see a doctor; he smiled and told her that she worried too much. Her anxiety ebbed as she went off to her job at Kmart, only to resurface when he didn't answer the phone during her lunch break.

When Regina rushed home a few hours later at the end of her shift, she found Jim sprawled across their bathroom tile. His eyes were wide open and he clearly recognized her, but his words were garbled. He couldn't tell her what was wrong or how long he'd been that way. She frantically dialed 911. Within a half-hour of his arrival at the emergency department, after a neurological exam and rapid CT scan of his brain, it was clear what had transpired: Jim, just a few weeks shy of forty, had suffered a massive stroke.

The doctors learned that Jim had high blood pressure that had been poorly treated, but found nothing else to account for his tragic fate. He had no heart problems. No clotting disorders. No aneurysms. No diabetes or high cholesterol. He didn't smoke, rarely drank, and avoided street drugs. Ultimately, as best they could tell, Jim mostly had a lot of bad luck.

About two weeks later, I stood at the foot of Jim's bed at Duke Hospital. Along with another first-year medical student, I was shadowing Dr. Wilson, a faculty neurologist, as part of a weekly seminar that introduced us to clinical medicine. This class was the highlight of our week, as it gave us a brief break from the lecture hall and laboratory, where we memorized biochemical pathways and microorganism names, and provided a peek at our future lives on the hospital wards. We wore perfectly knotted ties and crisp white coats for the occasion, trying hard to look like the doctors we would one day become.

Jim's future seemed far less promising than ours did. A big man, he had once been a football player. Now he could not move the right side of his body. His face drooped as saliva dribbled out of the corner of his mouth. His words came out choppy, like those of a toddler; when frustrated, he cried like a child in the midst of his "terrible twos." Given his lack of improvement, the doctors had begun to doubt that he could make any significant recovery. They were preparing to send him to a rehabilitation facility. This place also had a long-term care unit, where, if he made no real progress, Jim might spend the rest of his life. According to the nurses, Regina's visits were already becoming shorter and less frequent.

"It's a very sad case," Dr. Wilson said, as we left the room and walked to a nearby conference area to discuss our patient and his illness.

He started by telling us that stroke was consistently one of the top five causes of disability and death in America. Then he drilled us about the major risk factors, going back and forth between us in a competition of sorts. In eager medical student fashion, we rattled off the usual suspects: diabetes, hypertension, heart disease, advanced age, smoking, and high cholesterol. When it was my turn again, Dr. Wilson indicated that there was one important risk factor we had yet to mention. He looked at me with a worried frown. Come on, his look said, for you of all people, this should be easy. I sighed. I'd hoped it wouldn't come to this, but, as I was quickly learning, it always did.

"Race," I said, looking down at my dark hand against my pristine white coat. "Our patient is black."

"Exactly," Dr. Wilson responded, as if I'd now earned a top score on my exam. "Some would say that this is the most important variable of all."

He rattled off damning statistics about race and stroke: "The risk is twice as high for blacks compared to whites for those over sixty-five. And in younger groups, such as with our patient here, the ratio is more like three-to-one or even four-to-one."

I'd seen the impact of stroke on both sides of my family. When I was fourteen, my dad's brother—who would often drive five hours each way on a Saturday to visit us for a few hours—died within days of collapsing at his home, putting an abrupt end to his unexpected and always enthusiastic visits that I so enjoyed. A few years later, my maternal grandmother—Grandma Flossie—developed dementia from a series of minor strokes that slowly stole her mind and, eventually, her body. Like Jim, both had high blood pressure.

"Our patient's other major risk factor is hypertension," Dr. Wilson continued. "This also is much more prevalent in blacks—nearly twice as common. No matter how you slice it, race is a very big deal when it comes to stroke."

Dr. Wilson had hammered home something I would learn time and again, both at Duke and beyond: Being black can be bad for your health.

"Of all the forms of inequality," Martin Luther King Jr. told a gathering of the Medical Committee for Human Rights in 1966, "injustice in health is the most shocking and the most inhumane."

At the time of his remarks, the United States had begun to take several formal steps to end its century-long practice of state-sponsored segregation that had followed the end of slavery. In medicine, this meant that black people could begin to receive treatment side by side with whites rather than being relegated to separate and unequal facilities or sectioned off in run-down areas of white hospitals. Such practices had undoubtedly contributed to their poorer health, especially in the Deep South of Dr. King's time, where black people on average had a life expectancy nearly nine years less than whites. While the civil rights movement ultimately stirred remarkable racial progress in various areas of American life, many of King's concerns about health and health care remain valid to this day.

From cradle to grave, these health differences, often called health disparities, are found virtually anywhere one might choose to look. Whether it is premature birth, infant mortality, homicide, childhood obesity, or HIV infection, black children and young adults disproportionately bear the brunt of these medical and social ills. By middle age, heart disease, diabetes, stroke, kidney failure, and cancer have a suffocating grip on the health of black people and maintain this stranglehold on them well into their senior years.

Thus, it is no surprise that the life expectancy among black people, despite real progress over the last twenty-five years, still significantly lags behind whites. In suffering a crippling stroke at age thirty-nine, Jim had become another casualty of inequality, a fresh case that Dr. Wilson could use to illustrate the health burden of being black.

Three decades after Dr. King's 1966 remarks, I entered Duke University School of Medicine as one of a half-dozen black students on scholarship. With the scholarships, Duke sought to cast aside its history of racial exclusion and become a national leader in producing a new generation of black physicians who could change the face of medicine. My goal as I headed for Durham was much less ambitious and civic-minded. I simply wanted to make my parents proud of me and set myself up to earn a good living. Race-based concerns ranked low on my list of priorities.

But my professors couldn't stop talking about race. During my early months, as they taught us about diseases both common and rare, they inevitably cited the demographics, explaining which disorders were more common in the young or old, women or men, and one racial group or another. When they spoke about race, they would sometimes mention Asians, Hispanics, and Native Americans. Yet invariably, as it always seems to in America, their analysis came down to comparing blacks and whites.

It seemed that no matter the body part or organ system affected, the lecturers would sound a familiar refrain: "It's more common in blacks than in whites."

Each time the demographics of a new disease came up in a lecture, my stomach twisted. I knew where this was heading. Seated in a sea of mostly white and Asian faces, I wondered how this information affected their views of black people, whether they already had biases against us, and whether any of this impacted the way they saw me. This racial health data intensified my already uneasy feelings about my place at Duke. My classmates largely hailed from well-to-do suburbs and had attended prestigious, brand-name schools; I came from a working-class neighborhood and had attended a state university with little name recognition. Their parents all seemed to be doctors, lawyers, or professors. My dad didn't finish high school and worked as a meatcutter in a grocery store; my mom attended segregated inner-city public schools before embarking on a forty-year career in the federal government. From the moment I walked along Duke's manicured lawns and inside its Gothic buildings, I worried that I was at a stark disadvantage, both socially and academically.

Constantly hearing about the medical frailties of black people picked at the scab of my insecurity. Over time, I came to dread this racial aspect of the lectures so much that I felt intense, perverse relief whenever a professor mentioned that a disease was more common among white people. But this list was short and the refrain that accompanied it proved equally painful. For example, while breast cancer got diagnosed more often in white women, "black women who get this disease do much worse," the professors would say.

While I was learning about the health woes of my race, my own body began to betray me. The first sign occurred not long after I'd met Jim, the young stroke victim. As part of that same introductory course, my classmates and I learned basic medical skills by practicing on each other. One day, we measured blood pressures. My classmate frowned as she took mine. The reading was 150/95. Our supervisor, a family physician, rechecked and confirmed the reading. The doctor I saw soon afterward gave even worse news: My kidneys were showing early signs of failure.

To a twenty-three-year-old first-year medical student, high blood pressure and kidney disease sounded like a death sentence. Worst-case scenarios flashed through my mind: Dialysis. Kidney transplant. Transplant rejection. More dialysis. Infection. Death. Was I destined for a similar fate as my uncle and grandmother? Or something worse? Would I even reach fifty?

The image of Jim flashed through my mind. A few weeks after leaving the hospital and moving into the rehab facility, he died from a massive blood clot that lodged in his lungs. He had just turned forty. I drove home from the clinic picturing Jim in an open casket. But instead of a stirring eulogy and traditional funeral hymnals, I heard Dr. Wilson's voice reciting statistics on race and stroke.

As I struggled to make sense of the prospect of facing chronic illness in my twenties, I became consumed by the broader health problems of my race. Along with the many patients I saw who gave life to my professors' statistics came reports of prominent black men who had met similar fates. Harvard Law graduate and billionaire CEO Reginald Lewis died at age fifty from cancer, while football legends Walter Payton and Reggie White died in their mid-forties from rare disorders, just a few years before *60 Minutes* mainstay Ed Bradley succumbed in his mid-sixties to cancer. Journalist Ron Howell chronicled the premature deaths of his black classmates from Yale in a 2011 article for the university's alumni magazine that generated national interest. A large bank account, Ivy League schooling, Hall of Fame busts, and a quarter-century run on America's most-watched program stood no match against early death for these black men.

Why do black people suffer more health problems than other groups? What do these challenges mean in their everyday lives? How do their struggles play out before a largely white medical community? How can we begin to solve these seemingly intractable problems? Do I have a special role to play as a black physician? Confronting these questions has led me on an intellectual and emotional journey, one that I've tried to capture in the pages that follow.

I've divided the book into three sections, corresponding to the different phases of my medical life. Part I surveys my medical school years. Part II explores my grueling twelve months of medical internship as a newly minted doctor. Part III examines my subsequent years in psychiatry training and in early clinical practice. Throughout each stage, race played a recurrent role, at turns predictable and unexpected, often annoying, sometimes disheartening, and occasionally uplifting. By sharing my story, as well as the stories of some of the patients I've met over the past fifteen years, I hope to humanize the dire statistics and bitter racial debates and paint a fuller picture of the experiences of black patients, as well as that of the black doctors who navigate between the black community and the predominately white medical world.

In tracing my journey along the intersection of race and medicine at the end of the twentieth century and the dawn of the twenty-first, I make no claim to speak for all black physicians or black patients, yet I am confident that much of what I have written will ring true to their varied experiences. By putting human faces on these serious dilemmas, I hope to contribute to a much-needed public dialogue on improving the health of black people. Jim's fate—a young black person robbed of his future—is one that far too many of us suffer.

PART I

Disparities

People Like Us

It was a hot late-summer morning, a month into my first year as a Duke medical student. The classroom of nearly one hundred students buzzed with energy. After a few weeks of mostly tedious lectures that seemed no different from the science classes we'd taken in college, our professor had just finished the first half of his presentation on the case of a young boy with a rare childhood disease. A short film had brought the complex scientific data in our textbook to life in the words and actions of the boy and his parents. Following the video, the professor talked about promising therapies for this disorder. Finally, we were getting glimpses of the clinical knowledge that we'd come to medical school to learn. I could hardly wait for the second part.

But that wasn't the only reason that I suddenly felt better. My first few weeks at Duke had been an exercise in expanding insecurity as I learned more about my classmates. As one of a handful of black students, I naturally stood out, but race was just part of the story. In those early days, it seemed that all of my classmates came from professional, well-to-do families. My mom never entered a college lecture hall; my dad did not finish high school. While my brother, Bryan, had been the trailblazer of our immediate family in graduating from college, medical school was a different league. The majority of my classmates graduated from high-prestige colleges like Duke, Harvard, Yale, or Stanford. I'd gone to the University of Maryland–Baltimore County (UMBC), a young school with a limited national profile. Could I hack it at Duke? Determined to use this fear as a buoy rather than a deadweight that could sink me, I probably spent as many hours studying in that first month at Duke as I had my entire senior year of college.

The effort paid off. Our midterm scores had just come back, and, to my immense relief, I had done well, firmly within the top half of the class on each exam. As I stood to stretch during the break before the professor resumed his lecture, I was finally starting to feel comfortable, or at least what qualified as such for a first-year medical student.

The mid-class break offered time to use the bathroom, grab coffee, or simply remain in place and gossip. I preferred to move about, as the lecture hall, with its folding seats, dim lighting, and sticky floor, had the uncomfortable ambience of an old movie theater. On my way out, I chatted with a few people and overheard one group discuss plans to camp out for Duke men's basketball tickets.

When I reentered the lecture hall a few minutes later, Dr. Gale, our professor, headed in my direction. Ordinarily, he didn't socialize with students, so I expected him to walk past without acknowledgment. Instead, he stopped directly in front of me.

"Are you here to fix the lights?" he asked.

The sounds of the classroom seemed to vanish. So did my peripheral vision. Calm down, I told myself, maybe he was talking to someone else and only seemed to be looking at me. I glanced behind me. Nobody there. A few classmates were within hearing distance, but they seemed too engaged in conversation to notice us. Maybe with all the background noise, I had misheard him.

"Did . . . did you ask me about fixing the lights?" I said.

"Yes," he replied, irritation creeping into his voice. "You can see how dim it is over on that side of the room," he said, gesturing with his index finger. "I called about this last week."

Reflexively, I stroked my chin and looked down at my clothing to check if I seemed out of place. Clean-shaven, and dressed in a polo shirt and khaki slacks, I thought that I'd done a decent job of looking the part of the preppy first-year medical student. Obviously I had failed.

"No," I said, stumbling to come up with a reply. "I don't have anything to do with that."

He frowned. "Then what are you doing here in my class?"

My mouth went dry. Why had he intentionally singled me out in this way? Race was the first thought that entered my mind. I tried to summon an attitude of 1960s-era Black Power defiance, but what came out sounded like 1990s diffidence. "I'm a student . . . in your class."

"Oh . . ." he said.

Dr. Gale looked away, then walked off without another word. I staggered to my seat, sitting through the second part of his lecture like a robot, tuning out his voice. What had started out as a promising day was spoiled.

During lunch a few hours later, I replayed the encounter to three black classmates as we sat out of range of others in the cafeteria. I'm not sure what I was looking for, other than the chance to vent to people who might understand what I was feeling. Their response surprised me: Two of them burst out laughing.

"That's messed up," Rob said, almost choking on his hamburger.

"At least he thought you were a skilled worker," Stan said, as the two laughed harder. "He could have asked you to pick up his trash or shine his shoes in front of the entire class."

"That's not funny," Marsha said, glaring at them.

"What else are you going to do but laugh about it?" Stan shot back.

"He's right," Rob chimed in. "You know you want to laugh too."

Marsha started to say something about reporting the incident or confronting the professor, but her militancy evaporated as Stan and

Rob started quoting the comedian Chris Rock. I don't recall the specific joke, but it made me smile and calmed me down enough that I could eat my lunch. Racial insults—big and small—were a part of our lives and sometimes humor was the best way to deal with it.

Yet the good feelings didn't last. The afternoon lectures gave way to a different course, and with it, another professor. I could not concentrate at all. "Are you here to fix the lights?" played over in my mind. In high school and college, I had been mistaken many times for a potential criminal, hired help when I was a paying customer, and most favorably, as a six-foot-six budding professional basketball player. But it's one thing to be insulted by a stranger you'll never see again, and something altogether worse for your professor—who assigns grades that dictate your future—to cast you in such a limiting way.

Trying to apply reason to the situation, I told myself that at Duke, Dr. Gale saw many more black maintenance workers than black men in his class. And I also firmly believed that there's no shame in blue-collar work. My dad spent thirty-five years as a meatcutter at a grocery store while my maternal grandmother—Grandma Flossie—worked her whole life as a housekeeper, or in the parlance of her times, a cleaning lady. What bothered me was Dr. Gale's assumption that I had no business in his class unless I arrived in some service capacity. Sensitive as I already was about my place at Duke, this incident stabbed at the core of my insecurity. With one question, Dr. Gale had shattered my brittle confidence and my tenuous feeling of belonging at Duke.

In a color-blind world, Duke might well have rejected me; at the very least, its admissions committee would not have offered me a full-tuition scholarship to its medical school.

This troubling revelation occurred to me less than an hour into my first day on campus. The Duke Med Class of 2000 had gathered for the first time, crowded into an old lecture hall that was in its last year of use. It was a typically humid August day in North Carolina, with the temperature already approaching eighty-five degrees by mid-morning. Inside, an antiquated but powerful air conditioner chilled the room to the mid-sixties. Our eyes focused on the speaker who stood at a small lectern. An anesthesiologist by trade, she had short graying hair and spoke in a monotone that could put you to sleep without medicine. Nonetheless, the room crackled with tension. Our medical lives were about to begin.

"Congratulations," she led off. "I'm proud to say this is the most accomplished class we've ever had during my time at Duke."

Nervous laughter filled the room. On a scale of cutthroat competitiveness, future doctors are worse than Olympic hopefuls. Pre-meds arrive with better grades than those who attend law, business, or other graduate programs, and this is no coincidence. Although most schools deny it, getting into medical school is, to a large extent, about numbers. In keeping with our numerical obsessions, we craved our first glimpse of how we measured up against each other.

She began with our college grade point averages. "The mean was 3.7 on the standard 4.0 scale," she said, leafing through papers that defined our lives as data.

My GPA was higher, but I discounted this edge since I had attended a less prestigious college than almost everyone around me. That realization had sunk in months earlier, during my admission interview at Yale. "I'm not sure the grades from your undergraduate college reflect what you'll face here and beyond," an elderly surgeon told me, his faced lined with worry as he viewed my transcript. And with that swipe of his verbal scalpel, he cut my straight-A record down to what seemed a B-minus average.

Next up were our scores on the MCAT, the medical school equivalent of the SAT. "The average combined score was 34," our Duke professor announced.

I'd scored a few points below this class average. Based on percentile rankings that she went on to explain, my result was still as good as, or better than, those of a third of my classmates, but that did nothing to prevent my empty stomach from twisting into a painful knot. While admissions committees do consider other factors, I'm fairly certain that my community service record, leadership skills, and interview performance all rated average at best. These were not the talents that made Duke offer me a scholarship.

Things got worse as she boasted about the number of students from various prestigious colleges. "Twenty-five percent of the incoming class has an undergraduate degree from Duke," she said.

Another quarter came from the Ivy League, most either Harvard or Yale. Of the remainder, the vast majority hailed from other elite private colleges, such as Stanford and Johns Hopkins, or highly regarded state schools such as the University of Virginia or the nearby UNC–Chapel Hill. While I had considered many of those schools four years earlier and been accepted to several, I attended the lesser-known University of Maryland–Baltimore County. At the time, it felt like the perfect choice, as it offered a full scholarship, the opportunity for playing-time on a Division I basketball team, and was only a forty-five-minute drive to my parents' home. But now at Duke Med, I felt like a scrawny thirteen-year-old on a basketball court with grown men.

Why had Duke accepted me, and offered a full scholarship as enticement? As I played through the scenarios, affirmative action appeared to me the only answer. Seemingly dialed into my thoughts, the professor then turned to racial numbers:

"We have fourteen underrepresented minorities out of our total of one hundred students," she said, as she smiled broadly. "That makes this our most diverse class ever."

In academic circles, underrepresented minorities include blacks, Hispanics, and Native Americans; Asians are excluded from this tally because they enroll at colleges and medical school in very high proportion compared to their numbers in the U.S. population. In our class, all but one of these fourteen underrepresented minority students was black. Hispanic students tended to choose medical schools in a few large cities (New York) or states with large Hispanic populations (Texas, Florida, and California). At the time, North Carolina, and the city of Durham, had few Hispanic residents. Native Americans simply make up a very small percentage of the underrepresented minority pool, so they have little impact on the total distribution.

I scanned the room. About half the black faces clustered in a center area near the front, with the rest scattered, as I was, throughout the lecture hall. I had met most of them months earlier, during a weekend that Duke held for admitted black applicants. At the event, black medical students, resident doctors, and faculty all descended upon us to offer assurance that we would not be racially isolated at Duke. Along with the opportunity to meet and greet prominent people at the school, current black students had organized informal gatherings that featured common African-American themes: barbecue at the local park, pickup basketball games, and a venture to a trendy nightclub. They did everything to show that they wanted us badly.

Duke was not alone in its efforts to recruit black medical students. Johns Hopkins filled our recruitment weekend with similar engagements, and it had a few aces that Duke lacked. Levi Watkins Jr., a black cardiac surgeon who implanted the first automatic defibrillator in a human, led the festivities. Our experience culminated with brunch at the estate of Ben Carson, the famed neurosurgeon then known best for separating conjoined twins. Even then, his story of triumph over childhood hardship had spawned a career unto itself with lucrative speaking engagements and bestselling books. In our eyes, he was the Michael Jordan or Denzel Washington of black doctors. Seated in his elegant living room amongst black medical faculty, residents, and current Johns Hopkins medical students, we heard the implicit message loud and clear: As admitted applicants, we'd been invited to join an exclusive community. Friends of mine attended similar events at Harvard, Yale, and the University of Pennsylvania.

This preferential treatment from these elite schools stemmed from their perception of us as "the best black," a term coined by Yale Law professor and novelist Stephen L. Carter. In the post–civil rights era, college and professional schools still sought to enroll the best white students as they always had, but they also began a new, urgent mission: to bring the top black students into their halls. According to Carter, this aim resulted in a distinct set of standards where academically successful blacks were not judged against whites (or Asians), but rather against one another. "There are black folks out there. Go and find the best of them," Carter wrote, describing the mentality that he saw as pervasive across several areas of society. This approach to admissions explains why I received a full scholarship to Duke and was offered early acceptance to Johns Hopkins during my junior year of college.

Yet even with these aggressive efforts, the numbers of black students and doctors are low overall. Blacks constitute about 13 percent of the general U.S. population but a much smaller proportion of the physician world. In the mid-1990s, blacks accounted for about 7 percent of medical students; that percentage holds steady today. That figure includes three predominately black medical schools (Howard in Washington, D.C., Meharry in Nashville, and Morehouse in Atlanta) that currently comprise about 20 percent of the black medical student population. Some schools have just a few black students. What might those numbers look like without affirmative action? Perhaps the past holds some answers.

Before the social and political upheaval of the 1960s, black doctors were a rarity—comprising less than 2 percent of all U.S. physicians. The vast majority of these doctors were educated at Howard and Meharry (Morehouse was not established until 1975) with the expectation that they would provide medical care to segregated black communities. Of the prestigious white schools that did admit blacks, none could be called progressive in that era. Johns Hopkins graduated its first black medical students in 1967. The University of Chicago had just one black student in its Class of 1968. Harvard enrolled just two black students that same year. Yet Duke, from its founding in 1930, has dealt with a racial climate in many ways more intense than its peer schools.

Among elite medical schools—those regarded among the top ten in terms of selectivity, national reputation, and placement of graduates in prestigious clinical residency programs—Duke alone is located in the South. Like most southern hospitals and medical schools, it was fully segregated through the early 1960s until a constellation of events occurred. In 1964, the U.S. Supreme Court upheld a lower court ruling in a North Carolina case that struck down the separate-but-equal doctrine in hospitals. The subsequent Civil Rights Act of 1964 and enactment of Medicare in 1965 gave the federal government the leverage to force the hand of southern hospitals into integrating their facilities.

At the time of these radical developments, you could count the number of black medical students and physicians at Duke literally on one hand. "During the late 1960s, they basically enrolled just one black student every year," one black doctor from that era told me.

On the undergraduate campus, black students were not admitted to Duke until 1963, and their numbers were only slightly higher than at the medical school. According to those who lived it, overt prejudice in those early years on campus was rampant. It was represented by senior university officials' membership in a prominent local country club that excluded blacks. It also took the form of campus cross burnings and other racist acts. This combined racism—equal parts blatant and symbolic—fomented black student unrest that culminated in the 1969 nonviolent protest and occupation of the school's Allen Building, an episode largely credited with paving the way for Duke's entry into the modern multicultural era.

Yet the stain of Duke's racial legacy persists. In the late 1980s, well-known Harvard professor Henry Louis Gates Jr. was briefly a professor at Duke. He didn't stay long, feeling unwelcome, and later publicly referred to Duke as "the plantation." More recently, in 2006, Duke's racial problems resurfaced when three members of the near all-white men's lacrosse team were arrested and charged with the alleged rape of a local black exotic dancer. The case dissolved after the charges were shown to be false, but the race, gender, and class elements revived campus and community tensions while fueling decades-old stereotypes.

So while the days of cross burnings and swastikas are a distant memory, Duke still grapples with its legacy of racial discrimination. During my medical school interview at Harvard, I ate lunch with Kevin, a senior from Princeton who was the only other black person in the group of thirty or so applicants. We were considering all the same schools save for Duke. I told him how much I had enjoyed my interview at Duke and how beautiful the campus was.

"It's a great school," he conceded, "and it would be great to live in a place where it is seventy degrees in November." He then looked around to make sure that no one else was listening. "But you know how they don't have a good track record with people like us." I must have heard some variant of this comment a dozen times during that interview season. It was clear that many black students viewed Duke through a racially tinged lens.

A few years earlier, in an effort to combat this perception, the medical school decided to offer full-tuition scholarships to the handful of underrepresented minorities (primarily black) it saw as most desirable. Anyone who has known a medical student or recent graduate recognizes this award as the lottery ticket it is. With rare exceptions, the only way that future doctors can get someone else to pay for their education is to serve in the military or on some rural outpost for a handful of years after graduation and training. But Duke's offer came with no strings attached. At its essence, the scholarship was a form of recruiting reparations, a practical way to entice blacks students who might otherwise be scared away by stories from Duke's past.

And it worked. For me, the scholarship was the decisive factor in choosing Duke over Johns Hopkins, which offered more prestige, a slightly better track record of training and hiring black doctors, and proximity to my family. It also bumped Duke ahead of three Ivy

League schools on my list. I later learned that the free ride propelled the other five recipients to Duke for similar reasons. Back then, the scholarship was valued at $100,000 over four years, but factoring in interest rates for an equivalent loan over many years, it was more like $175,000, or even more. A lot of money for a group of people like us who'd never had much.

So there it was: Not only was I admitted to Duke, when in a color-blind world I might not have been, but I had arrived with a full-tuition scholarship in hand. Depending on your perspective, affirmative action had done its job, giving a working-class black kid the chance for an elite education, or affirmative action had reared its ugly head, taking a slot from someone else more deserving while possibly setting me up for failure.

In our initial week on campus, we accumulated all the trappings of first-year medical students: parking passes, ID badges, and bulky textbooks. Classes started the following Monday. As I nestled into a spot in the middle of the lecture hall, nearly a week after I'd learned how I stacked up against my classmates, I saw three unfamiliar faces seated together a few rows in front of me. Two were black. Were it not for this, I probably would have overlooked them, assuming they were classmates whom I had not met or had simply forgotten in the chaos of shaking so many sweaty palms during our orientation. However, the numbers of black students in my first-year class was small enough that I already had a mental catalog of their names and faces. These two—one man, one woman—were new to our select company.

During a short break between lectures, I leaned over to Greg, a native southerner who'd gone to college at the University of Florida. "Who are they?" I asked.

"I don't know for sure," he said, "but I have an idea. Let's ask Angela. I bet she knows."

We turned around and looked up at Angela, another black

classmate, who sat a few rows behind us. She was from New York and had gone to Yale as an undergraduate, where she'd been an English major. The gregarious type, she already had her finger on the pulse of medical student gossip. Later that day, as the three of us walked along a semi-enclosed path to the medical school bookstore, we asked her about the unfamiliar faces.

"They have to repeat first-year," she whispered.

"Why?" I asked.

"I guess because they didn't pass last year. What other reason is there?"

"That doesn't look good," Greg said.

"You're right about that," Angela said.

I agreed. Despite our varied backgrounds, we knew the stakes: Affirmative action may have done us a favor in admissions, but it certainly hurt us whenever a black student struggled.

"So who's the third person?" I asked, referring to the white person in that group.

"Her father is a tenured professor here," Angela replied.

"That sucks for her," Greg said.

As Daniel Golden detailed in his 2006 book *The Price of Admission*, elite schools are widely known to give clear admission preferences to the children of alumni and faculty. In contrast to race-based affirmative action, the beneficiaries in these instances are overwhelmingly white, a testament to the reality that these institutions were almost exclusively white during the pre–civil rights era.

"I think if it came to having to repeat a whole year, I would just quit," Angela said.

"That would make things look even worse," Greg said.

Over the next several weeks, I learned that minority-student struggles were indeed a real problem. A college friend at another elite medical school told me that three black students from the previous year had failed and were in her class, and that another had flunked out altogether. Other friends at different medical schools told similar stories. From what we saw and heard, white and Asian students were far less likely to suffer academically to this degree.

Our stories fit within a broader picture. The University of California, Davis (UC-Davis) medical school, ground zero for the famous 1978 U.S. Supreme Court *Bakke* decision that supported using race as a tool in admissions while striking down numerical quotas, conducted a twenty-year study of admitted students from 1968 to 1987. Those admitted under special consideration, meaning that traditional admissions criteria were not used in reviewing their applications, were far more likely to be black. Although they ultimately graduated at similar rates as the regular student body, medical school proved to be a struggle; they earned lower grades and were more likely to fail their general medical licensing exams compared to students accepted under general admissions criteria.

Defenders of affirmation action say that these studies of medical school classroom-based performance do not predict one's success as a physician; they argue that practicing medicine requires far different skills than answering multiple-choice questions. And perhaps they are right. No one can define a good doctor in the precise ways that tests identify good medical students. As Robert Ebert, the dean of Harvard Medical School from 1965 to 1973, who oversaw the school's implementation of affirmative action, asserted: "the purpose of medical education is not to pass the National Boards with the highest scores, but to send out physicians who answer the needs of our society for excellent care and quality research. A good doctor has nothing to do with how well he or she did on a test."

Yet this probably offered little consolation to the two black students who'd been forced to repeat their first year. It is often said that the hardest part of an Ivy League education is getting admitted. But for a significant group of black students, surviving medical school is a real hurdle. Some critics of racial affirmative action, such as Supreme Court Justice Clarence Thomas, contend that "stigmatized" black people are the real victims of racial preferences. Those in Thomas's camp assert that these black students' failures are largely due to a lack of adequate preparation or a mismatch between the student and the school they attend. Affirmative action supporters, on the other hand, are more inclined to believe that social aspects—such as feelings of cultural isolation faced by otherwise qualified black students—play a larger role.

During those first few months, as I was living the experience that so many had talked about in abstract and intellectual terms, I feared that both factors were working against me. As a black man from working-class roots and a state university, I worried about my future at Duke. Was I destined to become another academic casualty?

My racial anxieties intensified after Dr. Gale asked me to fix the lights in his classroom. Clearly, he didn't see me as a Duke medical student, nor was I confident that I could succeed at this level. According to Shelby Steele, a self-described conservative black scholar at Stanford University's Hoover Institution, this is one of the costs of affirmative action: It "nurtures a victim-focused identity in blacks" and increases their self-doubt as "the quality that earns us preferential treatment is an implied inferiority." Steele makes some valid points, but his theory did not predict how I responded to Dr. Gale.

The way I saw it, confronting Dr. Gale about the incident seemed like a bad idea because he had final authority over my grade. What would I say to him? How would I expect him to react? Likewise, I felt that reporting the incident to a medical school administrator would prove futile, and possibly even damaging to my future at Duke. His words hadn't been blatantly racist, and I envisioned that his middle-aged white colleagues would have had trouble understanding why I had interpreted them that way. These influential people were likely to perceive me as a hypersensitive, borderline-militant black male looking to make everything into a racial issue. Given my innate aversion to controversy, that wasn't the reputation I wanted.

Further, if I complained to the administration, exactly what result would I have sought? For Dr. Gale to give me a formal apology? To all black students at Duke? Would I have wanted him forced into racial sensitivity training? Or something more serious, such as suspension or removal from his teaching duties? I couldn't imagine any of that happening; all I could foresee were future repercussions against me if I was labeled a racial agitator. If that was the power to be had from exposing this encounter, or identifying myself as a victim, then I wanted no part of it.

Given Stan's and Rob's reaction to the incident—laughter—I doubt my other black classmates would have acted differently. And yet I was furious. I had to do something with that energy in my own way, to show Dr. Gale how wrong he'd been. So instead of taking my case public, I turned inward and did what any good medical student knows best: I studied my ass off.

Day after day, I spent just about every waking hour with textbook in hand. I was determined to prove to each of my professors— but especially Dr. Gale—that I wasn't a token student admitted to medical school by accident or pity. After class, I headed straight to the library, reviewing my notes and rereading the material until the wee hours of the morning. No matter how enticing the invitations to take a break with classmates, I declined. For those next several weeks, I slept only three or four hours each night.

Other black doctors have traveled this same terrain. In his memoir, *Brain Surgeon,* Los Angeles–based neurosurgeon Keith Black recounts a similar episode during his medical school years at the University of Michigan in the 1980s. While working under a young physician he perceived as racist, Black was assigned to present a case to the chairman of the department. He prepared more diligently than ever before. "Obviously the chief resident was going to be gunning for me," Black wrote, "but I decided that I would not live down to his expectations. It was time to stand and deliver." Black warded off his supervisor's attacks and impressed the chairman so much so that the chief resident had to give him the highest evaluation possible, setting Black on his path to neurosurgery. Ben Carson, in his first memoir, *Gifted Hands*, tells a remarkably similar story from his surgical internship of his perseverance in the face of a chief resident from Georgia who "couldn't seem to accept having a Black intern at Johns Hopkins."

In the days after the final exams, a nervous energy again pulsed through our class. With single-minded perspective, many of us attached the same importance to these results that a patient might to a skin biopsy or blood test. When word spread that the scores had been posted outside the main administrative office, we crowded around the 10-point-font printout that was stapled inside a large glass case. The report identified students by a number that had been given to us individually to maintain confidentiality. Along with our separate scores, the printout showed the class mean and graphed the results on a bell-shaped curve.

"There are some gunners among us," a classmate mumbled to her friends.

The word *gunner*, slang for a hyper-competitive student, was new to me. We were all overachievers in a broader sense, but it was socially unfashionable to appear too ambitious.

Ordinarily, I might have cared about that distinction, but I was too preoccupied with proving myself to Dr. Gale. I knew I had done well on his exam; nonetheless, I was surprised by the result: In my class of one hundred students, I had received the second highest score.

Since the final counted twice as much as the midterm, I hoped that I had earned Honors, the grade reserved for the top ten or so students, even though my midterm score was nowhere near the top. I carried my exam to Dr. Gale's office during his scheduled student hours to find out the verdict. His cluttered office was open for visitors. We were alone to hash out my fate.

This was the first time we had stood face-to-face since our exchange a few weeks earlier. His eyes darted away for an instant as he tugged at his shirt collar. I knew that he recognized me. Surely, he understood that our initial interaction was at least potentially insulting, if not something more. Were the roles reversed, I would have apologized profusely—if not at the time of the mix-up, then definitely the next time we spoke. But Dr. Gale had no such plan.

"How can I help you?" he asked.

I gave him my midterm and final exams and asked whether I had met the cutoff for Honors. His eyes widened as he looked at the final exam score. He removed his glasses and squinted before putting them back on to make sure his vision was not failing. He then stared at my ID card, to see if the name on the exam matched my Duke badge.

"Wow," he said, unable to conceal his astonishment. "I am very impressed that you scored this high. You've definitely earned Honors. You have absolutely nothing to worry about."

I had imagined this moment from the time I turned in the blue exam books the week before, playing out all the pointed things I might say to put him in his place. But now that it had arrived, all I could do was stand there mutely.

"Congratulations," Dr. Gale said, his excitement showing no signs of dimming. "This is really incredible. Would you be interested in doing research in my lab?"

In just a few weeks, I had gone from pariah to prize pupil. This unmitigated praise felt like another aspect of Stephen Carter's "best black" syndrome. The stereotype of black intellectual inferiority was so ingrained that for a black person to do as well, or better, than whites and Asians, they had to be "exceptionally bright"—earnest admiration and condescension wrapped in the same package.

I thanked Dr. Gale and told him I would consider his invitation, although I had no intention of doing so. I wanted nothing to do with a professor who could be so dismissive of me one moment, only to change his mind without apology, as if his earlier comments could be erased like chalk on a blackboard. I left Dr. Gale's office—the last time I ever saw him on Duke's vast campus—with a confused mixture of pride, relief, frustration, and bitterness. "Are you here to fix the lights?" stirred then—and still today—each of those emotions.

In the nearly twenty years since that episode, Duke has made clear strides on the racial front. Under the direction of admissions dean Dr. Brenda Armstrong, Duke has become one of the most racially diverse medical schools. Many of Duke's black graduates have gone on to specialize at highly competitive programs nationwide. Perhaps my success and that of others has enabled certain professors to embrace something once unimaginable.

At that time, however, I had no concerns for future black medical students. My victory was strictly personal. No matter what else happened, I had proved to myself, Dr. Gale, and any other doubters that Duke had not erred in accepting me. It didn't matter whether my classmates were Asian or Jewish, had gone to Stanford or Princeton, or had parents who were surgeons or law professors. I could keep up with them, and rightfully assume my own place as their peer. Affirmative action, despite its flaws, had worked. I had held up my end of the bargain.

But the good feelings didn't last long. As I transitioned from the classroom to the clinical setting the following year, I was about to witness the far greater struggles of black patients play out before me.

2

Baby Mamas

We heard the shrieks as soon as the automatic doors sprang open.

"Is that her?" I asked the nurse, hoping the sound had come from the waiting room television, but fearing that it came from the patient we were about to see.

"That's her," the nurse answered. "This ain't going to be pretty."

We hastened our pace as we approached her room in the labor and delivery triage area, where I was working overnight. Inside, a flurry of activity awaited us. Two nurses worked quickly, one inserting an IV into the patient's arm, the other adjusting the fetal monitor. A large plastic bag containing the woman's bloodstained underpants had been pushed into a corner. A small tank pumped oxygen through her pierced nostrils. A blood pressure cuff and pulse oximeter were connected to an overhead monitor that displayed her vital signs. Our patient looked sicker than I had expected.

She needed a doctor. But I was just a medical student, less than halfway through my second year of school. Just about anywhere else in the nation, that would have placed me in a lecture hall or laboratory doing the usual pre-clinical coursework known to all medical students. However, Duke condensed the traditional two-year classroom training into a single year, with students beginning clinical rotations a full year earlier than usual. The advantage was that it allowed upper-level medical students a full year for independent study; the downside was that it made us grow up quickly. Instead of looking at slides of diseased tissue under a microscope, I stood before a screaming patient who needed help.

Minutes before, I was as relaxed as a second-year medical student on overnight duty at the hospital can be. My classmate Roger and I were sitting in the staff lounge, our eyes on the twenty-five-inch TV. The college basketball season was in full swing and Duke, after a few years of uncharacteristic mediocrity, was back near the top of the national polls. The Blue Devils were in the midst of a big run when Carla, one of the nurses on duty, approached us.

"We got a call about a new patient who just arrived," she began. "I paged the resident, but she's tied up with another patient, so I figured one of you could start seeing her first."

Roger looked at me. He had taken the last case, an anxious woman whom our supervisor sent home after reassurance that she had not had a miscarriage. This new one was mine.

"What's the story?" I asked, turning down the volume on the TV.

Carla provided a quick synopsis. "It's a nineteen-year-old black girl with unknown pregnancy dates and history who comes in with painful vaginal bleeding."

For a seasoned physician, her description would have sparked immediate ideas about diagnosis and treatment. While I was years away from that level of skill, one thing that I had learned in my handful of months on the hospital wards was how to ask logical-sounding medical questions: "How far along does she think she might be?"

I knew that she had to be at least halfway through her pregnancy for us to be seeing her, as the emergency department downstairs handled cases under twenty weeks. Still, we needed a far better estimate. The timing would indicate whether the fetus could survive outside the womb, needed medication to hasten lung development, or might be delivered safely without any of these or other worries.

"She says she wasn't aware of being pregnant," Carla snickered, running her fingers through her reddish hair. "But from the looks of things, she's got to be five or six months along."

Fresh off a psychiatry rotation at a state institution, I instantly wondered whether our new patient had a mental illness. At the psychiatric hospital, delusions about pregnancy were not uncommon. Two women insisted that they were pregnant despite all evidence to the contrary, one going so far as to accuse me of being the deadbeat dad-to-be of her imaginary set of twins. This sounded like the same type of psychotic delusion run in reverse.

"Good luck," Roger said, turning back to the Duke game.

I followed Carla down a long hallway toward the labor and delivery triage area, where we evaluated new patients. Through a large window, I could see that the sun had almost set, with the moon emerging across the sky. The quiet of the adjacent waiting area reflected this peaceful scene, except that now it was punctuated by our patient's screams.

By the time we arrived in her room, the nurses had already done much of the initial care required to stabilize and monitor her condition. "Anything new?" Carla asked her colleagues.

"BP's a little low but stable," one said. "Just sent off stat labs. No fetal heart rate yet."

I looked at the woman. Her skin had a cluster of pockmarks on her left cheek. A small scar zigzagged on her lower chin. Thin lines stretched across her forehead. Her oily hair showed signs of early thinning. She was not yet twenty, but looked closer to thirty.

An older man, around fifty and smelling of cigarettes, stood in the rear corner. He had brought her to the hospital. "I'm her uncle," he told us.

We stepped outside the room while the other nurses tended to our patient. "Can you tell us what happened today?" Carla asked.

"She called me about an hour ago hollering and screaming. When I picked her up I seen she was bleeding too. I figured I could get her here faster than calling 911."

"Did she say if anything happened to her? Like an accident? Or someone assaulting her?"

He shook his head. "She just said she hurt real bad."

"Do you know anything at all about her pregnancy?"

"Nah," he said, as he looked away. "I ain't seen her in over six months."

"Okay, thanks," Carla said. "We're going to need you to stay outside in the waiting room. We'll come find you if we have any more questions or when there are any updates."

"I'm Leslie's only family," he said, stepping away. "Y'all please take good care of her."

Leslie. Until then, she had been an anonymous person with medical problems. Even at that early stage of my training, I'd grown far too comfortable categorizing people as organ systems or diseases. Much of it was simply modeling what I saw senior medical students and doctors do. On the chaotic hospital wards, this approach made it easier to keep track of the relevant medical concern while avoiding getting too attached to the patient. Without realizing it, I'd already done that with Leslie.

We walked back into the room. "I can take it from here," Carla told the other two nurses, who stepped aside. I introduced myself to Leslie, who sat uncomfortably in the bed at a slight incline. The nurses had dressed her in a baggy cloth gown, loosely draped over her abdomen and thighs to offer some privacy. Blue pads had been placed underneath her to absorb the small trickle of blood from her vagina. From what we knew thus far, she had not had any prenatal care. We were the first medical providers she had seen. "Are you the doctor?" Leslie asked me.

"I'm a medical student. I'm going to get things started."

"I don't want you touching me down there," she said, briefly distracted from her pain.

Like other male medical students on the obstetrics and gynecology rotation, I heard this reaction quite often. Even though it bothered me sometimes, I understood their perspective. A stethoscope across a gowned torso surely felt quite different to many women than being fully exposed to the eyes and hands of an unseasoned twenty-something man.

After my assurance that I would not examine her, Leslie agreed to let me ask her a few questions. Meanwhile, Carla made several adjustments to the fetal monitor, but could not pick up a fetal heart-beat. "Get Dr. Garner in here ASAP!" she said to one of the junior nurses.

The urgency in her voice made me feel like I should have been doing something besides asking questions, but that was all I really knew how to do. I started with the most obvious one:

"How far along are you?"

"I ain't pregnant," she answered, even as she was grimacing and writhing in intense pain.

My eyes went down to her abdomen, which protruded to the size of a volleyball. I wanted to ask her what else she thought might explain this, but that seemed a futile question. Instead, I focused on her symptoms of bleeding and pain, but the monosyllabic answers she gave between groans provided me with no helpful clues.

Despite her strange denial about being pregnant, Leslie did not seem acutely psychotic or manic like the women I had seen at the psychiatric hospital. So I searched for other explanations for her behavior. "Have you used any drugs recently?" I asked.

"No," Leslie said without hesitation.

Just to be certain, I then went through a typical list I'd heard other doctors recite: "Marijuana? Heroin? Cocaine? Meth? Pain pills?"

"No, no, no," she said, once again shaking her head.

She sounded convincing. Then again, she had also denied being pregnant. Either way, my brilliant idea had gone nowhere. "Do you smoke cigarettes or drink alcohol?"

"I had a cigarette a few days ago. But what's that gotta do with my pain?"

"Okay," a woman's harried voice interrupted me. We all looked toward the doorway, where Dr. Garner, my supervising resident, stood. At five-eleven, with short brown hair and broad shoulders, she struck an imposing figure. After introducing herself to Leslie, she turned her attention to Carla. "Let's type and screen her. She's going to need two units of blood."

Dr. Garner did a quick external exam, listening to Leslie's heart and lungs, feeling her belly, and inspecting her lower legs and feet for any signs of swelling or poor circulation, while simultaneously asking questions that produced no more information than mine had. All the while, Carla continued to adjust the fetal monitor in hopes of finding a heartbeat.

With Carla having no success, Dr. Garner wheeled over the ultrasound machine. She layered a thick gel on the handheld ultrasound probe, then rubbed it across Leslie's belly, moving it around so quickly that I could not tell what she saw. She was in no mood to slow things down for teaching purposes; her tense energy signaled that there was no time for that. "I think that this might be an abruption," she said to Carla.

Leslie was unlikely to recognize this word. It was shorthand for placental abruption, a condition in which there is premature separation of the placenta, the vital connection between the mother's uterus and the growing fetus.

"There's no sign of trauma," Dr. Garner said aloud, sounding as if she was going through a mental checklist. "And her blood pressure is normal."

These were two of the most common risk factors for placental abruption. Dr. Garner refocused on a third one. With a hard look at Leslie, she began to speak. "I can understand why you would want to deny using illegal drugs, but it's important that I know right now what, if anything, you might have used recently. It can tell us what might be causing this to happen and could possibly save your life, as well as your baby's."

Leslie stared at the wall behind us, her face revealing nothing. Dr. Garner pressed on: "My suspicion is that you might have used cocaine. Your symptoms sound like your placenta might have separated from your womb. Cocaine is a known cause of that."

Leslie shook her head as she continued to groan. Then, to my shock, Dr. Garner abruptly changed her tone. She took a step toward Leslie, and in a harsh voice suddenly demanded: "When is the last time that you smoked crack?"

Leslie looked directly at the doctor. Tears flooded her eyes. "Two . . . days ago . . ."

What? I could not believe what I'd just heard—neither the accusation nor the response. I'd never seen a doctor confront a patient that way. But it had worked, and like a typical self-centered medical student, a part of me felt embarrassed that I hadn't been able to get this same vital information on my own.

Yet Dr. Garner's approach troubled me. What was it about Leslie that made Dr. Garner so certain she used drugs? And crack in particular? Was it her appearance, her speech, her race? Some combination? Would Dr. Garner have done that to a Duke graduate student, even one whom she suspected might have snorted a few lines? Or to any patient who looked and acted middle class? What did it say about the vastly different ways that patients could be treated? Moreover, if Dr. Garner hadn't demanded answers, if she'd continued to accept Leslie's denials as I had, what might have happened?

My head swam with just as many questions about Leslie's mindset. Why had she lied to me, and then, at first, to Dr. Garner? Lying made no sense: The nurses had collected a urine sample and surely it would come back positive to contradict her denial. Then again, denying that she knew she was pregnant didn't make much sense either, so clearly she wasn't thinking rationally. And smoking crack while pregnant . . . didn't everyone know that was bad? Maybe she had to delude herself into believing that she was not pregnant in order to continue using.

Her face flushed with anger, Dr. Garner continued with the

ultrasound. She finally got a clear view of the fetus. "It looks to be somewhere around twenty-two weeks," she said.

She found no sign of fetal movement nor a heartbeat, yet she kept looking, in much the same way that I later saw doctors doggedly continue CPR when they knew that the patient was dead.

Finally, she gave up: "I'm sorry . . ." she began, as she removed the ultrasound probe from Leslie's abdomen and looked directly at her, "but your baby has died."

Leslie's groaning stopped. She looked up at Carla, then over to Dr. Garner. They each took one of Leslie's hands into theirs. In response, she began to wail again.

"No . . . no . . . my baby . . . my baby . . ."

Her moans expressed a profound sadness like nothing I'd ever heard. This young woman had known all along that she was carrying a child. She probably knew that smoking crack while pregnant was dangerous. But she had tragically underestimated the possible consequences.

At that point in my training, death had made only brief, detached intrusions into my medical life. The infamous first-year cadaver dissections, taking place as they did in the basement of a research building, with five students hovering over a formaldehyde-preserved body, felt more like a ritual or rite of passage than a true encounter with death. Our autopsy experience later that year—a postmortem examination of an elderly man who had died a few days earlier from a rare vascular disease—came closer to the real thing, but neither the physician (a pathologist) nor any of us students had known the man in life.

I inched closer to experiencing the personal side of death a few months later during my surgical oncology rotation. There, I followed patients with colon, pancreatic, and breast cancers whose long-term prognoses were poor. Even so, surgeon and patient seemed to have negotiated a silent pact never to look too far ahead, as if exploring that territory might get in the way of what could be done in the short term. Some of these patients probably lived for a few years, while others likely died in a matter of weeks; I never knew for certain, as I soon moved on to the next clinical rotation. Not seeing these deaths allowed me to suspend disbelief about their fates.

But Leslie offered no such escape. Her fetus was too young to have survived on its own, and as a result, in purely legal terms, would not have been considered a person at all. Yet Leslie's piercing cries made clear the emotional stakes: She had lost her child.

After briefly comforting her, Dr. Garner focused on the medical task at hand. While first trimester miscarriages could sometimes take place safely within a woman's home, the risks of carrying a larger dead fetus—infection and blood clots, among others—necessitated medical intervention. Dr. Garner gave Carla and another nurse medication orders to stimulate Leslie's contractions while also dilating her cervix. "Call over to L and D and tell them to get everything prepped for an IUFD," she said.

This acronym likely meant nothing to Leslie, whose deep cries had slowed to a whimper. But to me, calling the labor and delivery unit to prep for an intrauterine fetal demise communicated a clear and terrible message: We were getting ready to deliver a dead baby.

As an assistant nurse wheeled Leslie down the hall of the triage area toward the adjoining labor and delivery suite, we had a few minutes to collect our thoughts. The impact of what we had just seen hit everyone at once.

"This never gets any easier," Dr. Garner said. "Does it?"

Carla shook her head. "It's awful. But in a case like this, it's for the best."

Dr. Garner agreed and tried to convince me as well. "Even if we could have gotten a heartbeat and then delivered the baby alive, I doubt it would have survived more than a day," she said to me. "At this early a gestation, it didn't really have a chance."

We'd been taught that twenty-four weeks was the cut-off point for a viable pregnancy. We heard about a few cases of live deliveries at twenty-two and twenty-three weeks, but these infants rarely left the hospital alive; when they did, they were profoundly disabled. With that knowledge, I agreed with Carla and Dr. Garner. We were falling back on the familiar "he's in a better place" or "she's no longer suffering" clichés that surviving family and friends so often use for comfort after the death of an elderly or sick loved one. Or at least that was what I thought—until Carla kept talking.

"I knew she was a crackhead," she said. "I knew it. It's bad enough to ruin your own life, but to do that to your baby? That's just unforgivable. Even if she had carried this baby to term, it wouldn't have stood a chance. Like I said, what happened is all for the best."

My body stiffened. Dr. Garner, who was walking to the nearby sink to wash her hands, said nothing. Carla was voicing the fear and anger that pervaded the 1980s and 1990s: Crack-addicted moms—primarily poor black women—would birth a generation of "crack babies" who would grow up with serious developmental, psychological, and physical ills, strain limited social resources, and perhaps even threaten the safety of our society. It was in this spirit that a nonprofit California-based program in 1997 started paying drug-addicted women $200 if they agreed to use long-acting contraception or be permanently sterilized. This panic was also enmeshed with the politics of the war on drugs and the fight over abortion, most notably when the state of South Carolina enacted a policy in 1989 that brought criminal charges and punishments against women who used cocaine while pregnant. To many people at this time, pregnant women who smoked crack were true villains.

"Do you plan to talk to her about getting her tubes tied today?" Carla asked Dr. Garner.

Dr. Garner frowned. "She's nineteen. She just lost a pregnancy. That's probably not the most appropriate conversation to have with her right now."

Carla would not be deterred. "I disagree," she shot back. "I don't think we should take the risk of sending her out to get pregnant again. A few months ago, we had another crackhead here who delivered her fifth kid. All of them are in foster care, and I bet they all have some kind of serious disability. I don't think people like her should be allowed to get pregnant again."

Carla's view had once been official policy in North Carolina and in over thirty other states. Beginning in the early twentieth century, forced sterilization programs typically targeted criminals and those in mental hospitals, but North Carolina expanded its reach to include the poor, many black. All told, more than seven thousand people were officially sterilized under North Carolina's laws until the practice was abolished in 1974. While the government had repudiated this policy, Carla was not the first or last person I heard who continued to embrace it.

"We talked about that case on M and M [morbidity and mortality] rounds a few weeks ago," Dr. Garner replied. "That patient was almost forty and probably had CNS [central nervous system] lupus and neurosyphilis. This girl is healthy and still has time to get her life together."

"You're still new to this," Carla said. "You'll see. These crack people don't change."

"Or maybe you've been doing this for too long," Dr. Garner countered, visibly irritated, as she motioned for me to follow her.

Carla said nothing, although her narrowed eyes and clenched jaw suggested she had a good deal more that she wanted to communicate. She had worked in nursing for over two decades, much of it in obstetrics. I had seen how comforting she could be to women and their nervous family members, but as with many of us in medicine, drug addicts seemed to bring out her worst side. I wondered how long she had been so openly cynical and hostile toward drug-abusing pregnant women. More important, had her opinions affected her clinical judgment?

Leslie had come in with painful vaginal bleeding during a second trimester pregnancy; in hindsight, I wonder whether this was an appropriate case for a medical student to begin seeing without a physician present. Had Carla's negative assumptions about Leslie affected the way she communicated the urgency of the case to Dr. Garner? Would she have allowed potentially precious time to pass with a different patient, or would she have insisted that Dr. Garner, or even a more senior doctor, attend to Leslie immediately to salvage any chance of saving the fetus?

Had race played a role? Carla, a white woman from the Northeast, seemed especially focused on crack, a drug widely known to be used more often by black people. A national survey in the mid-1990s revealed that black women were ten times more likely than white women to use crack during pregnancy. The same survey, however, found that pregnant white women were more likely to abuse alcohol, a substance that can produce its own distinct set of severe problems: fetal alcohol syndrome. Would Carla have reacted the same way if Leslie had been a married, white suburban schoolteacher who drank three glasses of wine every night?

Much of the hysteria surrounding this feared crack-baby epidemic, which ultimately turned out to be more fiction than fact, fed off pre-existing negative beliefs about irresponsible black welfare moms draining the system. This seemed to be Carla's perspective. Yet if accused of racial prejudice or bias, Carla surely would have denied it. Her comfort in voicing her opinions around me indicated as much. She had always been pleasant with me, certainly not treating me any worse than my white or Asian colleagues. Nor had I seen her interact with minority nurses or other hospital staff with anything less than appropriate respect.

When it came to Leslie, however, Carla had a different attitude. And she was not alone. Dr. Garner had accused Leslie of drug use in a confrontational manner I have never seen from a doctor before or since. Years later, I would work in both private substance abuse and eating disorder clinics where some of the well-to-do clients were equally self-destructive, but no doctor there would ever have dreamed of being so aggressive. Still, to her credit, Dr. Garner did make an effort to defend Leslie and encourage Carla to see beyond her prejudices.

And, if I had to be honest with myself, I too felt disdain toward Leslie, perhaps on some visceral level, even more powerfully than Carla did. As a crack-abusing pregnant woman, Leslie had put the worst face of black America on full display for this white medical audience. Much of my life had been devoted to combating and defeating vicious racial stereotypes. But in witnessing the pathology of Leslie's behavior and the doctor's and nurse's reaction to it, I suddenly felt naked, as if someone had stripped me of my white coat and left both of us to share the same degrading spotlight.

So, while I thought of many things to say to Carla at that moment, I kept quiet, trailing behind Dr. Garner as we prepared to remove Leslie's dead fetus.

Leslie's room was at the far end of the hall in the labor and delivery area. It was about twice the size of her previous one in the triage wing, large enough to accommodate several medical providers who could tend to the delivering woman and, under normal circumstances, the first minutes of her infant's life.

Two nurses stood on either side of Leslie, as she stared vacantly from her bed at the overhead television. The local news report showed clips from Duke's basketball game. Earlier in the evening, watching this matchup had been the highlight of my day; now it held no more interest than looking at a group of random kids shooting hoops at a local park.

"How are you feeling?" Dr. Garner asked.

Leslie glanced up at her before looking back at the TV without saying a word. Unfazed, Dr. Garner explained what we needed to do and asked Leslie if she had any questions or concerns. More silence. Dr. Garner then turned to the older nurse. "How do things look?"

"She's starting to dilate. We've got a little time."

"Okay," Dr. Garner said. "Call me when it's getting close."

We turned around and walked back to the unit's central nursing station area, where the fetal heart rate output from each pregnant woman on the floor was displayed across several monitors. Dr. Stone, a senior resident and Dr. Garner's immediate supervisor, soon joined us. Dr. Garner updated him on the list of patients, including Leslie.

"What a mess," Dr. Stone said, shaking his head as he learned about Leslie's case. "I would've hated wasting my time operating on a damn addict for a baby with no chance."

It sounded like he was relieved that Leslie's baby had died when it had, as this outcome had spared him the trouble of having to perform an emergency C-section. After Carla's diatribe, his words didn't shock me. This was not the place for compassion if you had a drug problem. "Call if you need me," he said. "I'll be up for a while."

Dr. Garner was about to check in on a patient in the early stages of labor when the older nurse from Leslie's room approached her: "I think it's time."

Moments later, we sat at the end of Leslie's bed, ready to receive the motionless image we'd seen on the ultrasound. The labor-inducing medications had taken effect, and Leslie's contractions caused her to writhe in pain once again.

"I know this is hard," Dr. Garner said. "But I need you to push."

Sweat trickled across Leslie's forehead as she grunted and strained. Nothing came out. "Take a break and try again in a minute," Dr. Garner said.

During her next contraction, Leslie pushed again. This time, the tiny head was visible.

"Good," Dr. Garner said. "One more big push."

Leslie complied, and in a few seconds, a miniature infant was delivered into Dr. Garner's gloved hands. I looked down at it. This infant was less than half the size of the other newborns I'd seen during my rotation. Unlike all of the previous deliveries I had attended, Dr. Garner did not suction the baby's nose and mouth to remove excess fluid, nor did she rush to hand the child over to the nurses or the pediatrician. Instead, she used a cloth to wipe off the excess blood and other fluids and examined the silent, stillborn infant as if we were in a first-year pathology class.

"It was a male," Dr. Garner said to me.

My legs felt rubbery as my vision blurred. I had fainted in college during my first rat dissection but had never come close since. Only this was far more shocking: A tiny human life was gone before it had any chance. I needed orange juice or water, or better yet, a bed. I was about to tell Dr. Garner that I had to leave when the older nurse's voice distracted me. "She'd like to see it."

Dr. Garner looked up from her inspection. "Is she sure about that?"

The nurse nodded, her frown accentuating her heavily lined face.

"Okay then."

Dr. Garner handed the dead infant to the younger nurse, who cleaned him further and wrapped him in a fresh cloth so that only his small head was visible. She then handed him to Leslie. We knew what was coming, but her reaction was still heartbreaking.

"I'm . . . so . . . sorry . . ." Leslie repeatedly cried out, as she cradled her dead child in her arms. Inconsolable, her raw pain consumed all the air in the room.

The younger nurse began to cry—the first time I had seen a medical person cry in the hospital—as she and her older colleague cleaned the delivery area. Dr. Garner stood up and looked directly at me. She wanted to say something, perhaps to offer comfort that this was as bad as it got in medicine. Until then, my time on the obstetrics service had been a perpetual celebration of new life, and maybe she wanted to remind me of that. Instead, her eyes began to cloud as she gazed down at her bloody gloves. Without uttering a word, she walked away.

I wanted to escape too. But I could not think of anywhere to go to ease what I was feeling. So I stood there, frozen. As Leslie continued to cry, I realized that, despite our many assumptions and heated words, we knew very little about her. The initial medical urgency of her case and her unwillingness to answer questions had kept us in the dark. Now, with her pregnancy over, I wanted to understand what kind of life, what kinds of choices, had led her to become a pregnant crack abuser at nineteen. Alone with her grief, grappling with her horrible loss, Leslie, in her own way, was a lost child too.

While Leslie's case stood alone as the most disturbing during my time in obstetrics, it shared several troubling features with other patient encounters. A few weeks earlier, under the supervision of one of Dr. Garner's colleagues, I had rotated through prenatal clinics at Duke and at a handful of county health centers, both in Durham and in nearby counties. These sites offered the trade of services so commonly seen in poor urban and rural settings: The patients allowed us medical trainees the chance to learn and practice our clinical skills, while we provided medical care for which they might not otherwise have had access.

The women at these prenatal clinics were all black, just as they were at many community clinics back then, even those in cities that were 50 percent white. For prenatal visits, the demographic skewed young, mostly adolescent. Approaching my twenty-fourth birthday, I was still a novice when it came to sex, yet found myself in a white coat giving clinical services and medical advice to a group of sixteen-to-twenty-year-olds who, as pregnant women, knew more about sex—or at the very least, had more experience with it—than I did. I would have felt less ridiculous instructing Larry Bird on how to shoot a three-point jump shot or Tiger Woods on how to sink a winding thirty-foot putt.

But their real-world experience did not translate into mature decision making. At one clinic, about an hour from Durham, I interviewed an eighteen-year-old high school senior who was about twenty weeks into her first pregnancy. When I inquired into her overall feelings about the pregnancy, she gave the perfectly reasonable answer that it had come as a surprise but that she planned to make the best of things. Did she hope to continue with school or find a job after she settled into life with her baby, I asked?

"I'm not sure," she said. "I'm stayin' with my mom for now."

"Is the father around?"

"No. We're not together," she replied. "He said he ain't ready to be a dad."

A moment of silence followed while I jotted notes and tried to think of a transition from what I assumed was unpleasant news. But she had moved on. "Do you have a girlfriend?"

The pen slipped from my hand onto the floor. Afraid of what else she might ask if I said otherwise, I lied and told her I was dating someone. I became acutely aware of the awkwardness of being alone with her in a clinic room in which I was soon going to perform a pelvic exam. As male medical students, we'd been told to have a female staff member, usually a nurse, present whenever we examined a woman. That did not typically include the beginning question-and-answer part, but it was time to interpret things more strictly. "I'll be right back," I said, toppling over the chair as I dashed away in search of reinforcement.

Another woman at a different clinic—also under twenty, probably twenty-five weeks pregnant—avoided direct questions about me and instead asked if I knew any nice single black men at Duke or at other area colleges. She too had parted ways with her former boyfriend shortly after becoming pregnant. Over the next few weeks, I met several other young women who had similar stories and queries. As embarrassed as I sometimes felt, their questions about eligible men probably weren't the product of them being hyper-sexualized or immodest. I was there, I was black, I seemed to have a good future—so why not inquire about me and my friends?

Of the dozens of patients that I saw in those clinics, not a single one came with a man—no husband, no boyfriend, or anyone else with a Y chromosome. Nor did any report having a male figure that would be involved in their child's life. Each woman was destined to become part of an oft-repeated yet still staggering figure: More than

70 percent of black children are born to unmarried women. That's more than twice the rate among whites, and consistently ranks as the highest among all groups in America. Many people use these numbers as a statement about the breakdown of black families and communities, framing it as a criticism of welfare entitlements, hip-hop culture, and their purported contribution to moral decay. While those critics raise many valid points, the situation they describe is more complicated. For one thing, the statistics on single mothers include emotionally healthy, well-educated women with good salaries who seem fully capable of raising a child as a single mom. They also include stable couples that, for whatever reason, choose not to marry. Further, being married does not assure a healthier family: We've all seen or heard about marriages so chaotic or abusive that the kids would almost certainly be better off raised alone by the more suitable partner.

Still, it is hard to dispute that most black children born to young single mothers enter life at a distinct disadvantage. Nowhere was this more evident than in the teenage moms-to-be that I saw in these public health clinics; they were, in the detached terminology of the labor force, unskilled and uneducated. Born into poverty and lacking the resources to escape it, these young women and their soon-to-be children faced an assortment of challenges. And although the rate of teenage pregnancy for all groups declined for a fifteen-year period starting in the 1990s, the rates among black teens remained more than twice that seen among white teens.

The sobering medical and social realities of early pregnancy were cemented for me by Tanya, a sixteen-year-old girl who arrived at a Duke clinic as a walk-in complaining of early contractions. She had been seen once before at the same clinic about two months earlier, at the twenty-five-week stage. She looked so young that a part of me wanted to cling to the fantasy that her distended belly was a costume for a role that she was playing in a sex-education campaign.

Her mother sat beside her as I gathered the relevant history. Tanya reported having regular contractions for the previous four hours and thought her water might have broken. The medical issue at hand was whether she had gone into pre-term labor. As I looked down at the record from her twenty-five-week clinic visit, however, I realized that we needed more information. The report indicated that she had tested positive for gonorrhea and chlamydia. She'd been pre-scribed the appropriate treatments, but had not returned for a two-week follow-up visit as recommended to ensure that these potentially dangerous sexually transmitted infections had cleared such that her growing fetus was safe from any further harm.

Needing to navigate this delicate terrain, I asked Tanya if I could speak with her alone; she insisted that her mom stay with her. As gently as I could, I tried to ask her about these infections. But her mom cut me off before I got halfway through.

"She got all that taken care of," her mom said dismissively. "We're not here for that."

After finishing the interview, I left and found my supervisor at the nearby work area. He sat at a computer terminal with his old tennis shoes propped across a chair. I explained to him the present-ing concern, the history of infections, and the mother's resistance to discussing this.

"It sounds like she's scared and is pretending to be innocent around her mom," he said, "and her mom is in denial about what's been going on, but it's way too late for any of that."

I returned to the room with my supervisor, who confirmed the information I'd obtained, and more, in a fraction of the time. As he performed the pelvic exam, it took him less than a minute to decide what was next: "We need to transfer her to the labor and deliv-ery unit," he said to Tanya's mother, before standing up to look at Tanya. "You're in early labor."

Within five minutes, the nurses had situated Tanya in a wheel-chair, ready for transport to the main hospital. As they whisked her away, the resident told me that she was likely to deliver in the next day or two, meaning that, at thirty-three or thirty-four weeks, her child would be premature. Early births, 60 percent more common in black women than in white women, are a large contributor to the reality that, despite remarkable medical progress in the past thirty years, the infant mortality rate in the United States among blacks remains twice as high as among whites. In Tanya's case, her recent history of sexually transmitted diseases was a separate risk factor for premature delivery, a concern further complicated by her spotty record of prenatal treatment.

In the end, despite these many risks, Tanya delivered a borderline low-weight daughter otherwise in good health, and made it through the delivery unscathed. They were lucky. Tanya was still legally underage, however. Did she simply have poor judgment in picking a sexual partner, or had she been the victim of something more sinister? The next morning, the social worker, a middle-aged white woman, filled in the details. She did her usual rounds with the medical team, which on that day consisted of two thirty-something white female doctors. The father of Tanya's child had just turned eighteen, the social worker told us, which meant that no North Carolina statutory rape laws had been violated at the time of conception. Like the other boys I'd heard about in the community clinics, this one had no desire or intention to be an involved father.

I found myself becoming angry at this unnamed, unseen young black man as I thought about the absentee dads from my extended family and childhood neighborhood. While I knew all the usual explanations for this behavior—joblessness, alienation, and poor role modeling, to name a few—I still sided more with my parents' philosophy that it was truly a moral failing for a man to go about his life and not have anything at all to do with his children.

The social worker told us that Tanya lived with her mother and that together they would raise the child. Only they had company. Tanya's eighteen-year-old sister had a kid of her own. This placed their single thirty-five-year-old mother, herself a former teenage mom, as the head of a home with two small kids and two jobless teenagers living off public assistance. In becoming pregnant during high school, Tanya had followed the path laid out for her by her mother and sister. Maybe the pattern went back further.

Despite what seemed to be genuine concern for Tanya's situation, I felt increasingly distressed by the dynamics of three middle-class white women discussing the stereotypical perils—teenage motherhood, absentee dads, life on public assistance—of Tanya's black family. As I'd felt sitting in the classroom a year earlier listening to my professors recite statistics on race and health, I wondered if hearing about Tanya's family negatively affected their views of black people, or merely reaffirmed preexisting biases. I hated thinking and feeling this way, never more aware of the two worlds I represented.

In contrast to Tanya's family and the girls I met at the public health clinics, I'd mostly lived a prudish adolescence. Part of that stemmed from the influence of my parents, who preached abstinence-only and were unwaveringly conservative on all sexual matters. The rest was the result of my personality, which was profoundly anxious and socially awkward, especially around women. Despite being a popular basketball player, I was a college freshman before I kissed a woman, and several more years passed before I ventured into anything sexual. At times, I found myself more judgmental than white people might be, as these racial stereotypes about Tanya and others felt like they were also stereotypes about me—even though my life bore little resemblance to theirs.

Ultimately, however, the more patients I saw, the stronger my desire was to learn more about their surrounding worlds and how their environment influenced their overall health.

After delivering her stillborn infant, Leslie stayed on the postpartum unit for monitoring.

Over the next day, her blood tests all returned to normal levels and her vital signs remained stable. From a purely medical standpoint, she was ready to leave the hospital. But where would she go?

Was she ready to face her world, whatever it was, given what had transpired?

During morning rounds, we spent a significant amount of time reviewing her case. Barbara, the same social worker who earlier had revealed the pattern of recurrent teenage pregnancy in Tanya's family, once again took the lead. As before, her main audience consisted of two white physicians—an older man and a younger woman this time—while I listened in on their discussion.

Barbara had gotten some information from Leslie directly and the rest from the uncle who had dropped her off at the hospital. Her background was even more sordid than I imagined. She spent her first decade in an East Baltimore housing project, where her mom neglected her while hooked on heroin, and a series of her mom's boyfriends molested her. When Leslie was around eleven, her mom walked in on her having sex with her sixteen-year-old brother. She blamed Leslie, and severed all ties to her. Leslie then spent several years in the foster care system, where she endured more abuse until her uncle took her to live with him and his wife in North Carolina.

According to the uncle, she did well for a while, so much so that she talked about going into nursing and one day having her own family. But when her mom, clean from heroin after a prison stint, tried to get back into her life, everything fell apart. Leslie took up with a man who dealt drugs. She dropped out of school, and before long, broke off contact with her uncle.

"For the past year, she's been on the streets, prostituting herself for money and drugs," Barbara summarized.

We stood silently for a second or two before Dr. Adams, the senior physician, spoke: "It's hard not to feel sorry for her."

Dr. Raynor, the junior physician, and Barbara nodded in rueful agreement. While her stillborn child was the ultimate victim, after hearing her life story, we all felt that Leslie was a victim too. How could she get beyond this?

With Dr. Adams in the lead, we entered her room. Leslie did not respond, staring out the window at the prison-like view of brick buildings. The overhead television was tuned to a morning talk show.

"How is your body feeling?" Dr. Adams asked, choosing his words carefully, I suspected, to avoid any discussion about emotional or psychological concerns.

Leslie made eye contact with him for an instant then looked away. "Okay," she said.

"Are you having any pain?"

"Just a little," she said.

The two doctors did a brief exam, listening to her heart and lungs, feeling her abdomen, and briefly inspecting her pelvic area for any signs of continued bleeding or infection. Leslie was motionless, only shifting in compliance with the doctors' requests.

"Is there anything we can get you?" Dr. Adams asked.

She shook her head and continued to look at the television. He told Leslie that she was doing well from a physical standpoint and that someone would come by later to discuss the next steps. Leslie made no acknowledgment that she had even heard him. We then left to discuss her case outside the room.

"I think we should call Psych," Barbara said. "She may need to be admitted to their unit. I'm worried about suicide, given what's happened to her and how unresponsive she is."

"I agree," Dr. Adams said, as he looked to Dr. Raynor, who would carry out this order. "We've done all we can from our end. It's time for our mental health colleagues to take over."

After we finished seeing the remaining patients on our unit, I spent the rest of the morning and early afternoon in the hospital prenatal clinic. When I returned to the postpartum unit that afternoon, I met up with Dr. Raynor to get updates on our patients. As we talked, she saw a doctor carrying Leslie's chart to the physician workroom. It was the psychiatry resident; their team had just finished seeing Leslie. "So what do you think?" Dr. Raynor asked the psychiatrist.

"She's clearly depressed," he said. "We talked about her options, and she doesn't want to go to the state hospital. I don't think it would help her to force her to go there against her will."

During my rotation at this facility, the most common cases I saw were paranoid and indefatigable states of psychosis and mania. I tried to visualize Leslie in that setting; it seemed like a bad fit.

"The state hospital," Dr. Raynor said with a frown. "What about the psych unit here?"

"She doesn't have health insurance," the psychiatrist answered. "For those people, the state facility is the only option. Besides, I doubt our unit would have taken her even if she had insurance, given how prominent cocaine is to her presentation."

It's a common practice in the mental health world to treat substance abuse as a distinct entity from other mental illnesses, such as severe depression, bipolar disorder, or schizophrenia, although drug use frequently overlaps with these disorders.

"So what about a residential substance abuse program?" Dr. Raynor asked.

"As far as the twenty-eight-day private rehab kind, it's the same problem of her being uninsured," the psychiatrist said. "The state-run rehabs require her to get into outpatient counseling before they would authorize her treatment. That's what we will set her up with."

"So that's the best she can get?" Dr. Raynor asked, incredulous.

"Sadly, yes," he said, his exasperation indicating he felt the same frustration that we did. "The odds are stacked against people like her. We talked about her going to a women's shelter, as those sometimes can provide the needed structure and support, but she wasn't too keen on that. I talked with her uncle, who seems like a decent guy. He is willing to take her back, and she's okay with that. We'll get her an intake appointment set up. In the meantime, we recommend starting her on Prozac."

With that, Dr. Raynor began work on Leslie's discharge papers. It was time for her to leave. Under the current system, the hospital had done all it could for her. As we tied together the final loose ends, I thought back to the heated exchange between Carla and

Dr. Garner before we delivered Leslie's stillborn infant. Much of Carla's anger, and to a lesser extent Dr. Garner's and my own, had been targeted at Leslie for selfishly taking a drug that she must have known could be harmful to her growing fetus. But learning her life story had made that judgment a little less fair. The world she grew up in had clearly not been on her side. Perhaps nature had not been either, given her mother's heroin use and what is known about genetic predispositions to drug abuse.

Still, Leslie had chosen poorly, and her baby had paid the ultimate price. She would have to face the emotional consequences of what had transpired. As far as I could tell, the health care system—where she was easily maligned—wasn't prepared to provide her much help with that.

Within a few hours, Leslie's uncle and his wife came to pick her up. They both hugged her fiercely. One could hope that with their support, and with the mental health care we had initiated, this episode might trigger something within Leslie to steer her on a path toward a stable, drug-free life. But with the ashes of this trauma piled atop the many others she had endured in her short life, I wondered where she'd go from here. As a future physician, I was also beginning to think more about the limitations of medicine and where my responsibility to patients might begin and end.

3

Charity Care

T his is it?" I asked.
"That's it," Mike said. "It's a far cry from Duke."

Sharon simply nodded. We stood beside a cotton field, one hour away from the high-tech hub of Research Triangle Park, which was anchored by Raleigh, Durham, and Chapel Hill. Despite our proximity to the major universities and cosmopolitan residents of these cities, it felt, from my lens as a black northerner, as if we'd been transported back into a black-and-white photograph from the Jim Crow era. A tiny white home, nestled within a group of dingy trailers and makeshift houses, served as the building where we would spend the day treating patients. A small graveled area served as the parking lot. Flowing cotton fields and decrepit buildings filled out the canvas. My mind couldn't help but conjure up images of Ku Klux Klan rallies a half century earlier.

Although the clinic would not open for twenty minutes, about a half-dozen people stood waiting on the dusty porch. They were all black. While African Americans made up about half the town's population of two thousand citizens, every person who trekked up the creaky stairway that day was black. This was where the poorest residents came to get care.

Duke's relationship with the town and clinic dated back nearly fifteen years. For Duke, the project served two purposes: helping patients in an area chronically underserved by doctors, while at the same time giving medical students a practical way to build their clinical skills. For the patients, in a town with no physician and many people without health insurance, the clinic offered some residents their only opportunity to see a doctor. One Saturday each month, these two worlds joined hands.

Earlier that morning, I'd met Mike and Sharon, both third-year medical school classmates, in a parking lot adjacent to Duke Hospital.

"Is there a first-year student coming with us?" I asked Mike.

He shook his head. "It's just us. They're all too stressed about their micro test."

At Duke, third-year medical students formed the backbone of clinic operations. After an intense, compressed beginning to our education—we accomplished in two years what students at other schools did in three—the third year was pretty much ours to do as we wished. Most worked in research labs, as I did, to build our résumés for residency training. Several others went to UNC to earn a master's in public health, or to Duke's business school for an MBA.

No matter the choice, life was much less hectic than in those first two pressure-packed years. We worked between forty and fifty hours a week, with weekends and holidays off. We had time for sleep. Time for exercise. Time for travel. It was the closest most of us would come for many years to living a normal life.

Nonetheless, we were still medical students, and that meant we felt compelled to do at least some extra work to avoid losing a competitive edge. If we went a year without seeing any patients, many of us feared we'd be at a disadvantage when we returned to hospital duties as fourth-years, so we sought out clinical opportunities. It was easy enough to shadow doctors around the hospital, but with many years of specialty-based training ahead of me, I wanted to try something different—away from the high-tech world of what is called tertiary care medicine. The rural clinic, with its opportunity to learn outside Duke and with greater autonomy to build practical medical skills, seemed a perfect fit. Mike, the student leader for the group and future family physician, traveled there most months. Sharon and I were first-timers.

Within a few minutes, two others had joined us: Dr. Watson, a senior medical resident, and Dr. Kelly, a faculty member and supervisor for the day's activities. The group did not ordinarily include a resident doctor, but Dr. Watson, in the final months of her residency, was preparing to become a supervisor at the clinic. As we clustered around him, Dr. Kelly, a trim, graying endocrinologist, briefly explained our mission. "This is not like anything you'll see at Duke. Here you are treating people in their own community, without the luxuries we take for granted. Working in a place like this is part of what it means to be a doctor too."

The clinic was about five hundred square feet, the size of an urban studio apartment or a small single-wide trailer in this part of the world. It had been efficiently divided into three compartments: a makeshift waiting area in the front where a few patients could sit while the rest stood, a central space crowded with medical supplies and a cluttered desk for our supervisors, and two small examination rooms separated by dilapidated curtains.

The first person I saw was Pearl, a woman in her early fifties. She wore a baggy plaid dress that came down to her ankles. Tiny black moles were sprinkled across her forehead. Her eyes lit up as they met mine: "It's so good to see a young brother in a white coat," she said. "That don't happen much 'round here."

I smiled. In the two-plus years I'd been at Duke, I'd often gotten this reaction from black receptionists, nurses, phlebotomists, cafeteria workers, and cleaning service crew. They shared in my achievements and promise like an extended family. Along with the racial pride that came with their praise and adulation, however, I felt an added weight, as if my success or failure would reflect not just on me, but on those who had come before and those who would follow me.

"Where you from?" she asked. "You look like a boy from the suburbs."

The implication, as I heard it, was that a black person like me—clean-cut, college-educated, studying to be a doctor—did not come from an area like hers. Nor from the inner city. The odds stacked against those children—bad schools, broken families, negative peer pressure—were, with rare exceptions, too great. While I had grown up in a suburb, it probably wasn't the kind she had in mind. Mine was the segregated, working-class variety where some of my peers became teenage moms while others got busted for dealing drugs.

I politely answered Pearl's questions about my background and career interests before turning my attention to her: "So what brings you here today, ma'am?"

"I need my sugar checked," she said, holding up her calloused hand, pointing to the fingertips where diabetics prick themselves for blood. "I also wanna see if my blood's high."

She was referring to screening for diabetes and hypertension. I'd learned these colloquial references from extended family long before discovering the proper medical terminology. My maternal grandmother and her younger sister, both of whom lived in Washington, D.C., often talked about their health problems and those of other family members, gossiping that so-and-so had "high blood" and his wife "had sugar" and how they ultimately "weren't doing right." Listening to Pearl was like hearing an old recording after many years.

"Have you been diagnosed with either disease?" I asked her.

"The last time I was checked, they said I was on the borderline for both."

"When was that?"

"About a year ago. Maybe two," she admitted. "But I've been feeling fine."

"So what made you decide to come today?" I asked.

"My brother just started dialysis. His doctors said it's 'cause of his sugar and high blood, so I figured I better get checked out again."

"Do you take any medications?" I asked.

"I take a water pill once in a blue moon. When I start to feel my legs are swole up. They gave it to me when I came here the last time."

"Do you know the name of it?"

She shook her head. "It's a small orange circle."

That meant nothing to me. I said the names of some common medicines that are described as "water pills," diuretic drugs that make patients urinate and reduce bodily fluid volume, but Pearl looked at me as if I were speaking Chinese. While we shared the same skin color and lived in the same region, we were communicating in different languages. I knew the textbook names, while she knew what the pills actually looked like.

Unlike other clinics I'd rotated through up to that point, we worked without nurses, so I had to check Pearl's vital signs. I started off by measuring her height and weight. She was five foot four and weighed 210 pounds, her body mass index far above what my pocket guide listed as ideal. I was more than a foot taller, yet we made the same imprint on the scale. Her blood pressure and blood sugar were both high, measuring 160/100 and 275, respectively. After a physical exam—listening to her heart and lungs with my stethoscope and checking her feet for signs of swelling or poor blood circulation—I found Dr. Kelly, who sat in what amounted to a tiny cubicle.

"So what should we do for her?" he asked me.

"Well, she's not on medication for either hypertension or diabetes. So I'd probably start her on something for both. But we probably need to get some baseline labs first."

Dr. Kelly quizzed me on what blood tests to order and seemed pleased with my answers. He appeared less satisfied with my suggestions for medication treatments. I'd thought they were both standard drugs used for these conditions.

"Those drugs might be what we'd prescribe at Duke," he instructed me.

Out here in this clinic, however, we had other things to think about. For example, we didn't know whether Pearl had health in-surance and prescription drug coverage. And we wouldn't be able to see her again for at least another month, maybe longer, for follow-up tests.

This kind of concern had never arisen during my two-month family medicine rotation in Durham the previous year. There, in a private-practice setting, the only limitations in choosing a medi-cation for patients were their existing health problems. But here we were practicing a different type of medicine, one constrained by in-fluences beyond basic science.

Dr. Kelly examined Pearl and found signs of nerve damage in her feet. He was also concerned about possible early nerve damage in her eyes. Both were complications of diabetes.

"My Lord," Pearl said, as she began to fan herself like a woman in a hot southern church. "What's all that mean for me?"

"The most important part is getting your blood sugar under con-trol," Dr. Kelly answered. "We'll need to do some blood tests. You're also going to need a more specialized eye exam."

I wondered if the blood tests would show the early stages of kidney disease that had struck her brother, but Pearl's thoughts had moved away from her health: "I can't afford all that," she said. Pearl told us that she had once had health insurance, but lost it five years before when the company she worked for shut down. Her new fac-tory job didn't offer insurance.

Dr. Kelly looked disappointed but not surprised. "We'll do the best we can," he said.

While I drew her blood, Dr. Kelly wrote a prescription for the cheapest diabetic pill available and gave her a one-month sample pack of blood pressure pills we'd brought along. There was no guarantee that they'd have the same medication samples available the next time, he told her. We handed her a packet of test strips to check her blood sugar, as she told us that she could use her brother's machine. Fi-nally, we gave her the name of a clinic a half hour away where she could get an eye exam at little or no cost.

"Losing weight will also help out a lot," Dr. Kelly said. "I know it can be really hard."

"I need to start walkin' with my husband every morning. He's as skinny as I am fat."

We smiled and wished her well. "Thank you so much," Pearl said, giving both of us a vigorous two-handed handshake. "I'm gonna make sure I do right with this."

After she left, I thought about how different this treatment model was from what I'd seen at Duke. Pearl's medical care seemed so tenuous. As her medical providers, we were nearly ninety minutes away at Duke. And there would be no one here for another month, when a new medical student and physician would pick up where Dr. Kelly and I had left off. What if the weather was unusually bad that day or the medical team got a flat tire on the way to the clinic?

"What if she needs to see a doctor in the meantime?" I asked Dr. Kelly.

"She'll have to miss work and go to a walk-in clinic," he said. "Or, if she runs out of options, her nearest emergency room. That's what happens. She really needs a regular primary care doctor who can manage her diabetes and refer her to the appropriate specialists when needed. But I suppose if she had all of that, she wouldn't have come to see us in the first place."

Physicians and hospitals have been providing what we offered to Pearl and the other people at the rural clinic, charity care, for as long as doctors have been seeing patients. During the first half of the twentieth century, public hospitals became the most well-known American venues for delivering care to the poor; a handful have become famous (New York's Bellevue, Chicago's County, and Atlanta's Grady). Public hospitals began to decline after the mid-1960s passage of Medicare and Medicaid, as these programs provided public insurance that lower-income patients could use for treatment at private hospitals. Combined with other fiscal factors, many public hospitals over the last fifty years have contracted their services or simply closed. But the need for charity care has not declined during this period; if anything, it has grown.

Medicaid has never fully met the needs of the poor. Many "working poor" have jobs that do not offer private insurance and incomes that place them slightly above the poverty level, disqualifying them from Medicaid. Some states require certain groups (for example, single men) to be medically disabled before they can be eligible for Medicaid, regardless of their income level. Between 1987 and 1998, the year that I attended this charity clinic, the number of uninsured rose from 32 million to 44 million.

This environment has led to the evolution of what is called the health care safety net. Here, patients who fall outside the traditional health care marketplace receive services. Alongside public hospitals, academic institutions like Duke and UNC provide hospital-based charity care. In the outpatient sector, a patchwork of federally funded community health centers, public hospital–based clinics, locally funded state health departments, and volunteer-based free clinics provide basic medical services. It was in this sphere as a free clinic that the Duke-staffed rural health clinic operated.

Just a few hours into the Saturday clinic, three issues stood out in my mind. First, all of the patients were black, even though the region was nearly 50 percent white. Perhaps Duke had specifically targeted the area's black community. But it is known that black people are far more likely to be seen in safety-net settings. One national study found that poor blacks were four times as likely as the general population to receive care in safety-net clinics. Another study in rural Massachusetts observed that black residents sought care at a free clinic at nearly twice the rate of that region's general population.

Second, there seemed to be clear differences in the type of care that could be provided compared to what I'd seen at Duke. In recounting their respective outpatient experiences at Chicago's Cook County and New York City's Lincoln Hospital in the 1970s as doctors-in-training, physicians David Ansell and Fitzhugh Mullan describe clinics with: "no set appointment times . . . once they showed up, it was first come first served," with patients seeing different providers each time, provoking feelings that the care they delivered was part of "a separate and unequal second-class system." Neil Calman, a New York City–based family physician, echoed their sentiments in a 2000 essay where he described the challenges one of his patients, Mr. North, faced getting treatment for his heart failure: "There is absolutely no doubt that Mr. North is treated differently than my white, middle-class patients are treated," Calman wrote, expressing regret that "I cannot provide Mr. North with all that New York's great health care institutions have to offer." Several hundred miles away, Dr. Kelly and the clients at the charity clinic faced a nearly identical set of problems.

The third defining aspect of my experience at the rural clinic was the nature of the patient's concerns. Each had chronic medical problems either caused or worsened by the way they lived. Pearl's obesity surely contributed to her diabetes and hypertension. The next patient I saw was a smoker who came in with recurrent bronchitis; another one had developed numbness in her feet from not taking her insulin and enjoying too many desserts. They were like characters out of Henry Louis Gates Jr.'s memoir *Colored People*, who "drank on top of diabetes and would fry up ham and bacon and sausage for breakfast, directly defying doctor's orders." As one person after another came in with similar stories, it became tempting to place the blame for their health problems squarely and solely on their shoulders. Nobody was forcing them to eat at McDonald's and Bojangles' or watch TV instead of taking a long walk. No one had held a gun to their heads to make them start smoking cigarettes or keep doing so even as they coughed and wheezed.

This was a simple and detached way to look at things, and it was easy for me to embrace that limited perspective. I began to feel more frustration with each successive patient, a reaction intensified by my being the sole black provider there. As their medical providers, we could only help them so much; the majority of progress, such as eating better and exercising, they had to make for themselves. And most of them simply weren't doing it. Despite their apparent good intentions, I worried that my white colleagues—Sharon, Mike, Dr. Watson, and Dr. Kelly—had made unconscious or even conscious negative judgments about these black patients, and thus about black people in general. Or was I simply projecting my own racial insecurities onto them?

Despite what I'd seen, it was not until I met Tina, the last patient of the day, that I came to appreciate how the medical system itself is sometimes just as sick as its patients.

As morning gave way to afternoon at the clinic, patients filed in steadily. We took brief, separate lunch breaks in order to accommodate the thirty people who sought care. Dr. Kelly was briefly worried that we might have to turn people away until the inflow gradually slowed. At three o'clock, I checked in Tina, our last patient. On the surface, she seemed the healthiest of anyone I'd seen that day, but I quickly learned that she had two serious medical problems.

"I've been bleeding heavy with my periods and in between them," she told me.

With my limited knowledge of gynecology, I thought about the possibilities as I jotted down notes. I then looked up at her. Tina was nearing forty, but with bright teeth and smooth dark skin, she seemed a few years younger. She was dressed in a polyester blouse and blue jeans, the kind of neat but nondescript outfit you might find at a bargain store. She showed no outward signs of illness and reported no other health-related issues.

I took her vital signs. At five-seven and 140 pounds, she was slender in comparison to the other women I had weighed that day. Her pulse was steady and calm at 70 beats per minute. Her temperature and breathing rate were also normal.

In order to measure her blood pressure, I had to switch from the large cuff that I had used all day to the smaller, standard-sized one. The result I got was abnormal. Was this cuff broken?

"Does your pressure run high?" I asked, as I pulled the stethoscope from my ears.

"Not that I know," she said, a slight frown emerging across her brow. "Is it high now?"

"Let me try again," I said, without answering her question.

I was more careful this time, slowly deflating the pressure gauge. But the result was the same: Her pressure was 190/110, well above the 140/90 threshold for diagnosing hypertension.

"Your pressure is pretty high right now," I said.

She pursed her lips, using her forearm to wipe away the sheen on her nose. She'd come to the clinic worried about her irregular bleeding and was learning of an entirely different problem.

"When is the last time you had it checked?" I asked.

"I don't know," she said. "I guess when I was in the hospital with my youngest."

"How long ago was that?"

"She just turned six a few weeks back," Tina said, as she smiled for a brief moment. "They said it was high when I was pregnant with her, but it came down after I delivered her."

Before I could ask anything else, Dr. Watson, the resident supervisor, came over to me. With a few strands of reddish hair having escaped from her loose ponytail and her eyeglasses resting on the bridge of her nose, she looked as if she'd spent the day poring over textbooks. She readjusted her glasses as she introduced herself to Tina.

"Is everything okay?" I asked, wondering if she'd been listening in and I'd made an error.

She nodded. "Tell me what you have so far."

I briefly explained what I knew and showed her the vital sign measurements.

"Since this is the last one," Dr. Watson began, "how about we do this one together?"

That was her way of saying everyone was tired and wanted to go home. Mike and Sharon had finished with their patients; Tina was the only person standing between us and the trip back to Durham. And even though I had a year of clinical medicine under my belt by then, a good resident could still get more information from a patient than I could, in half the time.

I followed Dr. Watson and Tina into a dinky examination room. Its flimsy, makeshift walls and shower-curtain door offered visual privacy but no sound protection. This was not the place you'd want to reveal intimate details about your sex life or problems with your bowel movements. In a soft voice, I asked Tina more details about her health history and current habits. She did not take medications or supplements. "Do you drink alcohol?" I asked.

She shook her head. "Not at all. Never liked the taste. Don't smoke or use drugs either," she said, anticipating my next questions before I could ask them.

She did drink two large cups of coffee each day. While she avoided the saltshaker, she did not monitor the sodium content of her food. She rarely exercised.

"Have you had any headaches or blurry vision?" I asked, trying to determine if she had experienced any symptoms associated with a persistently high blood pressure. She shook her head once again. "Does anyone in your family have high blood pressure?" I inquired.

"My dad," she said with a wistful look. "My mom always said I was more like him."

Her father had been diagnosed in his fifties and was on two blood pressure medicines; she also had an older brother with hypertension. Since both men were overweight, smoked cigarettes, and drank alcohol, Tina had always figured that high blood pressure was not going to be a problem for her, at least not until she was much older.

Dr. Watson then took over as she inquired about the bleeding issue. Not only were Tina's periods heavier and longer-lasting than usual, but she was having some spotting in the intervening days. This had been going on for about six months. "Have you been on birth control pills, or anything like that, for contraception, in the past few years?" Dr. Watson asked.

"No," Tina said. "I got my tubes tied after my daughter was born."

"How many times have you been pregnant?" she asked.

"Twice," Tina said, smiling again. "I have a seven-year-old boy and a six-year-old girl." Aside from the brief interval with an elevated blood pressure, Tina's pregnancies had been uncomplicated, with two normal deliveries. She'd never had any surgeries or other gynecological procedures.

After a few more questions, we stepped out so Tina could change into a paper gown.

The room was too small for me to stand over Dr. Watson and observe the pelvic exam, so I waited outside. When Dr. Watson finished, I stepped inside as Tina sat up on the exam table. Dr. Watson then delivered her diagnosis: "You've got something that we call fibroids."

"What's that?" Tina asked, with genuine puzzlement on her face.

Dr. Watson explained that a fibroid was a benign tumor that enlarged her uterus—in Tina's case to the typical size for a woman sixteen weeks pregnant—and caused her bleeding. In my head, I ran through what I knew about this disorder, which, like so many others, fit the painful racial profile so familiar to me. Not only are fibroids two to three times more common in black women than in white women, but studies suggest that in black women fibroids develop at an earlier age, grow faster, and are more likely to cause symptoms requiring surgical treatment. No one knows exactly why.

"Tumor," Tina said with obvious worry. "Is that the same thing as cancer?"

"Yes and no. The vast majority of the time they are benign— meaning that they don't spread or cause any problems after we remove them. This is a very treatable condition."

Dr. Watson reviewed the treatment options, which ranged from taking medication, to surgical excision of the individual fibroids, to a full-fledged hysterectomy.

"What do you think I should do?" Tina asked.

Tina's hopeful eyes suggested that she trusted Dr. Watson's opinion. In response, Dr. Watson curled in her lower lip for a second. She stepped closer to Tina and lowered her voice. "Given the size of what I felt, you'll probably need a hysterectomy. I can refer you to a specialist at Duke to discuss your options, unless there's someone closer that you would prefer to see."

"For something like that," Tina answered, "I want to go to Duke."

"Okay," Dr. Watson said. "But we'll have to treat your high blood pressure first."

She asked me to check Tina's pressure again. It had gone down to a less dangerous level, now about 180/100. But it was still far too high.

"Do you have a family doctor that you can see in the area?" Dr. Watson asked.

"No," Tina said, as she looked down at her lap. "This is it. I don't have no insurance."

"But you have small children?" Dr. Watson said, more a plea than a question, as a streak of red flushed her cream-colored cheeks. Low-income parents of young children are a preferred group for Medicaid, which covers more than 50 million people in the United States each year.

"I got temporary Medicaid during my last pregnancy," Tina said. "My girl is still on it, but they cut me off not long after she was born."

At that point, we had not gotten a full "social history," as it is called in medicine. Specifically, we knew nothing about her work or marital status. Without thinking, I had filled in those gaps with stereotypical assumptions. First, I concluded that the reason Tina was uninsured was that she didn't have a job. Second, as she wore no wedding ring, I'd assumed she was a single mom. But I was wrong on both fronts. Tina worked at a local convenience store. Her husband of ten years worked with his brothers in a small home repair business. Neither job came with health insurance. Their combined income, she told us, was around $25,000 per year. Medicaid cut her off because "they said we made too much money."

She and her husband had looked at a private plan, but realized that they couldn't afford the premium and still pay their other bills. So, comforted that their children had health coverage, Tina and her husband went through life praying not to get sick.

I drew blood as Dr. Watson counseled Tina on ways to reduce her salt/sodium intake. We then went to the medicine cabinet in search of free pills while Tina produced a urine sample. But Tina had the misfortune of being the last patient of the day, and like a shopper arriving late to a post-Thanksgiving Black Friday sale, she was out of luck. In this case that meant missing out on much-needed medicine rather than failing to score a discounted fifty-inch television.

Instead, Dr. Watson wrote a prescription for a diuretic pill, which would cost just five dollars a month. She explained that someone would contact Tina with the lab results, and that Tina should return to the next free clinic the following month. With the clinic now closed, we packed up our medical supplies and personal belongings. Before we left the building, Dr. Kelly wrapped up the day as he began it: "I hope everyone took something positive from this experience today. I hope that in whatever field you choose, you devote at least some of your time to caring for people who otherwise couldn't afford to see you."

We all nodded in agreement and approval, as if our leader had preached a medical gospel. I had gone through my first day of hands-on medicine in months, and been reminded of what I enjoyed about it: the data of vital signs and lab tests; the intricacies of the human body seen through the physical exam; synthesizing these findings into a treatment plan. But mixed with these thoughts about process and analysis came concerns about the people we'd seen.

Would Pearl lose weight, take medicines, and stave off the complications of diabetes and hypertension that struck her brother? Would the man with recurrent bronchitis quit smoking? And Tina? Could we get her blood pressure under control? Would she be able to get surgery?

After saying our good-byes to the doctors in the gravel parking lot, Sharon and I got into Mike's car for the drive back to Durham. We took in our dilapidated surroundings one more time. "Being here really does make you appreciate what you have," Sharon said.

"Amen to that," Mike replied.

But as the single-lane road became a two-lane highway and then a three-lane interstate, we gradually put the day's patients behind us.

Two years earlier, during my first year of medical school, I sat nervously in an exam room at the student health clinic. A nurse had just left the room. She had confirmed the high blood pressure readings that a classmate had discovered a few days before during our weekly introduction to medicine course. Dr. Katz, a small-framed, middle-aged man with short brown hair and large glasses, entered the room and scanned the nurse's notes before asking me the same questions I would ask Tina two years later. My answers were simple: Other than mild scoliosis, I didn't have any health problems. I didn't smoke, drink, or use drugs.

"Do you have a family history of high blood pressure?"

I nodded. About twice a month after Sunday church, my mom would drive to my grandmother's second-story, one-bedroom apartment off Georgia Avenue in Northeast Washington, D.C. One afternoon, when I was about ten or eleven, my grandmother had cooked salty ham, and this led to a heated discussion with my mom about how my grandmother had not been taking her blood pressure medication or cutting back on high-salt foods as her doctor had recommended. My grandmother argued that the medication made her go to the bathroom all night, and, in her usual blunt style, announced that she had no plans to stop enjoying the foods she'd eaten her whole life. Frustrated, my mom backed off, realizing that there was nothing more that she could do. That was the last time I remember them talking about her high blood pressure.

On the other side of my family, I didn't yet know about my dad's hypertension, because he'd avoided doctors for more than three decades. When he was finally diagnosed, he wound up requiring three different medications to control his blood pressure. But I did know that his older brother, who died from a stroke when I was four-teen, had hypertension. Like my grandmother, he apparently had not followed medical advice either.

Despite this family history, I had not expected to find myself in this position, certainly not in my early twenties. "How's your diet?" he asked.

Terrible, I admitted. I'd grown up eating whatever was placed in front of me—and then seeking out more. My mom worked long day-time hours and my dad worked nights, and healthy homemade meals were the exception rather than the rule. Ready-made processed meals, fast food, and buffet restaurant trips were dietary staples. Every so often, my mom would go on a Weight Watchers diet and eat health-ier foods, but that didn't impact me. Since I was very tall and skinny throughout childhood (I stood six-five and weighed 160 pounds at age sixteen), what harm could come from two foot-long steak subs, an extra-large pepperoni pizza, or a half-dozen hot dogs?

This eating pattern only worsened in college, as I tried to add weight to keep from getting pushed around during basketball games. Even with an extra thirty pounds, I still fell within the normal weight range for my height, so I saw no reason to cut back. This approach to food continued upon my arrival at Duke, where each day brought dinner at a regularly rotating group of fast-food spots. Just as in col-lege, I rarely drank more than a glass of water daily, and I could go several days without eating a fruit or vegetable (not counting French fries and potato chips). However, with a myopic focus on weight as my barometer for wellness, I'd chosen to ignore basic nutritional facts and believe that I was perfectly healthy.

Dr. Katz performed a basic physical exam that he said was normal. He then sent me downstairs to the lab, where a pimply-faced young phlebotomist took two tubes of blood from my arm and sent me to the adjacent bathroom to collect a urine sample.

The following day, I returned to see Dr. Katz to get the results. He wasted no words: "Your creatinine is 1.6."

I took a deep breath. Serum creatinine is the baseline test used to assess kidney function. The upper limit of normal at Duke's lab was 1.3. Something was wrong with my kidneys.

I searched his face for reassurance, but he looked down at the lab report before speaking. He had more bad news.

"There were also traces of protein in your urine," he said.

A detectable level of protein in the urine, known as proteinuria, is another sign of kidney disease. My face fell into my hands. Worst-case scenarios flashed through my mind.

Sensing my distress, Dr. Katz tried to calm me down. Even though he spoke for several minutes, I made out only the bare outline of what he said. Something about restricting sodium intake and supplementing basketball with other aerobic exercises, such as jogging or swimming. At the end, he told me to check my blood pressure weekly and return in a few months for repeat tests.

The day before, Dr. Katz had said that my heart and lungs sounded normal. But as I stepped outside the clinic into the crowded parking lot, my heart pounded as if it were going to explode from my chest. My shirt was soaked with sweat. I could barely breathe. Although I had never experienced one before, I knew I was having a panic attack.

During the ensuing sleepless night, my mind flooded with images of my grandmother. Around the age of seventy, her memory began to fail rather abruptly—likely from vascular dementia, the result of decades' worth of mismanaged hypertension. At age seventy-three, she suffered a massive stroke and was later found to have heart failure, which was also related to her hypertension. In those few years, she'd been reduced from the spirited person I'd loved so much to someone barely recognizable: crippled on one side, needing aides to clean her, babbling about places from her childhood and people long dead. Was that my future too?

From that point forward, hypertension became my obsession. For weeks, I spent hours in the medical library reading everything I could about it. Hypertension is the prototypical disease when it comes to black health disparities. It's about 50 percent more common in black people than in whites, afflicting nearly two out of every five adults. It also strikes black people at a younger age, and blacks are less likely to have their blood pressure adequately controlled. Consequently, hypertension tends to run a more aggressive course in black people, increasing the risk of several other diseases that are also more common in blacks (e.g., stroke, kidney failure).

The reasons offered as to why black Americans suffer so severely from hypertension are as diverse as the fields represented. The psychologically oriented journals cite the stress of American racism. Evolutionary scientists theorize that among African slaves, the ones best able to retain water survived the harsh Atlantic journey, passing on their genes, which later proved problematic in the modern world. Public-health writers comment on the various inequities in our health care system and cultural differences in dietary and physical activity patterns.

Regardless of the cause, or causes, I wanted answers, a fix for my problem. Armed with data from several research studies, I set about changing my life. I started regular grocery shopping for the first time, being sure to eat fresh fruits and vegetables on a daily basis. I replaced soda with water. I supplemented basketball with running on a treadmill and stretching exercises. Within three months, my weight was unchanged, but my blood pressure had dropped to a normal 120/80. From then on, I knew it would be my blood pressure, and not my weight, that would define how healthy I was.

Later on in medical school when the time came to choose a research project, I jumped at the chance to work in a behavioral medicine lab led by Duke psychologist James Blumenthal that studied lifestyle-based approaches to treating hypertension and heart disease. There, I saw patients, both black and white, reduce their blood pressure through eating better, exercising more, and learning basic stress management techniques. This experience reinforced my own commitment to live a healthier lifestyle.

When I saw Pearl and Tina at the rural health clinic, I was not just another medical student seeing black patients with poorly controlled blood pressure. I stood before them face-to-face with my family's past and perhaps my own future.

Despite our similar health struggles, I quickly recognized the many advantages that I had over Tina, Pearl, and so many others. For starters, I understood the language of medicine. Terms like glomerular filtration rate, thiazide diuretics, and calcium channel blockers were part of my growing medical vocabulary. The patients at this clinic had limited formal education. Tina had a high school diploma; Pearl hadn't gotten past tenth grade.

At Duke, I had access to three campus gyms along with several nearby grocery stores and restaurants that served healthy items. Tina and Pearl were constrained by fewer exercise and healthy-food options where they lived. And while I had no money to my name, my social status as a medical student placed me in daily contact with physicians and other medical professionals who could help me navigate the best practices and expose me to the latest medical advances. Tina and Pearl were from families and communities cut off from these advantages.

A 2005 *New York Times* article vividly illustrates this dramatic influence of social class as it follows the journey of three New Yorkers—one rich, one middle class, and one working class—who each suffer heart attacks around the same time. In describing their uneven recoveries, in which the wealthy person is left better off, the middle-class man fighting through a setback, and the working-class woman struggling with increasingly complex medical and social problems, the author observed: "class informed everything . . . from the emergency care each received, the households they returned to, and the jobs they hoped to resume. It shaped their understanding of their illness, the support they got from their families, their relationships with their doctors. It helped define their ability to change their lives and shaped their odds of getting better."

I saw a similar contrast between me and the women at the rural clinic. As a Duke student, I had health insurance. I didn't have to think about seeing the doctor or filling a prescription; everything was covered. For each clinic visit, I'd see Dr. Katz and enjoy the benefits of a stable doctor-patient relationship. Tina and Pearl had to go to a monthly free clinic where doctors rotated each month; this meant they had to "start over" with the hopes that the next doctor would be as caring and competent as the previous one. While Tina's initial blood pressure pill was cheap, Dr. Watson worried that her blood pressure was so high that she would likely need a second or even third medicine that could each cost in excess of $50 or more every month.

So while Tina, Pearl, and I were all black and hypertensive, the similarities ended there.

Given these glaring differences, it should come as no surprise that the poor and uninsured as a group have worse health outcomes and higher death rates than people with health insurance. A 2002 Institute of Medicine report noted that in one study over a seventeen-year period, adults who lacked health insurance at the outset of the study had a 25 percent greater chance of dying than did those who had private health insurance. A major 2001 study found that a lack of health insurance is associated with an increased risk of decline in health for adults over age fifty. Diagnoses are delayed, and chronic conditions are poorly managed. Both factors result in a dizzying array of medical complications on the way toward a premature death.

As with so many societal problems, blacks as a group suffer to the largest extent, being nearly twice as likely as white Americans to live without health insurance. And while obtaining health insurance alone does not fix the health problems of the poor, it makes a real difference. A 2007 study found that previously uninsured adults, in particular those with cardiovascular disease or diabetes, reported improved health over a seven-year follow-up period after obtaining Medicare coverage at age sixty-five.

Back in the late-1990s, Tina was one of approximately forty million uninsured Americans, a tally that climbed closer to fifty million over the ensuing decade. Though I'd heard snippets about the uninsured in college during the fight over the failed 1993 Clinton health plan, I had ignorantly allowed myself to assume that they lacked health coverage because they didn't work, and that they ultimately received medical care as part of our social welfare system. Because of my growing interest in the topic, I later learned that more than 70 percent of people who are uninsured are either working or, in the case of stay-at-home spouses, live under the same roof with a working person, and that having health coverage could be the deciding factor in whether a person sought health care, or if they could even receive services.

But I didn't know any of that when I met Tina. During the previous year of clinical rotations, we had a week or two devoted to an overview of the U.S. health care system. Although I vaguely recall some mention of how the United States lacked universal health coverage in comparison to Canada and Western Europe, the discussions seemed focused more on how managed care organizations potentially threatened our future autonomy and incomes. Or maybe the instructors had tried to teach us about the uninsured but I had simply tuned that part out, dwelling instead on topics related to my own self-interest. In the hospital setting, where most of our rotations took place, I rarely knew whether the patients had insurance or not; the ethos, at least in theory, was that people received the same level of medical care no matter their finances.

Nor did my family life offer any awareness about the uninsured. My parents and brother all had jobs that came with stable health plans. My grandmother also had employer health insurance, and Medicare by the time she developed serious health problems. Despite working-class roots, I was shielded from the trying experience that someone like Tina could face. How could someone play by the rules as she had—marry, have a family, have a job—and not be able to receive decent health care for a problem, such as fibroids, that was not of her own making? This was a problem that our country should have solved long ago.

When I came back to the free clinic once more that year—about three months later—I didn't see Tina. I had no way of knowing whether that was good news or bad news. Perhaps she had gotten her blood pressure under control and undergone successful surgery for her fibroids. Or maybe one of her problems had caused a heart attack, stroke, or a life-threatening hemorrhage. I could only hope that she had filled our prescription and was on the path to a healthier life.

Over the next several months, as I returned to the hospital wards and clinics, I saw two women very similar to Tina. They both lived in rural towns comparable to where I'd met Tina. Francine, an unusually tall woman in her late forties, visited a local clinic after several months of heavy vaginal bleeding. She was approaching menopause, and sensed that something was wrong, but she avoided seeing a doctor until she developed intense pelvic pain. Uninsured just like Tina, her initial concern was the cost of this medical visit, but Francine soon had far bigger worries: Doctors diagnosed her with widely metastatic uterine cancer.

Stephanie, a struggling, thirty-something, self-employed hairstylist, collapsed at work during a stressful day. She was initially taken to a local hospital and told she'd suffered a stroke. She was then transferred to Duke where she stayed for a week. The doctors did an extensive workup to determine a cause for her stroke; hypertension was the only identified risk factor. She'd had bad side effects from two older, cheaper blood pressure medications and, without health insurance, couldn't afford the newer one that worked well without problems. Thankfully, despite the severity of her initial symptoms, she made a full recovery.

For Stephanie, the silver lining of getting sick in such a drastic way was that it resulted in her getting insurance. She became eligible for Medicaid and could now afford doctor's appointments and the two new medications she'd been prescribed. In short time, her blood pressure came down dramatically. However, it is just as easy to imagine that Stephanie could have had a worse outcome, even a tragic one. Her stroke could have caused permanent paralysis, loss of speech, the inability to swallow, memory loss, or severe depression. It could have simply killed her. These doomsday scenarios, all too common, especially in black people, would have occurred in large part due to her being poor and uninsured.

In the end, while Stephanie ultimately got the care that she needed, this outcome spoke less to the quality of our system than it did to her own good fortune. Francine was not so lucky. Where Tina fell on this spectrum is something that I've wondered about ever since.

For all the billions of dollars in the health care industry, it seemed that there had to be better ways to promote community health. What could be done about all the people in rural North Carolina and beyond, the millions living outside the reach of health insurance and medical charity? Did the government—and wealthy institutions like Duke—have any responsibility to reach them? As a future black physician, did I have some special obligation?

4

Inner-City Blues

A s I sat alone flipping through a coffee-stained textbook in the hospital conference room, Dr. Collins, the resident doctor on duty, opened the chipped wooden door. "We've got a case of acute chest pain coming in," he said, excitedly.

I shared his energy. In my fourth and final year of medical school, chest pain was probably the one clinical problem that I understood best. As a second-year student, I received my highest evaluation on the general medicine rotation where cardiology was a core subject. During third-year, I'd gained additional knowledge working in a clinical research lab that studied heart disease. Earlier in my fourth year, I'd spent a month in the cardiac intensive care unit where I'd also done well. At the time, among the array of clinical specialties, cardiology seemed the logical choice for me.

After just a few days on my new emergency medicine rotation in Atlanta, however, the confidence I'd built at Duke had begun to fade. This place—the crowds, the filth, the despair—overwhelmed me. So the thought of evaluating chest pain felt welcome, like a chance to play on familiar turf.

"What's the story?" I asked Dr. Collins.

He told me that the patient was a fifty-year-old woman who'd developed chest pain while arguing with her son that morning. The electrocardiogram (EKG) obtained by paramedics at the scene showed some abnormalities, but not the classic findings of an acute heart attack that required immediate cardiac catheterization or clot-busting drugs.

I grabbed my temporary ID badge off the ink-stained table. It proclaimed that I was in Atlanta, but I might as well have been in a foreign land. The setting—Grady Memorial Hospital, an inner-city public hospital—bore little resemblance to what I'd grown accustomed to at Duke. Grady's emergency department (ED) took up about three times more space than Duke's ED, yet stepping inside it felt like being on a crowded elevator. Everywhere I looked I saw patients. Some were in the single and double-bed rooms I'd seen at Duke, but most were in the hallways. Gurneys were stacked along both sides of the hall like parked cars on a city street.

The patients on this day ranged in age from eighteen to eighty-six. All were black. Some were quite sick—a homeless man with AIDS wore a special blue mask to prevent him from sneezing and coughing particles possibly infected with tuberculosis. Others were there for mundane problems better handled elsewhere—a thirtyish woman with a sore throat, a forty-something man with a sinus infection. A few were downright scary—a heavily tattooed twenty-five-year-old in a bright prison uniform, handcuffed to a bed-rail with a corrections officer standing over him, receiving treatment for a hand infection he sustained after knocking out someone's front teeth.

Why was I in an inner-city emergency department? Why had I left the comfort of Duke?

The answer was simple and complicated: love. For the first two years of medical school, my social life consisted of the occasional awkward first date that rarely resulted in a second one. My fortunes changed during my third year, as I started dating Kerrie, a student in the class above mine. She was originally from Jamaica but had spent most of her childhood in Florida. I was smitten by her photogenic smile and radiant eyes as well as her soft-spoken, understated style—she didn't wear heels, makeup, or tight-fitting clothes. We'd chatted from time to time earlier in medical school, but our schedules and social lives didn't line up until her final year. One date turned into two. Soon, we saw each other every day. We had a lot in common; we enjoyed basketball, tennis, and watching TV medical dramas. More important, she shared my insecurities about being a black student at Duke from a working-class family. I was in love for the first time.

But our courtship hit a roadblock. She'd already signed on to begin her three-year internal medicine residency in Atlanta at Emory, the school where she'd also attended college. Just a few months into our relationship, she moved six hours away. Trapped by the brutal schedule of her internship, we decided I should sign up for a visiting clerkship in Atlanta. She'd completed an emergency medicine rotation at Grady/Emory the previous year and suggested I do the same. Since Duke did not have a training program in this field back then, it was an easy sell with the curriculum office. Persuading myself that I could actually do it was proving harder. Taking in my surroundings and the ways they differed from Duke, I wasn't sure I'd make it.

Dr. Collins and I entered the room as two paramedics transferred our patient from a gurney onto a hospital bed. Because of the urgency of chest pain and the need for cardiac monitoring, she had been placed in a single room. The man who had previously been there, and had recently awakened after an accidental overdose, was pushed out into the hallway alongside dozens of other patients. He was no longer sick enough to need a private room.

The paramedics summarized what they knew about our patient, Lucy. Her chest pain had come on abruptly, about two hours earlier, while she was arguing with her son because he'd gotten into some kind of trouble. She had high blood pressure and diabetes, but no record of heart disease. They'd given her the standard medications for someone with chest pain, which had eased but not fully relieved her distress.

Dr. Collins ran his fingers through his sandy-blond hair as he looked at the EKG, taken a few minutes earlier. The narrow peaks spiked in rapid succession. A few were followed by abnormal dips resembling the profile of someone with a double chin: Lucy's heart wasn't getting enough oxygen. Based on the data, Dr. Collins barked out orders to a nurse: blood tests to see if Lucy had had a heart attack; a drug to slow the heart rate and lower her blood pressure; another drug to thin out her blood. Lucy was going to need admission to the hospital.

He then turned from the medical facts to the patient. Lucy was fifty but looked sixty. Her hair was thin and graying. She weighed far too much; her arms were the size of legs and her legs as thick as old tree trunks. Her abdomen seemed as if it had been inflated under high pressure. Her body had put her heart under immense strain.

"Hello ma'am, I'm Dr. Collins."

"Lucy," she said, in a frail voice we strained to hear amidst the cacophony of beeping monitors and the background bustle of the emergency room. "I need to go home."

I recalled what I knew about mental stress and heart disease. Extreme emotional stress, such as in response to an earthquake, had been shown to increase rates of heart attacks in the immediate aftermath. During my previous year in the behavioral medicine clinic, I'd learned that less dramatic but nonetheless mentally stressful scenarios could trigger cardiac events too. I wondered what kind of trouble Lucy's son had gotten into. At this moment, however, it didn't matter.

"We're going to do everything we can to get you back home," Dr. Collins said. "But you're at high risk for having a heart attack, so you're definitely going to need to be admitted."

She tried to protest, perhaps having expected to stay only a few hours. But she was too weak and scared to fight. "Okay. I'll do what you say. Just help me, doc."

We'd been taught throughout medical school about the inherent power imbalance between helpless patient and learned physician. Our instructors implored us to respect this status and to use it responsibly—for good rather than simply for our own benefit. We were reminded what an honor and privilege it was to have someone rely on us in matters of life and death. Some doctors appeared to thrive under this pressure, but as Lucy transferred her fear into our hands, it seemed to me that this privilege could just as easily be an overwhelming burden.

Dr. Collins took his stethoscope from a pocket of his white coat to begin his physical exam just as a nurse started to draw blood. Before they could do either, Lucy's body went limp.

"Lucy!" Dr. Collins called out.

Her eyes did not open. He tapped her face and pinched her hand. No response. He put his fingers on her neck. No pulse. He put his ear to her chest. No breathing.

At that same instant, the cardiac monitor alarm activated. I felt my own heart pounding. On the screen, Lucy's heart rhythm was no longer merely fast. Instead, it showed a classic case of ventricular fibrillation, a life-threatening pattern that any fourth-year medical student could recognize. Her heart had stopped pumping blood to the rest of her body.

"Open the cart," Dr. Collins screamed. "It's a code."

Within seconds, the room filled with doctors and nurses. One doctor placed a rubber mask over Lucy's nose and mouth and squeezed a bag to force oxygen into her body. A nurse performed rhythmic chest compressions as if guided by a metronome: one, two, three. As they cycled back and forth, Dr. Collins prepared the defibrillator; its shock was our best chance to get Lucy's heart back in rhythm.

After several months rotating on general medicine and intensive care units, I'd witnessed enough of these codes to know that they rarely worked the way they did on TV medical dramas of the era like *ER* or *Chicago Hope*. Only once had I seen a patient survive such heroic efforts. As physician Danielle Ofri writes: "The majority of times we start a code, we know it's futile." But absent a do not resuscitate (DNR) order that we sometimes used with terminally ill patients, we were obligated to proceed.

"Everybody clear," Dr. Collins yelled, an order for everyone to step away from Lucy to avoid getting a jolt of electric current.

He charged the paddles. I held my breath. Lucy's limp body went through three sequentially higher-current shocks to no avail. After the three failed shocks, Dr. Collins directed the nurses to administer various drugs through Lucy's intravenous lines while basic CPR continued. Nothing worked. Finally, after what was probably twenty minutes, Dr. Collins announced: "Let's call it," he said, shaking his head. "Time of death, ten-thirty a.m."

The extra doctors and nurses left as quickly as they'd come, back to see other patients, leaving the primary nurses to clean up the pile of medical debris—syringes, test tubes, wrappers, and gauze pads—that every code leaves behind. These nurses moved quickly in their tasks, as did Dr. Collins in starting the death-related paperwork. How did they feel about what we'd just seen? There seemed to be no time for self-reflection. Before long, another person would need the room. The wheels of the ER could not stop for Lucy.

In death, Lucy had become part of a set of troubling racial data. Black women are more likely to die from heart disease than white women at all ages; this disparity is more prominent in women under sixty-five. In life too, Lucy had been a walking billboard for health disparities: hypertension and diabetes are far more common in blacks compared to whites, and black women are almost twice as likely as white women to be obese. Together, hypertension, diabetes, and obesity had surely conspired to cause the heart attack that Lucy suffered right before our eyes.

From what I'd seen there and elsewhere, she probably hadn't been getting the care she needed. Some of that was likely the health system's fault—impersonal, inefficient, inferior care. But much of it surely stemmed from Lucy's cultural surroundings—unhealthy diets, less exercise, and a lower likelihood of following medical advice. All too often, patients at Grady delayed treatment until forced to come to the emergency room. By then, it was often too late.

These public health facts and debates were far from my mind at that moment. Instead, I kept thinking about how her chest pain began during an argument with her son. This dispute had ultimately been the trigger, or tipping point, in her rapid descent from life to death. According to the paramedics, he had gotten into some serious trouble.

As I stood next to Dr. Collins while he completed a "death note" summarizing the medical events of that morning, the charge nurse approached us: "The family is in the waiting room," she said.

Dr. Collins looked over at me and back to the nurse. "Tell them we'll be right there."

A few minutes later, we stood face-to-face with Lucy's family. They met us in the main waiting area, where dozens of black people crammed their bodies onto rows of hard vinyl seats bolted to the floor. Pam, Lucy's older sister, took the lead. Her complexion was a shade lighter, but the resemblance between her and Lucy—broad nose and thinning hair—was evident. They shared a body type too: Pam's short frame carried 100 pounds more than needed. Behind her stood Lucy's daughter Wanda, a mid-twentyish, trimmer version of her mother and aunt. Missing was the son who had helped set off this chain of events. Wondering where he was seemed easier than thinking about what Dr. Collins had to say.

"How's she doin'?" Pam asked Dr. Collins after he had introduced us.

Her wide stare, sweaty brow, and shallow breaths revealed her panic. Dr. Collins paused as he measured his words: "Let's talk where we can have a little bit of privacy," he said. "Please follow me to the family conference room."

Pam and Wanda held hands. They knew this was bad news. I struggled to stay calm as we stepped toward the conference room, knowing that this family would soon be devastated.

Before we could close the door, Pam demanded to know about her sister: "Tell me how she is doing."

Dr. Collins glanced at his hands briefly. He then looked up to Pam and then to Wanda. Finally, he took a deep breath. I braced myself for their reaction. "I'm sorry to say that things did not go well . . ." he began.

"What do you mean?" Wanda asked, her eyes pleading. "She's still alive, right?"

"No . . . I'm afraid not," Dr. Collins said softly. "We did everything that we could, but she went into cardiac arrest and died about thirty minutes ago."

"Lord Jesus . . ." Pam moaned, her knees buckling slightly for an instant.

"This is . . . bullshit . . ." Wanda screamed. "What kind of damn hospital is this?"

By this time, I'd seen enough misery and death to know that anger and blame were natural reactions for many people. But Dr. Collins seemed unfazed.

"We're very sorry for your loss," he gently answered. "I can assure you that your mother received the best care possible." I silently agreed. Everything they'd done here was exactly how I'd seen it work in the state-of-the-art cardiac care unit at Duke. Sometimes medicine is simply powerless against the wickedness of disease.

"This is Tony's fault," Wanda said, rapidly shifting the target of her fury. "That dumb ass. Mama told him to stay out of trouble, and he couldn't keep his stupid ass straight."

We figured she was talking about Lucy's son. "Can you tell us what happened this morning?" Dr. Collins asked. "We heard that there was some kind of dispute?"

Pam's rapid breathing made me fear that she might soon need medical attention herself. Leaning against the wall for support, she managed to compose herself long enough to answer, "Tony . . . Tony's her son. He been in a lot of trouble. He was on probation. But almost done. He was at a party last night. Somebody got shot. They arrested him this morning. Lucy . . . Lucy's chest started hurtin' right after they took him away."

Pam broke down in spasms of tears and moans. Wanda reached over and hugged her. Dr. Collins and I looked at each other, helpless.

Though we were standing in an emergency room, and Lucy had died from a medical problem, its context was social. The stress of her son becoming a statistic, another black man locked up, had been too much.

Neither of us could relate. Dr. Collins later told me that he'd grown up in an all-white Connecticut suburb and attended private schools his entire life. The most heartache he'd ever caused his mom was marrying a Protestant girl (he was raised Catholic). Although my origins were grittier, I had always stayed out of trouble.

Dr. Collins answered Wanda's questions about her mother's care. He did his best to explain what had likely happened to her heart. By the time he finished, Pam had regained some of her composure. "Can we see her?" she asked softly.

"Certainly," he said.

We led them to the room where Lucy had been treated. Since the end of the code, the nurses had largely restored it to its prior appearance. At the center, Lucy's body was covered with a white blanket from the neck down.

We remained outside while they entered. As they approached, a nurse stepped aside. Pam immediately rushed to the head of the bed, while Wanda hesitated and stood back. As she ran her hand across Lucy's face, Pam leaned over the lifeless body. "Oh Lucy . . . my baby sis . . ." she cried out, sobbing.

Wanda's anger abruptly washed away: "Mama . . ." she wailed, as she fell to her knees.

I was intensely uncomfortable in the midst of their sorrow, as though I needed to step away and pretend that it never happened. This was the sort of situation our professors didn't—or perhaps simply couldn't—adequately cover in their textbooks or lectures. I looked over at Dr. Collins to gauge his reaction, but his poker face gave no clue to his emotions. As sister and daughter moaned in grief, we stepped away and headed to the main area in search of our next patient. There were other people waiting to be seen. We'd done all we could for Lucy, and it hadn't been enough. I hoped it would be different with the next patient.

The four-week emergency medicine rotation took me through day and evening shifts in a variety of settings—an academic hospital, a small community hospital, and a children's hospital. But I spent the majority of my time where I'd met Lucy and her family—at Grady Memorial Hospital, Atlanta's public hospital and primary trauma center.

Grady reflects the best and worst of American medicine. Founded in the early 1890s shortly after the death of its namesake Henry W. Grady, a prominent Atlanta journalist and businessman, Grady had a core mission to provide emergency care for the entire city. And it has done that over the years, sometimes to national acclaim. During the 1996 Summer Olympics, more than a hundred people injured in the Centennial Olympic Park bombing were treated at Grady. Less than a year before my arrival, a securities day trader in the city's up-scale Buckhead district went on a shooting spree and killed nine people in two buildings. Seven of the twelve surviving victims were taken to Grady. Not long after I passed through Grady, supermodel Niki Taylor sustained near-fatal injuries in a car accident, spending nearly two months there on her way to recovery. If you were shot, stabbed, or otherwise critically injured in or near Atlanta, Grady was the place where you wanted emergency treatment.

From its outset, Grady's other core mission has been to provide care for the poor. And here too it has received national attention, but not always the flattering kind. During the period of my medical and graduate training between 1996 and 2007, Grady was caught in the vortex of political and economic forces that caused hundreds of public hospitals in the United States to close: rising numbers of uninsured and Medicaid patients, stagnant or decreasing state and federal budgets, and increased competition from private hospitals for paying customers who subsidize charity care. Each year, Grady lost millions of dollars. By 2007, it owed more than $70 million to Emory and Morehouse, whose medical schools supply the hospital's doctors. Grady was on the brink of financial collapse. And while good doctors like Dr. Collins meant that individual patients, such as Lucy, received top-notch care at Grady, problems were evident. Major publications featured stories about the hospital's impending demise, the kind that had befallen D.C. General Hospital in 2001 and Los Angeles's Martin Luther King Jr./Drew Medical Center in 2007.

But at Grady, the patients kept coming. Throughout the early 2000s, the emergency room averaged about three hundred visits per day. More than half of those patients had no insurance; an additional third were on Medicaid. Almost all the patients were black. Despite its shortcomings, Grady remained the best hope for people in dire financial straits.

Even more important to its survival, Grady remained the destination of choice for those with life-threatening wounds, and the Atlanta area had no shortage of such cases. During this same time period, between 3,000 and 3,500 trauma victims were admitted to Grady each year. About two-thirds of them suffered from blunt trauma—usually a car accident—while the remaining third came in with gunshot or stabbing injuries.

I saw one such victim, Sean, midway through my rotation. I'd been assigned second shift in the trauma wing. At first, things were so slow that Dr. Mason, the faculty supervisor, and Dr. Stephens, the third-year emergency medicine resident, spent several minutes talking about the current NBA season. Gradually, the conversation shifted to medicine. They asked me about my career goals. I told them that I was leaning toward cardiology but was planning to stay in school a bit longer to study health policy or public health. Seeing how difficult Kerrie's medical internship had been—thirty-six-hour shifts were common—gave me pause about jumping headfirst into that life. I wanted to have a satisfying career without torturing myself.

"Sounds like you're in the right place," Dr. Mason said. "Get a degree in public health. Emergency medicine is a good fit with that. Especially for people like us and our community."

"People like us"—I'd last heard that expression four years earlier, when I stood in a similar position, back then applying to medical school. On both occasions, the focus rested more on my identity as a fellow black person than as a future medical colleague.

Dr. Stephens agreed with his boss. "I thought about doing radiology or dermatology, you know, the specialties that pay a lot without you having to work too hard. But those were kinda boring. And they're removed from the day-to-day life of black folks. I wanted to get my hands dirty while being in a position to try and make a difference for my community."

At Grady, unlike at Duke, I regularly worked with black doctors. I estimated that about 20 percent of the doctors were black; whereas at Duke, the number was less than 10 percent. Part of the discrepancy was the emergency room setting, which likely drew black doctors for the reasons Dr. Mason and Dr. Stephens stated. Morehouse, a predominately black medical school, also sent its doctors to Grady. Moreover, Atlanta's reputation as a mecca for well-to-do blacks also added to the hospital's appeal to black doctors. Dr. Mason, from Queens, New York, and Dr. Stephens, from Chicago, trumpeted the philosophy often used to justify affirmative action in medical school: black doctors were more likely to practice in areas that served black patients.

Our conversation about race and medicine was abruptly halted as a nurse approached us: "Got a GSW on the way," she said.

Despite enjoying crime and medical shows, I didn't recognize the abbreviation at first—GSW was short for gunshot wound—because I hadn't seen any cases at Duke.

"How old?" Dr. Stephens asked.

"Eighteen," the nurse replied. "He took at least one to the abdomen."

Dr. Mason shook his head. We rushed to the trauma bay, where nurses and a respiratory therapist checked various equipment and supplies in preparation for the patient's arrival. About five minutes later, the paramedics wheeled Sean into our area. He was awake, but barely, his eyes flickering open and shut. He'd likely gone into the early stages of shock.

Dr. Stephens, two paramedics, and a male nurse carefully but quickly moved him from the gurney onto the trauma bed as Dr. Mason supervised their actions. We were soon joined by a trauma surgeon. With three doctors on hand and at least that many nurses, I stood toward the rear as they rapidly assessed Sean from head to toe. Dr. Stephens used industrial-strength scissors to cut through Sean's bloodstained Air Jordan sweatshirt and Nike sweatpants. A nurse hooked him up to a cardiac monitor, inserted a second IV line, and drew blood. Dr. Stephens then inserted a large caliber IV into the femoral vein in Sean's groin area that allowed rapid replenishment of blood and other bodily fluids. Dr. Mason shouted orders for medications and X-rays.

"What happened?" the trauma surgeon asked.

A fight had broken out on a basketball court in one of the worst neighborhoods in the city. Somebody came back with a gun and started shooting.

On the X-ray it looked as if one bullet had punctured the inner depths of his abdominal cavity while the other hadn't. The doctors wouldn't know for sure until they opened him up, so Sean was rushed to an operating room. I followed Dr. Mason and Dr. Stephens into the physician work area as they began the paperwork.

"Is he going to make it?" I asked.

"Fifty-fifty," Dr. Mason said. "It's a damn waste. He should be thinking about college."

But we all knew the painful reality. For black male teens, homicide is the leading cause of death; for all other teenage groups, accidents (primarily motor vehicle) are the biggest killer. We didn't know for certain the race of Sean's shooter, but more than 90 percent of the time, young black homicide victims are killed by another black person. Sean's shooter, if caught, would be headed to prison. There, blacks make up more than 40 percent of inmates, compared to just 13 percent of the national population. In the span of only a few weeks, I'd seen violence disrupt the lives of Sean and the family of Lucy's son Tony. College—which had placed me, Dr. Stephens, and Dr. Mason on the path to success—appeared beyond their reach. We had succeeded while so many of our brothers had been left behind.

It was a familiar story. In my neighborhood, two boys, both just a few houses away from where I lived, wound up doing serious time for drug-related crimes. I'd also had relatives on both sides of the family find their way to prison. Sampson Davis, an emergency room doctor raised in Newark, talks often about his narrow escape from a life of crime. In his memoir *Living and Dying in Brick City*, Davis returns to Newark after medical school only to discover that one of his childhood buddies had died, at the hospital where Davis was working, from gunshot wounds: "Why? Why me? Why had I survived? Why had I made it out?" he guiltily wondered.

Many black men face this dilemma, both in public and in private. Wes Moore, a Rhodes Scholar and White House Fellow, explores this subject in depth in his memoir of the divergent path his life took compared to a young man from his community who shared his name. Physicians Ben Carson and Otis Brawley, in their respective books, recount their own escapes from the poverty of Detroit to prestigious colleges and successful careers. The common thread for each was a belief that education would transport them beyond their surroundings. Dr. Davis summarizes this recurring theme as he writes of his return to Newark as a doctor: "I would see lives that might have been saved if the industrious young men landing in my emergency room full of bullet holes had learned and believed that education offered a better alternative."

Before Atlanta, I'd typically been the only black person on the medical team as we stood witness to the disparities that afflicted black people. I never knew for certain how white and Asian doctors felt about some of the black patients that we saw, the ones who abused illegal drugs, were more prone to early pregnancies and sexually transmitted disease, the ones who were perpetrators and victims of senseless violence. Did they secretly think, as Sampson Davis feared: "What's wrong with those people?" Or were we projecting our own insecurities onto them?

For that matter, I wasn't sure how black doctors really felt either. In the company of white doctors, whenever the topic veered toward race, a handful of black students and doctors were inclined to speak up and point to the legacy of slavery and Jim Crow as the cause of what they saw with black patients. Others, myself included, usually kept silent, figuring little good could come from fanning racial flames. But here at Grady, in segregated company, we could let down our guard.

"You know at some point, we've got to stop blaming white folks for all of our problems," Dr. Mason said. "We're our own worst enemy."

"You're right," Dr. Stephens replied. "A lot of us could be making much better choices."

"Don't get me wrong," Dr. Mason said as he looked at me. "I'm not a right-winger. Pulling the rug out from under our community isn't the answer either."

They went back and forth for a while. They believed, as I did, that while government efforts to help poor black people sometimes failed, the obligation to keep trying remained. Local governments, in concert with nonprofit groups and the private sector, had to work smarter, they said, to reach them, to help them make better decisions. But what did that mean in the realm of health care? And was this social responsibility part of our role as doctors?

I found out a few days later that Sean had survived. He suffered no major complications. If his post-operative course went smoothly, he had a good chance for a full recovery. This spoke to the excellent trauma care he'd received, the kind that the Atlanta area had relied on Grady to provide for decades. Ultimately, the value of Grady was such that it was deemed too important to fail. In November 2007, after much contention, the hospital's leadership was transferred from a politically appointed board to a nonprofit corporation that, within a few years, steered the hospital from the verge of financial ruin to solvency. Grady, top-notch trauma center and massive safety-net hospital, was here to stay.

Yet as vital as Grady was to the Atlanta area, it felt as if we at the hospital were only scratching the surface of larger health issues. Sean's second chance would not have been possible had the bullets traveled a slightly different trajectory. What could be done to reduce the chances of more young black men becoming GSW statistics? What was happening outside Grady's walls to cause the carnage we saw inside it every day? As my month in Atlanta drew to a close, I got a firsthand look at the surrounding world that fed its patients to Grady.

During my final week, I spent one day experiencing the life of a paramedic. This was required of all students on the rotation to expose us to the first step in emergency care. I began the day irritated that this exercise would replace an ER shift. The smell and feel of the ER had grown on me and my clinical skills had rapidly improved: I had stitched lacerations, drawn arterial blood tests, and assisted on lumbar punctures. What could I learn from paramedics that a doctor couldn't teach better?

My two paramedic guides—one white, one black, reminiscent of many buddy cop shows and movies—were unaware of my condescending attitude and eagerly greeted me outside the main Grady Hospital emergency room. Both were in their forties and a little soft and wide around the mid-section. They wore their usual work garb—dark slacks and shoes and a short-sleeve shirt with a sewn-on patch indicating their official title.

"I know where we have to go first this morning," Ron, the black paramedic said, with a gap-toothed smile.

"This should be fun," replied his partner, Kurt. "Let's do it."

I had no idea what they had planned at my expense. I crouched into a seat behind Ron, who took the wheel. It was my first time inside an ambulance. On the surface, it wasn't very impressive: it rode like the van my high school basketball coach had driven me to practice in every day. Behind me, however, I saw the tools of medicine: a defibrillator, several bags of intravenous fluid, a folded gurney. What must it be like, I wondered, to lie back there, semi-conscious, bleeding, in intense pain, with strangers hovering over you, rushing to a hospital with sirens and flashing lights, not knowing if you were going to survive? Would you worry about family? Friends? Your accomplishments and failures? Or whether you'd had enough faith?

We parked at a local fire station where Ron and Kurt gave me a brief tour of the facility. They explained how they often worked together with firefighters as first responders. Ron stepped into a small office and emerged with a well-worn basketball in his hands.

"Let's see what you got," he said, motioning to the basketball hoop in the parking lot.

Ron suggested that we play 21, the popular playground game I'd grown up with, but Kurt reminded him that the last time they'd done that, Ron had injured his back and missed a week of work. So instead, we settled for a few games of the much less strenuous H-O-R-S-E.

Afterward, we stopped for doughnuts and coffee, surely negating any benefit from our twenty minutes of light exercise. As they traded sarcastic stories about their work and families, I felt as if I'd been transported onto the set of the popular TV show *Law & Order* with Detectives Briscoe and Green. My initial reservations were fading; I was having fun.

Just as we finished eating, we received our first call of the day: "Old guy with chest pain," said the dispatcher on the other end. "He's fully conscious."

"We're on it," Ron said, as he turned to me. "Bread and butter."

We trotted back to the ambulance, where Ron pushed an orange button that generated the siren and its accompanying flashing lights.

I felt a rush of anticipation. Many times, I'd been in my car and pan-icked at the sound of an approaching ambulance, desperately trying to decode in which direction the siren was heading. As it finally whisked past, I'd nudge myself toward the steering wheel and grip it with both hands, trying to insulate myself against its deafening blare. Now, from inside the ambulance, I saw this same reaction in other drivers. The world looked different from here, as if the other cars were operating in slow motion, our flashing and beeping put-ting them in a state of confusion.

Our drive took us through a run-down area of check-cashing joints, liquor stores, and fast-food stops. Steel bars covered the win-dows to deter would-be burglars. About a half-dozen black men be-tween twenty and forty years old congregated in a pothole-infested parking lot. They smoked cigarettes while laughing and talking. The scene reminded me of childhood trips with my mom through New York Avenue on the way to my grandmother's apartment in Northeast Washington.

This commercial strip gave way to an area of old houses, the kind that were probably once part of a nice community but had fallen into disrepair as the surrounding neighborhood declined. After park-ing outside the address the dispatcher gave us, we hurriedly unloaded our supplies—a gurney and two large bags of tools—and jogged up the narrow driveway. An elderly black woman wearing a white bathrobe opened the front door. Her hand trembled as she pointed to a room inside the home. "He's in the kitchen."

"Are you his wife?" Kurt asked.

She nodded. "Is there anyone else who lives here with you?" he asked.

She shook her head. "When did all this start?" he asked.

"About a half-hour ago," she said. "I was making breakfast."

"How old is he?"

"Seventy-two."

"Does he have heart or lung problems?"

"No."

"Does he take any medications?"

"They're on the kitchen table. I gave him an aspirin when his chest started hurting."

In thirty seconds, he'd gotten the information it often took me at least a few minutes, sometimes longer, to obtain. We found our patient in the kitchen, his torso folded over in pain, forearms criss-crossed as they rested against the wooden table for support. Dressed in a checkered robe, plaid pajamas, and black slippers, he looked as if he'd been sitting down with the newspaper over a cup of coffee. Chest pain had intruded on his morning routine.

Kurt asked the man a few questions while measuring his vital signs and placing rubber tubing in his nostrils that hooked up to an oxygen tank. Ron reviewed his medications. We carried him to the living room where we put him down on the family couch. His EKG was normal so they gave him a nitroglycerin tablet to ease his pain and got him ready for transport to the emergency room. I asked if we were taking him to Grady.

Ron shook his head. "He has Medicare since he's over sixty-five. Most hospitals happily take it. We'll go somewhere closer. If he was one of the young jokers we passed on the way over here, he'd have to go to Grady."

Emergency departments are obligated by law to evaluate those who show up at their doors. But that doesn't stop them from screening out people before they arrive. According to Arthur Kellerman, former chair of Emory University's Department of Emergency Medicine (during which time he also worked as an attending physician at Grady Hospital), some hospitals will operate under case-by-case or selective diversion, where they can limit or weed out certain patients by diverting ambulances elsewhere. Kellerman speculated that it is a way for the hospital to conduct a "wallet biopsy"—accepting paying patients while rejecting nonpaying ones. Medicare, although not as desirable as private insurance, pays doctors and hospitals better than Medicaid, and certainly more than the hospital gets from uninsured people, many of whom pay little or nothing at all.

These uninsured patients invariably wound up at Grady, and many of them were the ones who filled its waiting room beyond capacity.

Once we got to the private hospital, we handed our Medicare-insured patient off to a charge nurse and physician. Kurt delivered a bullet-point summary that gave all the relevant information in less than thirty seconds, a stark contrast to the several-minute variety often expected of medical students. Their competence and efficiency impressed me. I had underestimated their medical knowledge and the extent of their responsibilities.

Just minutes after leaving the local hospital, we received a call about an alcoholic man who reported being suicidal. Ron made a U-turn and took a winding city road into another gritty area. There we drove past a dingy rent-by-the-hour motel from which a young black woman in high heels, a short skirt, and bright lipstick emerged. A few miles later, we found our patient on the sidewalk next to a food joint. With his leathery skin and lined face covered with gray stubble, he looked the part of someone who spent his days submerged in alcohol. The restaurant manager had called 911 after the man vomited while standing in line. Evidently, he was a frequent-flyer to the paramedic team, as Ron called him by name.

"Are you ready to get your act together, Gordon?" Ron asked.

"Yessir," Gordon said, his hands shaking.

Ron looked over at Kurt, who shook his head. "No reason to bullshit me. We're going to take you to the hospital either way. But you're wasting your time and everyone else's if you're just going to be right back here in a few days."

"No," Gordon protested. "I'm ready. I can't keep goin' on like this."

"Let's hope you mean it this time."

Kurt handled the medical side, checking Gordon's blood sugar and setting up an intravenous line for fluids, while Ron completed the paperwork.

"That might have seemed harsh," Ron said, "but hand-holding doesn't work for addicts. I've been there. Got fifteen years clean time. I never got quite this bad, but I was pretty close."

The contrast between Ron and Gordon at that moment made it nearly impossible to imagine one in the other's shoes: alcohol and drugs stripped away people's dignity in a way that few other things could. We dropped Gordon off at Grady, as he had nowhere else to go. He'd been there many times before, Ron and Kurt said. Usually he'd demand to be discharged after drying out so he could go back out and get drunk.

The pace slowed for most of the early afternoon, enough that we went back to the fire station and played more basketball until Ron started breathing too heavily. We traveled to a few other calls where we were secondary backup, but the injuries were so minor that our help wasn't needed. Finally, a little more than an hour before our shift ended, the dispatcher called us. "Domestic assault," she said. "Knife-related injuries."

"We're on our way," Ron said, as he fired up the siren again.

"This should be fun," Kurt said, when he heard the dispatcher announce the location.

We merged onto the highway, which by midafternoon was already starting to be jammed with Atlanta's notorious traffic. With little room to navigate, Ron took to driving on the bumpy shoulder. About ten minutes later, we exited into a wooded area that, at first glance, looked as if we'd left the city limits and entered into the semi-rural suburbs. For a split second, I allowed myself to imagine we were headed toward a mansion or gated community. But based on the day thus far, I sensed otherwise. As the towering trees parted, our destination came into view.

"Ah," Ron said. "Ain't nothing quite like the projects."

I'd seen my share of harsh housing projects growing up in the Washington, D.C., area and in college in and around Baltimore, but I'd always viewed them from inside a moving car at a distance. Through the lens of my childhood, "ghettos" were the areas my parents and neighbors had moved from in search of something better in the suburbs. "Projects," on the other hand, were something altogether worse; they were the places that led to D.C. being dubbed the country's murder capital in the late 1980s and early 1990s, and later made Baltimore the centerpiece for the critically acclaimed TV crime drama *The Wire.*

We parked about fifty feet away from a rusted metal trash bin surrounded by broken bottles, cigarette butts, and fast-food bags. Nearby, two young boys, probably no more than ten or eleven, threw an old football back and forth, seemingly oblivious to the hazards around them. The complex housed a half-dozen or so dingy, two-story brick buildings, each about the width of a basketball court. They were set on a hilly two or three acres of what was once a completely wooded area, giving the impression that the developers were trying to isolate its occupants like prisoners or psychiatric patients. The building design only added to this feeling, with its dark metal doors and wire-mesh windows, the kind I'd seen on locked wards to keep patients from escaping or leaping to their deaths. Weeds and bare dirt filled what should have been grassy areas. I doubted that a grounds crew ever made it out here.

Nearly twenty years after its popular release, this scene brought the lyrics from Grandmaster Flash's seminal 1982 rap hit "The Message" into my head.

Broken glass everywhere
People pissing on the stairs, you know they just don't care

A skinny, unkempt, wrinkled-looking man stood in a dirt patch, staring at us. My mind flooded with a sequence of negative assumptions: he was either an alcoholic or drug abuser; he had schizophrenia or some other mental illness; he had HIV, Hepatitis C, or syphilis. Was it my medical training that caused me to see him as a list of potential health problems rather than as an individual? Or was it the many ways in which I'd been indoctrinated by both white and black people, throughout my life, to see poor blacks as inferior and susceptible to so many problems? My reaction troubled me. What good came from thinking this way?

"You should probably stay here," Ron said. "Make sure nobody runs off with this thing. Just don't look scared and they'll leave you alone. Be sure to keep the doors locked just in case."

I wasn't sure if they were trying to protect me or their property.

"I'd take off the white coat," Kurt said. "And your necktie. Don't want them thinking you're a rich doctor or anything."

In other circumstances, the comment might have made me laugh. The white coat had been given to me by the school, and I'd purchased the necktie on sale for less than ten bucks. I only had fifteen or twenty dollars in my pocket. I didn't even own a credit card or cell phone.

"I thought this was an assault," I said, as I looked around. "Shouldn't the police be here?"

"Sometimes we're the first on the scene," Ron said. "This sounds like a fairly minor domestic incident. That's pretty low priority for them. They've got bigger fish to fry."

As they locked the ambulance doors behind them and headed toward the unit to assess our patient, I fought the urge to follow them. My reaction surprised me. It wasn't as if I was afraid of black people. My childhood neighborhood, for as far as I could travel on foot, was so thoroughly black that it might as well have been legally segregated. And that enclave was certainly not immune to some of the problems of urban life.

In Durham too I'd had contact with poverty and crime. While Duke paid for my tuition, I was on my own with room and board. In an effort to keep down the size of my future loans, during my first year I'd settled into a low-rent apartment complex with a class-mate. Although the area surrounding our ground-floor apartment was poorly lighted, I never felt physically threatened, day or night, not even after our unit was burglarized while we were at school taking our exams. My roommate and I both figured that the perpe-trators had pegged us for uppity Duke students and learned our daily routine so they could break in while we were away. They were probably furious to discover how little we owned.

But that brush with crime involved personal property, not threats to physical safety. In this secluded housing project, in contrast, I could almost feel the ghosts of past violent crimes. Along with Washington, D.C., Atlanta had one of the highest crime and murder rates in America during the 1980s and 1990s. As I took in my surroundings, I couldn't imagine a more likely place for bad things to occur. Just as I'd been unaware of the full extent of the paramedics' medical acumen, I'd also managed not to understand how dangerous their jobs could be, entering into the same situations and neighborhoods as cops, only without a weapon or bulletproof vest.

As darkness began to fall, I steadied myself by watching the two boys who were playing football. The image made me think about my childhood, playing basketball for hours at a time in my backyard or at the nearby playground, imagining myself as Dr. J, Magic Johnson, or Michael Jordan. While modest, my surroundings were, for the most part, clean and safe. The young boys here had to sidestep shattered glass and feasting rodents while acting out their athletic fantasies.

Eventually, Ron and Kurt emerged from the apartment building. A young woman walked between them like a criminal suspect being escorted by cops. She wore a ragged sweatshirt and paint-stained jeans, her natural hairstyle shorter on the sides than on top. With a gloved hand, Kurt applied a gauze pad to the left side of her neck. He walked back to the rear of the ambulance while Ron entered on the driver's side.

"More crazy shit," Ron said to me, as he took off his gloves and shoved them into a red biohazard bag. "She got stabbed with a dirty needle by some other crazy chick down the hall. Both of them are probably junkies. Fightin' over some punk-ass dude."

As we drove away, taking the woman to Grady, the two young boys continued to throw the football back and forth, now under the glow of a dimly lit streetlight. I wondered if someone—a parent or older sibling—had an eye on them to make sure they stayed safe. I tried to imagine my ten-year-old self in their shoes. How might my life have turned out differently had I grown up there, with a mother like the one we were hauling off to Grady?

On the way to the hospital, the people and the problems I'd seen that month flashed through my mind: Lucy's poor health and premature death triggered in part by her son's latest legal problems; Sean battling life-threatening gunshot wounds rather than college-prep classes; and all the other patients whose array of health problems had as much, if not more, to do with socioeconomic factors than with the medical conditions that I'd learned about in textbooks.

Graduation was just a few months away. I'd entered medical school focused on my own academic accomplishment and other selfish rewards of life as a future physician. But four years of medical school, where I'd witnessed the health problems of black patients and experienced my own, had changed my perspective. I wanted to find some way to help make life better for the Leslie's, Tina's, Lucy's, and Sean's of the world. Only I wasn't sure where to begin.

PART II

Barriers

5

Confronting Hate

On a humid Tuesday morning, Chester arrived at a busy Durham emergency room. While the other patients around him made the usual requests for pain medications, diagnostic tests, and reassurance that they were not about to die, Chester gave an entirely different kind of demand.

"I don't want no nigger doctor," he said to a nurse on duty.

I was about a month into my yearlong medical internship, the time when aspiring physicians make the abrupt, brutal transition from knowledge-seeking medical student to first responder at the scene of a three a.m. cardiac arrest. I was struggling with this adjustment along with the rest of my colleagues, my mind focused on the objective analysis of lab tests, EKGs, and chest X-rays—medical tasks that had nothing to do with race. But Chester's words had unceremoniously shoved me out of 2003, and back into a world that felt more like 1963.

I'd continued on at Duke for my internship, having grown comfortable with the medical center and North Carolina. The day before meeting Chester, I had arrived an hour prior to the start of my initial shift on the general medicine service, determined to make a good first impression. At the hospital, alone in the physician workroom, I used the down time to review the charts of the patients whom I had inherited from the previous intern.

By this stage of my training, I had developed a familiarity with the chart notations and abbreviations that had once looked like inscriptions from ancient times. As I skimmed through their medical records, I understood the basics of my patients' medical problems. But it turned out that this working knowledge and my early arrival offered no preparation for the onslaught that ensued the minute my shift started.

At exactly eight a.m., my pager chirped with a numerical message. I dialed the four-digit extension. "Hello, this is D . . . Dr. Tw . . . Tweedy."

"Are you sure?" the nurse asked.

My delivery still needed work. "Yes," I answered.

"Are you the Green-Two Intern?"

My name was irrelevant. It had been replaced by a seven-digit pager ID and color-number scheme. I knew I had been assigned to the Green medical group but could not remember the team number. I looked at the top of the printout on my clipboard, which contained all of our patient and team information. Yes, I was the Green-Two Intern.

"Mr. Jones and Mr. Patrick both need something for pain," the nurse told me.

My mind went blank: Who were these people?

I scanned the printout again. One person had been admitted for pneumonia, the other for antibiotic treatment of a diabetic leg ulcer. Audrey, the second-year resident who would be my supervisor for the month, was on the phone with another doctor. I had spent my initial few weeks of internship on a specialty consult service, where, given the complexity of the patients, a senior physician made all the decisions while I stood back in the role of glorified medical student.

But they held much higher expectations for us on the general medicine unit. These were "our" patients, and something as basic as ordering pain medicine fell within our responsibilities. With Audrey occupied, I faced my first solo decision as a doctor. And I whiffed.

"What do you think I should give them?" I asked the nurse.

As soon as the words left my mouth, I wanted to pull them back. The nurse laughed. "You're the doctor," she said.

My mind raced. For my own pain, I might take acetaminophen (Tylenol) or ibuprofen (Motrin), or Oxycodone if things got really bad, such as after my knee surgery. But these patients had more complicated issues. Both had histories of alcohol and drug abuse. One had liver failure, the other bleeding ulcers. Because of these problems, I knew my options were limited—but suddenly I couldn't quite remember which drugs were a bad fit for which condition.

I frantically scanned their medical records again as I tried to recall the dosage frequencies for common analgesics. After agonizing a bit more, I settled on an appropriate drug for each: Tylenol for the one with bleeding ulcers, Motrin for the one with liver disease. For a few seconds, I felt a measure of pride; I had done the work of a real doctor. By the time I'd written the orders, however, three other numerical pages had come through. Each call required me to do something I had never done before; evaluate and treat a high potassium level (which can damage the heart), prescribe an insulin regimen for a new diabetic, and interpret the results of a urine test and prescribe the proper antibiotic. Over the next few hours, I scrambled to stay afloat. The system was treating me like a doctor, only I didn't feel like one at all.

I called Kerrie on the drive home at the end of that first day. We'd gotten engaged a few months earlier. She was working extra evening and night shifts at a local hospital to finance our wedding. I told her how stressed I felt. "Hang in there," she said. "It's only going to get worse."

She was right. The next day brought the start of my first thirty-hour shift. By the late morning, I was slowly feeling a little more comfortable with my new job, as I started to get to know our patients. But as my anxiety began to settle, Audrey, the second-year resident, burst into our workroom, her 100-pound frame opening the door with enough force to scatter papers across the floor. I flinched.

"We've got an admission," she said.

"What's the name?" I asked, prepared to write this information on my clipboard.

She frowned. "I forgot already," she said, shaking her head in disgust. "Anyway, he's a seventy-something white guy with shortness of breath, fever, a white blood cell count of twenty [thousand], a creatinine of 2.5, and an oxygen saturation of eighty percent on room air."

Interns were not the only people reduced to colors and numbers. From her description, I knew that our patient was showing signs of infection as well as injury to his kidneys. Along with Gabe, the medical student on our team, we took the stairs down to the emergency department.

"We're from Green-Two," Audrey told the ED doctor on duty. "Which one is ours?"

"Over there," he said, pointing to the room closest to the nursing station. "Good luck."

I looked at the chalkboard and saw Chester's name. Just as we were about to meet him, a middle-aged ED nurse approached me. "Watch out for that one over there," she said in a thick Caribbean accent.

"What's wrong?" I asked.

I expected her to say the patient was agitated, confused, or some combination of the two. Instead, she leaned toward me and lowered her voice. "He asked a white nurse why there are 'so many niggers' working here and said he did not want any 'nigger doctors' taking care of him."

"What?" I asked in disbelief, barely able to get out this single word. "He said that?"

"Verbatim," the nurse said. "We ought to kick his ass out on the street."

I glanced over at my colleagues, both of whom looked horrified. Although we were still relative strangers, I had spoken with them long enough to form first impressions. Gabe was a nature-loving type from California who had gone to college at UC-Berkley. Audrey was Jewish and very interested in women's health issues. Both seemed to have progressive sensibilities, and they bristled at Chester's language.

Audrey stared at me, wounded. It took a few seconds for her to regain her composure. "Don't worry," she said. "You don't have to go in."

"I'll be fine," I said, forcing myself to breathe slowly. The idea of caring for a sick person was daunting enough without this other element. "But maybe you should do the talking."

With Audrey leading the way, we approached Chester's bedside. He looked the part of a hospital patient, dressed in a gown, his body connected through plastic tubing to an oxygen tank, a liter of IV fluid, and a bag to collect his urine. His abdomen protruded as if carrying a full-term child, a sign of liver disease or perhaps simply a lifetime of bad eating. A scraggly beard covered much of his ashen face. He smelled as if he had gone days, maybe weeks, without a bath.

After Audrey made introductions, Chester grimaced and strained to lift his head off the pillow. His voice was feeble and raspy. "Where's my real doctor?" he asked.

It is not uncommon for patients to question the skills of interns and residents and ask to see their supervisor. But because of the nurse's advance word, his request took on a sinister tone.

"We are your doctors," Audrey fired back. "And I am the one in charge."

Chester looked past her, his eyes settling on me for an instant, his face a nasty scowl, before they rested on Gabe. "I only wanna deal with you."

Gabe was just two years out of college, and with his deer-in-the-headlight gaze, looked as if he still belonged there. No patient could possibly mistake him for being our leader. Evidently, Chester didn't just hate "nigger doctors," but female doctors too.

Audrey clenched her right hand so hard that she snapped the hook on her ink pen in half. "I'm in charge," she asserted again, "so you can either answer my questions now or we can find you another doctor, which could take hours."

Chester looked around in silence as if weighing his options. Finally, his discomfort trumped his prejudice. "What do you wanna know, lady?"

Audrey gripped the pen tighter. "How long have you been having trouble breathing?" she asked.

"I . . . I don't know."

Audrey waited for him to say more. When he did not, she looked at me and sighed before turning back to him. "Did it start today? Yesterday? Last week?"

"Longer," he replied. "Maybe a few months. But it's gettin' worse."

Along with a lung problem, shortness of breath is a classic symptom of heart disease. She asked him about chest pain: "Yeah," he said.

She tried to get a sense of where in the chest the pain was, whether it was constant, and when he had first noticed it. But Chester couldn't offer any useful answers. Nor was he able to tell us about any previous or current medical problems. Since this was his first admission to our hospital, we had no prior records. It appeared that he had gone years without seeing a doctor, and was, as I would discover was the case with many people, seemingly detached from his own body.

Audrey continued to question him until, like a witness on a painful cross-examination, Chester put his hands over his face: "I feel bad all over. Can't ya'll just fix me?"

We gave up on the interview. We took turns doing a physical exam: tapping, poking, and prodding his fragile exterior and listening for problems that could be heard but not seen. His EKG and early blood tests didn't suggest a heart attack, so our attention focused elsewhere. His lungs sounded as if they were badly congested. With his fever and cloudy chest X-ray, pneumonia was the most likely diagnosis.

"What an ignorant asshole," Audrey said, as we left the ED and headed upstairs.

"You handled him pretty well," I said.

"You too," she replied. "I'm really sorry about what he told the nurse."

The last thing I wanted was for her to feel sorry for me or think of me as some kind of racial victim. "It's okay," I said. "He didn't seem to like you that much better."

We shared a quick laugh. I spent the next hour or so entering Chester's treatment orders and writing his admission note in the chart while answering nursing pages about my other patients. A second new patient arrived shortly afterward, this one healthier and able to give us a coherent story that made our work easier. And he seemed to have no problems with me or Audrey. A few minutes after I had finished his paperwork and was set to take a short break, a fellow intern entered the workroom.

"I need to sign my patients over to you," he said.

I looked at my watch. It was shortly after five p.m. "Okay," I said, feigning calm.

This was standard practice. Someone had to be responsible for the patients on the teams who were off duty, otherwise each intern would be on call every night. He showed me his list of patients, which contained their names, diagnoses, medications, and active issues. One person needed his blood drawn at nine p.m. to measure how well his blood thinner was working. Another needed blood culture samples taken to rule-out an infection if she developed a fever. A third was getting an emergency head CT scan after falling in his bathroom, so I needed to review the results with the on-call radiologist. Over the next forty-five minutes, two other interns tracked me down with their lists. One had five patients, the other ten. More blood draws and blood cultures and images to review with the radiologist. My head started to throb.

By the time all the interns had checked out their patients, it was nearly six p.m. My appetite was shot, but I rushed to the cafeteria and forced down a greasy hospital-issued steak that was my last opportunity for any food for several hours. As I returned to the ward, my stomach rumbled in much the same way it had before a basketball game or important interview. This time, though, the stakes were much higher. I was responsible for more than thirty patients, many seriously sick. One of them could easily die from something I did or failed to do. Doctors aren't alone in facing life-and-death scenarios on the job, but I couldn't imagine an inexperienced pilot being left to fly a commercial jet solo.

Fortunately, no one died or came close to it on my first night. In fact, nothing occurred that was beyond my level of training. But that didn't mean things were easy. The workload was steady as I admitted three more people while covering the other teams' patients. Between trips to the emergency department, the radiology suite, and back to the medical ward, I must have logged five miles on foot while trying to stay alert on a sleepy brain. In the end, I didn't sleep at all. I might have had twenty minutes here or there to shut my eyes. The hospital had a room where we could sleep, but I never found it. As the sun shone through dingy hospital windows the next morning, I felt my body shutting down. My joints ached. My muscles trembled. I needed a bed.

Never before had I pulled a true all-nighter. Even in medical school, where I worked diligently to prove to Dr. Gale and others that I belonged at Duke, I made certain to get at least a few hours of rest each night. As long as I could remember, sleep had been a top priority. When friends in high school and college bragged about staying up late, I frequently slept eight or nine hours each night; rarely did I get less than six or seven hours. Yet here in my new life, this luxury was simply not possible. I felt like punching a wall.

When I left the hospital later that afternoon, I was so frayed that my encounter with Chester felt like a distant memory. But he would soon return to the forefront of my thoughts.

I was an official M.D. when I met Chester. That meant that I had spent two of my required four years in medical school completing rotations across a variety of fields, such as surgery, pediatrics, and neurology. During those years in the hospital and clinic, I worked with hundreds of patients and families, but always under the clear direction of at least one physician. No one mistook me for their doctor, nor did I have that responsibility.

At least once a day during my rotations, my race would come up in an interaction with patients. The racial conversation was usually implied rather than explicit, as one person after another, usually white, took one look at me and inquired about my basketball skills.

Most asked: "Did you play ball?" The more presumptuous asked: "Where did you play?"

Others offered career advice: "You're wasting your time in school. You should be playing in the NBA."

"A tall black like you with long arms and legs should be on a basketball court and nowhere else," an elderly man once said to me, much to the dismay of his more-tactful daughter.

Some simply refused to believe that I didn't play for Duke. "What is Coach K really like?" a UNC–Chapel Hill fan asked me. "Is he really as much of a jerk as he seems to be?"

The truth was that I'd only had two passing encounters with basketball coaching legend Mike Krzyzewski—once outside the hospital and another time at a campus gym—and both times he seemed quite pleasant, in clear contrast to how he sometimes came across during games on television. But I was wasting my breath trying to explain that to this die-hard Tar Heel fan.

"How on earth do you balance your hospital schedule with all your games and practices?" another patient's wife inquired, the lines on her face conveying deep concern for my well-being.

One day, as I was heading from the medical ward toward the cafeteria, a middle-aged man approached me, his hands shaking, his voice trembling. "I don't normally do this, but you look like a famous basketball player I've seen on TV," he said. "Can I have your autograph?"

He must have thought that my white coat and necktie ensemble was my Clark Kent cover to disguise my true identity as a basket-ball superhero. I politely refused to autograph his napkin, telling him that he had mistaken me for someone else, but he probably thought I was displaying the kind of elitist snobbery that many associate with Duke.

Rarely did these sorts of comments, when taken in isolation, re-ally bother me. Like many stereotypes, this one had some truth be-hind it. After all, black players make up more than 75 percent of NBA rosters, six times our numbers in the general population. And back then, I was a youthful, slender, six-foot-six former hoopster. It was not as if they were asking a five-foot-five guy with stubby fin-gers and a beer gut if he could do a 360-degree dunk simply because he was black.

Yet along with some people's certainty that I could dribble and shoot came, at least to my thinking, an assumption that I was a dumb jock. In other words, athletic talent, at least for black players, was inversely proportional to native intelligence. This perception had followed me since high school. Back then, while discussing the prospect of college, one of my coaches flat-out predicted that I couldn't score better than 800 on my SAT (the older version was based on a 1600-point scale), even though he knew I had a near-perfect grade point average in a magnet-school curriculum in which students rou-tinely scored above 1200. A few years later, during a basketball camp, a college coach refused to believe my actual SAT score, suggesting at first that I had misread the score before later accusing me—in front of a handful of other coaches and players—of lying to make myself look good.

So as patients and families asked about my athletic résumé, I wor-ried less about their perception that I must be a good basketball player than I did a question specific to my future: Would they doubt my ability to be a competent doctor? If so, would that hinder my career?

I was not alone among black students when it came to facing lim-iting stereotypes. Pete, who was a few classes ahead of me at Duke, told me that more than once both nurses and patients had mistaken him for a patient escort even though he always wore a necktie and white coat. His classmate Susan one-upped him: After she'd finished performing a physical exam at a man's bedside, he asked her to take away his tray and bring him coffee. When she refused, he told her that she was not doing her job and that he would report her to her supervisor. Their stories sounded uncomfortably like another version of Dr. Gale asking me to fix the lights in his classroom. No matter the successes that led us to medical school or our achievements there, it seemed some segment of the population would never fully recognize us.

The insults didn't stop once you became a doctor. During her child psychiatry fellowship at Duke in the 1970s, Jean Spaulding, the first black woman to attend medical school at Duke, encountered a family that didn't want her to treat their grandchild: "Oh no," they said. "She's a black person, and she can't treat our grandson." Another black doctor described a scenario in recent years where the chief of a clinical service walked into a patient room in his white coat, flanked by several white residents and medical students, only for the woman to ask him to take her tray away, as she had assumed he worked in the cafeteria.

Nor were these stereotypes restricted to the South. Otis Brawley, executive vice president of the American Cancer Society, and Pius Kamau, a Denver-area thoracic surgeon and newspaper columnist, have recounted similar experiences with patient and family prejudice in their writings. Brawley, while a medical resident at a Cleveland hospital, describes caring for a terminally ill man whose family repeatedly questioned his "credentials, competence, and education." Kamau, while on duty one day, discovered that his new patient, critically ill, had a swastika tattooed across his chest. After fixing "hate-filled eyes" on Kamau, the young man refused to acknowledge him, choosing to communicate to the doctor through various white nurses and other staff, "as if I spoke in another language," Kamau wrote.

Dr. Marcella Nunez-Smith of Yale explored this issue in a 2007 project where she conducted detailed interviews of twenty-five African American physicians practicing in the New England states. The study revealed a recurring theme of black doctors facing discrimination from some of their white patients. As one medical subspecialist phrased it: "We have just met and they want someone else. I don't think that most patients want to discriminate against me . . . but patients sometimes expect us not to do a good job or as well as somebody else would do."

A pediatrician offered a more blatant story: "I was removed from taking care of a white individual. The division chief and I talked later. The parents were uncomfortable with me taking care of their child. They told him they didn't think I would be capable because of my race." Nunez concluded that the pervasive nature of negative race-related experiences leads to "racial fatigue" that contributes to higher rates of job dissatisfaction and greater changes in career trajectory among black physicians. A life in medicine was tiring enough without the added baggage that race sometimes brought with it.

By the time I met Chester, I had certainly heard about other doctors' experiences with patient prejudice and had experienced it in a more benign form myself during medical school. Neither context, however, had prepared me for the day when Chester demanded "no nigger doctor," nor how that request would shape the aftermath of our initial encounter.

I was no longer a medical student whose only real objective was to learn. I was a doctor. Despite my inexperience, I would be the one nurses called when an issue arose with Chester. I could order tests and prescribe or withhold medications that directly affected his well-being. How would Chester cope with this situation? Would he request another doctor? If not, would he continue to refuse to speak with me? Would he allow me to draw blood or do other procedures on him? Would I have to deal with a family full of people who shared his prejudices?

On the night of his admission, Chester had drifted in and out of consciousness, the result of his combined kidney failure and pneumonia. The next afternoon, the medicines we administered had started to take effect, treating his infection and gradually restoring his kidneys to working order. By the following morning, his third day in the hospital, he was wide awake.

When I arrived at the hospital that morning, I met with Sanjay, a fellow intern who had been on call overnight and covered my patients. He still had on a hospital-issue scrub top from the night, having had no chance to freshen up and change back into his shirt and tie. He scratched at his five o'clock shadow as he gave me updates on my patients. He told me that one of them—a young man with a blood clot—had developed mild chest pain. He'd done the necessary workup and everything had come back fine thus far. Sanjay commented that this man wasn't very nice, which was true. I told him, however, that he was lucky he didn't have to go see Chester.

"What do you mean?" Sanjay asked.

I told him about Chester's "no nigger doctor" comment. "That sucks," he said, wincing. "If it makes you feel better," he said, "the last time I was on call, I saw a real racist asshole too."

"What happened?" I asked.

"He asked me where I was from. I told him New Jersey. He said: 'You must mean New Delhi. I've never seen anyone from New Jersey who looks like you.' Then he laughed out loud. He's lucky I'd already drawn his blood. Otherwise, I might have made it extra painful for him."

I cringed. Sanjay's parents had come to the United States from India and settled in New Jersey several years before he was born. He had lived his entire life in America. He liked rap music, football, and science fiction movies. He was as American as anyone else, only some people couldn't get past his physical appearance. Up until then, I'd been so focused on the challenges black doctors dealt with that I hadn't given thought to what other minority doctors might face.

Audrey, my resident supervisor, arrived in our workroom a few minutes later along with Gabe, our medical student. She looked totally refreshed, her body seemingly accustomed to the quick recovery required to survive on the hospital wards. Gabe and I, novices to this way of life, looked and felt as if we needed a few more hours of sleep.

"Where do you want to start?" I asked, as I scanned the list of patients on my clipboard.

"We might as well get the worst one out of the way," Audrey said.

We all knew whom she meant. The three of us headed down the hallway where we passed by hospital staff going about their duties. At least half of the nurses who gave medications and the phlebotomists who drew blood on our unit were black. The nurses' aides, who measured vital signs according to doctors' orders, were exclusively black. Chester had come to the wrong hospital if he hated black people. And then he'd had the bad luck to wind up in the care of the one medical team that had a black doctor. He probably thought that he was in hell.

We took a collective deep breath and entered Chester's room. "Good morning," Audrey said.

Chester gave a silent, forced grimace, clearly unhappy to see we were still his doctors.

A middle-aged woman and young man sat at his bedside. She gruffly introduced herself. "Molly," she said, frowning at us. "I'm his oldest girl."

She wore a T-shirt that proudly displayed the Confederate flag. Her face had the weathered look of someone who'd spent too much time in the sun, smoked too many cigarettes, and drank too much alcohol. "This is my son, Thomas," she told us.

The young man nodded. He had a crew cut and thin forearms covered with menacing tattoos. His shirt pocket flaunted a smaller Confederate flag. To my sensitized eyes, he looked the part of a virulent racist. Instantly, my own racial prejudice arose, as my imagination put him in an old pickup truck, heading to a roadside bar where he would get drunk and get in a fight over a girl who wore too much makeup.

With manners similar to her father, Molly derisively asked: "Who's in charge here?"

Audrey dispensed with pleasantries and explained Chester's case in cold, clinical terms. At that point, we were confident that his kidney failure was secondary to his pneumonia, and we were still trying to determine if there was some other problem taking place with his lungs. Molly challenged her at first, but Audrey maintained an attitude that conveyed "I know what I'm talking about" as she replied to every question. After a few minutes, Molly and her son seemed satisfied that Chester was getting good medical care, even if they disliked who was giving it.

As we stepped outside the room and headed to see our next patient, Audrey made a fist. "Ignorant jackasses," she said. "I think we should trade patients with another team. At least two of the teams here have only white men. We might as well give these fools what they want."

I was dismayed at this idea. A change in teams would mean notifying our supervising faculty physician along with one of the senior chief residents, not to mention forcing this bigoted man and his progeny onto someone else. Even if Audrey was the one making the request, I knew that our supervisors would assume that I was the one behind it. At that stage of my career, at the bottom of the physician totem pole, dealing with a racist family sounded infinitely preferable to drawing more attention to myself than I invariably did. I preferred to just suck it up and move forward, just as I had with Dr. Gale during my first year of medical school. Once again, I feared developing a reputation of being hypersensitive on racial matters. So I convinced Audrey that we would be fine. All we had to do was stick to the medical facts, as she had proved with Molly. "You're right," she conceded.

Each day, I updated Chester's family on his progress. The visitors expanded to include a sister, another daughter, and a few grandchildren. Whatever doubts the family may have had about me they kept to themselves, perhaps comforted in knowing I was supervised by someone they saw as competent. Gradually, while tending to Chester's physical ills, his family provided me with a view into his life. He had been married for fifty years and took care of his wife in her final months after a stroke. They had three daughters and seven grandchildren. He worked in a textile factory most of his life. He loved fishing.

About a week and a half into his stay, Chester finally acknowledged me when I asked him one morning how he felt. "Okay, doc," he said. "I think I'm gettin' better."

I felt a sense of calm rush through me now that he had recognized me on my own terms. On the overhead television, a sportscaster from ESPN was projecting which teams had the best chance to win the World Series. I decided to try to connect with him.

"Do you like baseball?" I asked.

"Love it. Ever since I was a little boy," he said. His eyes lit up. For a few moments, an old man in a decaying body tapped into his youth.

"Who's your favorite team?" I asked.

"The Braves," he said. "Even going back to when they was in Milwaukee."

At the time, the Braves were a powerhouse team. But they were also known for their biggest star for two decades, Hank Aaron, a legend who faced racial insults and death threats in the 1970s as he approached, and eventually surpassed, white slugger Babe Ruth's home-run record. How did Chester reconcile his love for this team with his hatred for blacks? Maybe in the same way that I sensed he was grudgingly coming to accept me as his physician.

A few days later, his oldest daughter Molly began to soften too, as she asked about my personal life for the first time. "Do you know what kind of doctor you wanna be?"

"I'm not sure," I said. "Maybe a heart specialist."

"You should be a surgeon," Molly said. "You're good with your hands."

I smiled. The day before, I'd drawn blood from Chester after the phlebotomist had failed. In truth, however, I had a nervous temperament that would have doomed me in surgical training. But with Chester, my needle sticks were smooth. Being challenged had brought out my best.

"You got a family?" Molly asked.

"Molly," Chester admonished, as if his daughter was still a small child. "You ain't supposed to ask doctors personal questions like that."

"It's okay," I said. I told her that I was engaged and hoped to have children one day.

"I'm sure you'll be a good dad when the time comes."

Tension oozed from my back and shoulders. For the first time, I felt relaxed around them. Suddenly I was having a regular conversation with regular people, not feeling like I was running from a mob that wanted to see me locked in jail or strung from a tree.

Jean Spaulding described developing a "wonderful relationship" with the family that initially refused to have her treat their grandson. Neurosurgeons Ben Carson and Keith Black described similar breakthroughs in their early years as doctors. In his book *The Big Picture*, Carson recalls encounters with patients at Johns Hopkins who "obviously came in with a bias against people of my race," highlighting the gratitude most of them felt after he had treated them or their children. Black recounted a particularly stunning interaction during his neurosurgery training at the University of Michigan. "I would like to thank you for two things," the patient said to him: "one, for saving my life, and two, for changing my point of view. Before you took out my brain tumor, I didn't like black people." Decades later, I was navigating the same path that each of them had traveled, and finding it no less rewarding.

But as Chester's prejudices eased, his body rapidly failed him. Within a few days, his kidneys, after early improvement, began to shut down again. He also developed a multidrug-resistant infection in his bloodstream that, along with his kidney failure, led to a dangerous acidic state in his blood. A CT scan of his internal organs confirmed our worst fears: His pneumonia was the complication of an aggressive cancer that had spread throughout his body.

The verdict was in: Chester was dying, and dying fast. The only question that remained was whether he could go home to spend his last days with family or would instead die in the hospital under a black doctor's watch.

During Chester's extended hospitalization, I admitted another man who openly doubted my competence because I was black. Only in this case, the patient was black too.

I had just come back from my morning outpatient clinic when the nurse paged me about Robert, our new patient. "He's a tough one," she said.

"What do you mean?" I asked, feeling the earliest signs of a tension headache.

"Sickle-cell patient in a pain crisis," she said. "He wants high doses of IV narcotics. But he's also got a history of cocaine abuse."

People with sickle-cell anemia have a reputation in the medical community for what is called drug-seeking behavior. With an illness that is biologically based and very painful, these patients are often prescribed high-dose opioid painkillers that would render ordinary people unconscious. I had briefly rotated through a sickle-cell clinic in medical school, but the people that I saw there didn't fit the drug-abusing stereotype. If anything, they wanted to minimize their pain medications while their doctors encouraged them to take more. They took care of their health, held steady jobs, and seemed to have stable families. In the words of the doctors treating them, they were "high functioning."

However, I saw the contrast when I rotated through the Grady emergency room. There, the sickle-cell patients engaged in common drug-seeking behavior: requesting early refills with stories about "lost" or "stolen" prescriptions, demanding a specific type and dose of medication, and traveling from one clinic or emergency room to another in search of their favorite drugs.

From the nurse's description, it sounded as if Robert veered more to the "difficult" side. When I walked into the room, he was at the sink washing his hands. He was five-nine and weighed less than 150 pounds. Plastic tubing that connected to an IV pole snaked into his vein and delivered narcotics, fluid hydration, and antinausea medicine. When I introduced myself, he immediately interrogated me.

"Does anyone in your family have sickle-cell?"

"No," I said. This seemed to me a fair question, since it's far more common in blacks.

"What do you know about the disease?" he asked.

I suddenly felt defensive. In a casual conversation, I could have recited at least a dozen facts, but I stumbled under his scrutiny: "What do you mean?"

His sneer was penetrating. "Man," he said, shaking his head. "Ain't this some shit?!"

"What do you mean, sir?"

"C'mon man, we both know what the deal is. I'm sure you did good in school and everything, but they're passin' you off on me. And they think I won't care because I'm supposed to be a dumb nigger. Go tell your boss I don't want no black doctor."

I was suddenly aware of how tight my tie felt around my neck. "But sir . . ."

"I didn't come all the way to Duke to see no black doctor unless he's some kinda expert. I could have stayed home if I wanted to see a country ass doctor. I ain't gonna be no guinea pig."

Dazed, I retreated a half-step. I felt my heart thump and blood pulse through my ears. In the clearest of terms, Robert was saying that black doctors were incompetent, and that I was the latest example.

It had been years since I had heard this stated so bluntly. Growing up in a working-class black community, subtle and not-so-subtle references to black inferiority were everywhere. Whether it was a communal preference for Asian merchants over black ones, or my grandmother's assertion that a Jewish doctor was better than a black one, the feelings of inferiority infected me like a disease that kept recurring, no matter how much I washed my hands, got the proper rest, or took the right medicines. With years of success, however, I had started to fight off this virus and develop at least a partial immunity against further attacks. But Robert had essentially coughed this nasty germ right back in my face.

In *The Big Picture*, Ben Carson recounts the difficulty he sometimes faced in earning the trust of certain black patients early in his medical career, writing, "They automatically assumed I had gotten my position not because I was qualified but because I helped meet some quota." Otis Brawley, who trained a few years after Carson in the mid-1980s, echoed these feelings: "Black patients' prejudice against black doctors endures, now more as a fear that you got where you are not by brains and rigorous training but because of an affirmative action program." Nearly two decades later, Robert seemed to be reading from this same self-doubting racial script.

In addition, with his use of "guinea pig," Robert was also trumpeting the pervasive belief held by many blacks that the medical system wants to experiment on them. This is not bizarre paranoia; it is history. The Tuskegee syphilis study remains the classic example. There, the federal government staged an experiment where they watched hundreds of black men suffer and die from syphilis over a forty-year period (1932–1972) without treating them, even after curative treatment (penicillin) became available in the 1940s. These men were not told that they were in a research study. Nor were they ever told that they had syphilis or warned about possibly transmitting it to others. In recent years, popular works have explored how the Tuskegee study was not an isolated incident, but rather part of a larger sordid history of research abuses toward black Americans.

Even in present-day medicine, faint echoes of experimentation linger, as medical students and residents at many programs hone their skills on a disproportionately poor and black patient population. So for Robert, the son of modern-day sharecroppers, raised in a rural region of North Carolina in the era of Tuskegee, the idea of an inexperienced black doctor being responsible for his care had him on the attack.

After my initial stumble, I rallied and rattled off various data about sickle-cell anemia. For every question Robert had about one of his medicines, I answered, confident of my medical knowledge. This test of my competence probably took five minutes, although it felt much longer.

Evidently, he was impressed. "Forget what I said about changing doctors," he said. "We'll see how things go."

Over time, Robert seemed to look forward to our visits as he opened up to me about his life. He was divorced; he had a seventeen-year-old son who was being recruited to play college football. We shared a passion for Al Green's early music. On the medical side, his symptoms steadily improved. By the end of a full week, he was ready to go home. On the day of his discharge, he pulled me aside after the rest of the medical team had moved on to the next patient.

"Sorry how things started with us," he said.

"No worries," I said, as we shook hands. "Take care of yourself."

"I wouldn't mind havin' you as my doctor when you get all finished up."

Robert had paid me the highest compliment a patient could. Still, I was left with a bitter aftertaste. A white doctor might surely catch grief from a prejudiced black patient, just as I had from Chester and his family. But I could not imagine a white patient ever telling a white doctor that he wanted to switch doctors for no other reason than their shared skin color. In some ways, this rejection was more painful, given what it said about how we felt about ourselves as a race.

With each passing day, it became less and less likely that Chester would leave the hospital alive. As days turned into weeks, Audrey became more involved in face-to-face interactions with the family. She wanted the daughters to sign a DNR order, which meant that when the inevitable came and Chester's heart and lungs stopped working, there would be no electric shocks or breathing tubes. Along with our faculty supervisor, she spent nearly a half-hour one morning with the family discussing this order.

Later that day, one of the daughters asked me for my thoughts. My instinct was to deflect the topic back to Audrey and our supervisor, but she already knew their opinion and wanted mine. I was so caught up in the strain of my clinical duties that I failed to see this as a sign of their trust in me until later.

"I guess in the end," I started hesitantly, "you have to decide what you think he would want as opposed to what you might want for him or for yourself in his place. But that's hard."

His daughters ultimately agreed to sign the DNR order. A few days later, Chester went into cardiac arrest. It happened on a Saturday morning when I was exhausted, my goal to complete my rounds quickly and get home before noon. Audrey and Gabe were off, so aside from the distant supervision of our faculty physician, I was on my own. I received a page from one of the nurses just as I was getting ready to leave. "Your patient in room twenty-six has died," she said without emotion.

That was Chester's room number. "What?!" I said. "When did this happen?"

"His family just called a few minutes ago to say he had stopped breathing."

I was about to scream in panic and rage before I remembered that this was the point of a DNR order: to allow the patient to die without tubes or electric jolts. "What do I need to do?"

"You have to pronounce him and make it official," the nurse said.

"I'll be right there."

In medical school, I had seen many doctors in these situations. Some exhibited grace and compassion, while others were simply inept or too detached to provide any comfort. Now it was my turn.

When I arrived at Chester's bedside, his family filled the room. Cloudy eyes turned toward me. I recognized his sister, daughters, and a few grandkids; the rest were unfamiliar. I introduced myself to those I didn't know as I made my way to Chester. His eyes were closed; a blanket covered him from the shoulders down. He had not been dead long enough to look different from how he appeared in life. My medical job was easy: I had seen it done more than a dozen times in medical school. I pulled back the blanket and placed my stethoscope over his chest, where I held it for thirty seconds—no heartbeat. Then I put my fingers across his neck while my ear moved close to his nose and mouth: he had no pulse and was not breathing. The outcome was clear: Chester was dead.

I looked up at his family, scanning from one to the next. "I'm sorry for your loss." After I let that linger for a few seconds, I spoke again: "Does anyone have questions?"

I had grown so accustomed to asking this to family members of the living that it slipped from my mouth. *You idiot*, I silently berated myself. What question could they possibly have other than: *Why couldn't you save him?* Suddenly on the defensive, I braced myself for racially tinged criticism. But what came from their mouths was the opposite of hate:

"Thanks for all you did for my daddy," Molly said.

"We really appreciate all the time you spent with him," the youngest daughter added.

"Thanks, sir," said Thomas, the grandson who, at first, with his Confederate-flag clothing and scary tattoos, had looked to me like a budding neo-Nazi. "My granddaddy liked you."

I nodded, speechless. It was all I could do to leave the room without stumbling against a wall. Their kind words were what families used when they felt their loved ones had been treated with dignity. I'd never expected to hear those words from Chester's family.

I was proud of the way I'd handled Chester's case, but I was also left with a twinge of guilt. Though I was certain I had worked as hard as I could, motivated in part to show Chester and his family that

I was a competent doctor, I knew that my clinical diligence ultimately had as much to do with wanting to impress Audrey and my other supervisors. Despite the flashes of humanity that Chester showed me toward the end, based on initial impressions, I had regarded him and his family as beneath me.

As many people do, I had countered prejudice with prejudice. In my eyes, Chester and his family were high school dropout, Dixie-flag waving, trailer-park trash. From childhood, the black community and the broader society had nurtured these feelings. Without much thought, I had adopted them as my own.

Yet here was Chester's family, heirs to his bigoted ways, offering nothing but gratitude. I now saw how even racists such as Chester were capable of making genuine, human connections with those they professed to hate. Whether that meant I could now come over for dinner or marry their daughter I have no way of knowing, but ultimately, I had played a vital role in something even greater—life and death itself—and Chester's family had left our encounter grateful for what I had to offer them.

6

When Doctors Discriminate

A few months after Chester's death, I got a close-up view of racial prejudice clothed in white coats.

It was midafternoon at the hospital. After a busy morning where I'd worked alone managing our patient caseload, the pace had gradually slowed. I was able to write my daily progress notes for the nine patients on our medical service without interruption, a rare occurrence. I was even able to sit down for a peaceful lunch in the cafeteria. My pager went a full hour without beeping. Fearing that I might miss an urgent call that one of my patients was in dire distress, I double-checked to make sure that the pager's battery hadn't died.

Finally, it went off. "Are you the intern covering for the Med-One team?" a nurse asked when I returned the call.

Bruce, a fellow intern, had been on call the night before. He'd left an hour earlier due to new national guidelines that capped hospital intern shifts at thirty hours, sparked in part by stories of tired doctors hurting patients. Before that, thirty-six-hour shifts were commonplace. Someone had to cover his patients, and on this day, that was me. "Yes," I said.

"Mr. Warren is ready to be discharged," she said, "but no one has written the order."

I'd seen Gary Warren earlier that day, during morning rounds when another resident and intern had presented his case to our faculty supervisor. He'd come in with chest pain; the last I knew, he'd had two normal EKGs and two sets of blood tests that showed no sign he'd had a heart attack. When the team had seen him that morning, they were waiting for one more blood test. If that came back normal, they were going to discharge him home.

Bruce had forgotten to enter the discharge order in the rush to finish his work and go home. I wanted to be upset, but when I'd made the same mistake, someone had covered for me. Besides, it was an easy task. I pulled up Gary's chart to enter the order. Then I saw it.

The discharge summary listed not just chest pain but a psychiatric disorder. Gary was a thoughtful man who seemed to have no more of a mental problem than I (or any of the doctors who treated him) did. Like me, he was black. The traces of anger that I had felt earlier after we saw him that morning resurfaced and bubbled over. My fellow doctors had jumped to a ridiculous conclusion—and as far as I could tell, it was largely based on race. They were branding Gary with a label that simply didn't fit. This looked like a textbook portrait of racial bias—and I was about to sign off on it.

Throughout medical school and the first half of my medical internship, I'd been witness to the pervasive health problems that black people experienced. Poverty topped the list of culprits. Both at Grady and at Duke, I'd seen how poor black people were more likely to be fat, more likely to have been abused, and less likely to comply with medical treatments. With Tina at the charity clinic and in several other patients, I saw how lacking insurance undermines health, even for those who escape the other afflictions of poverty.

But I had never seen any examples of a doctor's racial bias inflicting medical harm.

Nonetheless, during my years in training, the scientific literature was flooded with articles on the subject. In 1996, Dr. H. Jack Geiger wrote an editorial in the *New England Journal of Medicine* (*NEJM*) where, after reviewing several studies, he questioned whether "racially discriminatory rationing by physicians and health care institutions" was a cause of racial disparity in the health care system. Three years later, the *NEJM* published a widely reported article that suggested that women and blacks with chest pain were less likely to be referred for the best cardiac care, though they later took a step back from the full claims of the study. In 2002 the Institute of Medicine added fuel to the discussion with their book *Unequal Treatment*, in which they concluded: "Although myriad sources contribute to [health] disparities, some evidence suggests that bias, prejudice, and stereotyping on the part of healthcare providers may contribute to differences in care." Throughout these years, a plethora of studies described racially disparate treatments and outcomes.

For many black Americans, these reports—whether the results were large or small—merely reaffirmed long-standing perceptions. Acclaimed writer John Edgar Wideman, in his 1984 family memoir, *Brothers and Keepers*, writes of the misdiagnosis and death of a family friend in 1970s Pittsburgh through his mother's voice: "Shame the way they did that boy. He'd been down to the clinic two or three times but they sent him home. Said he had an infection and it would take care of itself . . . you know how they are down there. Have to be spitting blood to get attention . . . when they finally took him to the hospital, it was too late. They let him walk the streets till he was dead."

Henry Louis Gates Jr. writes in his childhood memoir, *Colored People*, of his adolescent encounter with a physician who discounted his painful hip as "psychosomatic," telling his mother: "Because I know the type, and the thing is, your son's an overachiever," referring to Gates's ambition to be a doctor. According to Gates, "back then, 'overachiever' designated a sort of pathology, the dire consequence of overstraining your natural capacity. A colored kid who thought he could be a doctor—just for instance—was headed for a breakdown." Gates's mother later took him to another hospital where he required several surgeries for a slipped epiphysis (a fracture through the growth plate), a condition that resulted in his having leg-length differences that required the use of a cane and an elevated shoe for assistance throughout his adult life.

In his memoir, Wes Moore recounts how his dad was taken to the emergency room in a state of confusion. There, the doctors asked Moore's mother: "Does he have a habit of exaggerating? Is there anything going on in his life that would force him to make up symptoms?" before sending him home with a prescription to "get some sleep." Moore's father died just a few hours later at home from what later was found to be a case of acute epiglottitis. Moore sums up the way that he feels race and class influenced the doctor's care of his father: "My father had entered the hospital seeking help. But his face was unshaven, his clothes disheveled, his name unfamiliar, his address not in an affluent area. The hospital looked at him askance . . . and basically told him to fend for himself." Various medical scholars and authors have provided historical context to these anecdotes, chronicling the abuses that black people have faced from the medical profession dating back to slavery.

This history wasn't covered in any formal way during medical school. Nor had I experienced anything egregious that would call to mind this dark past. I'd seen nothing like the case that future Surgeon General David Satcher wrote about in 1973, when he described a black woman who had nine consecutive pelvic exams by physicians and students without being told whether her exam was normal or abnormal. Or a scene that occurred at Los Angeles County + USC Medical Center in the 1980s where a black administrator at the school was reportedly told by an ER doctor after breaking her arm to "hold your arm like you usually hold your can of beer on Saturday night." My main encounter with racial prejudice—Dr. Gale asking me to fix the lights—took place in a classroom setting.

Even when Dr. Garner brazenly accused the pregnant Leslie of cocaine abuse, what seemed like a verbal assault had actually been clinically useful; she had managed to extract vital information about Leslie's drug use where my gentle probing had failed. Moreover,

Dr. Garner defended Leslie against the racially charged assertion of the nurse who wanted Leslie sterilized. By and large, the white doctors whom I'd worked with treated black patients with complete fairness and respect. Dr. Watson and Dr. Kelly from the charity clinic, with their devotion to helping the poor and uninsured, stood out as the prototypes.

Nor do I recall any black classmates telling me stories of black patients being shortchanged because of their skin color. Perhaps we were all too busy worrying about ourselves, securing good grades and recommendations, to notice. It's also possible that our medical knowledge in these early stages was not sophisticated enough to decipher subtler forms of medical discrimination. Or maybe our very presence kept the white doctors honest.

In truth, at that stage in my training, I hadn't bought into the whole discussion of "discriminating doctors," seeing it mainly as the talk of academic types in search of grant money, or, as conservative medical writer Sally Satel would argue, those seeking to advance a political agenda. While I'd clearly seen how poverty adversely impacted the care that many black people received, this seemed to me an indictment of the health care system and broader social inequality rather than the thoughts or actions of any individual doctor.

But when I met Gary, I saw how doctors, in my view, could discriminate against a black patient.

I saw Gary around the halfway point of my internship. I'd spent the previous month on the neurology ward where I found the subject matter interesting and welcomed the less hectic pace. Like a golf scorecard, 70 (hours per week) sure beat the 80-plus customary on the general medicine ward.

"Welcome back, Dr. Tweedy," a senior nurse said, flashing a crooked smile as I stepped off the elevator onto the unit. "I know you've missed us."

"I've been thinking about you every day," I replied. "But you don't want to know what."

The nurse laughed. I'd taken the advice of many senior residents to be nice to the nurses, as they held the power to make an intern's life even more miserable than it already was. If a nurse didn't like you, they could wake you anytime they wanted, using the need for an unimportant order—say a three a.m. call for Gas-X for a patient who was sound asleep—as the ostensible reason. Getting on the nurses' good side prevented most of that. Being friendly also made them more willing to go the extra mile for you wherever they could.

I was alone as the day began, my supervising resident downstairs in his weekly outpatient clinic. That left me to manage our load of patients. Earlier in the year, the prospect of working by myself during a busy weekday would have overwhelmed me. Now six months into my internship, I could order surgical consults, coordinate radiology studies, and interpret blood and urine tests rapid-fire without flinching.

At ten a.m. we rounded with our attending faculty physician, a daily event where the teams in training—each consisting of a resident, an intern, and a medical student—review the list of patients with their senior physician supervisor. Ideally, the attending physician turns discussion about some or all of the cases into teaching exercises. In medical school, I'd always enjoyed the meetings, as they allowed me to show what I knew and gave me an opportunity to learn new things. Now, as an intern, attending rounds felt like a waste of time, a nearly two-hour delay in my day of drawing blood, writing notes, ordering tests, prescribing medications, and answering page after page to put out an inevitable series of fires.

Our sister medical team—with whom my team shared the conference room and the senior physician—had been on call the previous night, which meant they had new admissions to review.

"Good morning, everyone," Dr. Rhodes, our attending physician said as he entered our workroom. "How was the night?"

"We got five," Carl, the resident replied, a half-empty coffee cup in one hand and a chewed-up pencil in the other. He probably hadn't slept more than an hour—two at the most. "But one is on their way to surgery and the other one can probably be discharged today."

Along with the more noble goals of learning and helping people, most residents and interns wanted to keep their number of patients low. Fewer patients usually meant fewer calls and less paperwork, and that could mean the difference between a seventy-hour week and a ninety-hour one. The ideal was an admission that could be transferred elsewhere or discharged home within twenty-four hours. Getting two such cases in one cycle added up to a good night.

"Another day at the office," Dr. Rhodes said. "Let's review the possible discharge first."

Carl turned to Bruce, the intern on his team. I'd worked with Bruce earlier that year. He'd gone to medical school in Ohio and had told me he wanted to become a gastroenterologist. He began his summary of the patient's case.

"Mr. Gary Warren is a fifty-five-year-old African American male."

This three-pronged age-race-gender description was the traditional way to present a case. Once again the only black person in the room, I wondered if anyone else there had ever given thought to this method and shared any of my concerns. Age was obviously important to know; the cause and severity of chest pain in someone sixty-five years old had different implications than it did when presenting in a twenty-year-old. Gender too had important distinctions; lower abdominal pain in a woman meant considering the pathology of completely different internal organs than did the same complaint in a man. But why did it matter so much whether the patient was white, black, or something else? Did this way of presenting cases assume that race should automatically color the way a doctor approached a patient's chest pain or achy stomach?

The presentation continued. Aside from high blood pressure and his near pack-a-day smoking, Gary had been in good health. This was his first time in a hospital. The day before, for the second time that week, he had developed chest pain near the end of his shift at a hardware store. His initial tests were normal. The team was awaiting a third normal test result, which would rule out an acute heart attack. For the moment, Gary seemed safe.

"Very good," Dr. Rhodes said after Bruce had finished. We sat silently while waiting for him to direct the discussion or move on to the next patient. Dr. Rhodes was a nephrologist, a kidney specialist, who spent most of his time in the research lab. But he knew clinical medicine. We talked about the blood pressure medicine options that we had, comparing their pros and cons, and discussing the different effects that they had on the heart and kidneys. "Let's go see him," Dr. Rhodes finally said.

Gary's room was at the far end of the hall. He looked like the healthiest patient on the ward. He was neither skinny nor fat. He didn't have tubes going into his nostrils or penis. He sat comfortably on his bed. The combination of eyeglasses, goatee, and receded hairline gave him a scholarly look. Aside from the hospital-issued gown and the partially covered wires of his heart monitor, he could have been your average middle-aged black man lounging at home on a leisurely Saturday morning.

His attention was focused on the overhead TV, where a reporter talked about potential Democratic presidential contenders and their stances on the Iraq War. Gary turned down the volume and sat up on the edge of the bed, surrounded by our fleet of white coats, his chocolate scalp glistening under the fluorescent lights. I was the only member from my team, as the resident had taken our medical student with him to his clinic. Dr. Rhodes introduced himself to Gary, after which Carl took the lead.

"As I mentioned earlier this morning, we're confident that you didn't have a heart attack," he said to Gary. "Based on your history, we don't see any reason for you to have a catheterization right now; instead, we'd like to have you come back in a few days to the Heart Clinic for a stress test."

As I stood there listening to Carl, I thought back to what I'd heard about black people with chest pain being less likely than whites to get referred for the best cardiac testing and interventions. However, I'd seen doctors at this hospital recommend stress tests rather than cardiac catheterization for white patients as well. This approach seemed less like prejudice than a function of the difference between a public hospital where the doctors were paid on salary and cost-containment was high priority, and a private facility where doctor's income and hospital revenue was based largely on the number of patients seen and tests performed. Either approach, carried to their extremes, could be harmful.

"In the meantime," Carl went on, "we've identified a few things for you to address. Number one is smoking."

"You don't have to say more about that one," Gary said, confidently. "I already decided. I won't be doing that again. I stopped for nine months a few years ago, so I can definitely do it."

Carl and Bruce smiled. Doctors loved it when their patients agreed with them. They told Gary they would prescribe him nicotine patches to jump-start his tobacco-free life.

"We'd like you to take an aspirin each day," Carl continued. "We're also going to give you some nitroglycerin tablets. You can take these if you experience any chest pain."

Gary had received both treatments in the emergency room and his pain had gone away. "That sounds like a good idea," he said.

"The next concern is your blood pressure," Carl said.

"I haven't been taking good care of myself," Gary conceded.

"We'd like to start you on a daily medication."

Carl gave the name of a common drug. It was cheap, effective, and relatively safe. Gary nodded in silence as he scratched his beard, like a professor or psychiatrist in deep thought: "I'd like to hold off on that," he said finally.

Plenty of people don't like taking blood pressure pills. Some cause fatigue. Others cause dizziness. A few kill erections. They can end up feeling worse than they did without them.

Carl sighed. He'd hit a familiar stumbling block. He explained the need for medicine: "Your blood pressure is averaging around

150/100 here in the hospital. The cutoff for high blood pressure is 140/90."

"I understand," Gary said. "But I'd prefer to try lifestyle interventions first."

Carl ran his fingers through his thinning hair as he looked over at Bruce, who arched an eyebrow. "What do you know about lifestyle interventions?" Carl asked Gary.

From a young doctor's perspective, most patients whom we saw in public hospitals and clinics who declined medications seemed equally unwilling to make healthful life choices. "Lifestyle interventions" was not part of their vocabulary. But Gary was different: "Based on my numbers," he said, "it seems that I have mild hypertension. My understanding is that diet and exercise changes can be tried for a while before starting medicine. I have a lot of room for improvement with both."

I smiled. For years, I'd seen many black people undermine their health, whether it was the people with diabetes who refused insulin and kept eating doughnuts as they lost all their toes, those with heart failure who continued smoking cigarettes (or crack), or the patients with Hepatitis C who still drank a pint of vodka every day. Some lacked knowledge, while others lacked willpower. Gary seemed to have both in ample supply. From my perspective, it felt good to see.

The other doctors had a different reaction. Carl and Bruce looked at each other in wonder as if Gary had developed a cure for cancer. They glanced over at Dr. Rhodes, who seemed equally bemused. "That's mighty impressive," Dr. Rhodes whispered to Carl.

Granted, this was more medical knowledge than the typical patient in this setting offered, but it didn't require an M.D. or Ph.D. to grasp. Duke was one of the pioneers of the DASH (Dietary Approaches to Stop Hypertension) Diet—a program shown to lower blood pressure. Between the hospital and local clinics, it was easy to come across patient-education pamphlets that provided the exact information Gary recited. For all these doctors knew, Gary, or someone close to him, might have been in one of these studies.

"It's great that you know all of this, but most patients in our experience here find it very hard to accomplish much through diet and exercise," Carl said, rubbing the back of his neck. His smile and warm energy had vanished. Gary was no longer being a "good" patient, the kind who did what doctors told them.

"That's because they don't take it seriously," Gary countered. "I know I didn't when my family doctor told me I had borderline high blood pressure, but I will now. You can bet on that."

Carl turned to Dr. Rhodes for help. It was time for the boss to take over. At a slender five-nine, Dr. Rhodes was much smaller than Carl or Bruce or me, but there was no mistaking who was in charge. The white coats revealed our hierarchy; his knee-length coat conveyed seniority; Carl's stopped mid-thigh and Bruce's and mine were waist-length. Dr. Rhodes maintained good eye contact and spoke with confidence. He stepped forward. "Mr. Warren, it sounds like you know quite a bit about hypertension."

Gary put his palms on the bed, arms straight, and sat up even straighter, like a student on good behavior at his classroom desk. He glanced at us before looking up at our supervisor. If we were the teachers, he knew Dr. Rhodes was the principal.

"My family doctor gave me some pamphlets when I saw him last year and my pressure was up," Gary replied. "Like I said, I didn't take it as seriously as I should have. I sorta lost track of things, you know, getting busy with life. But this has been a wake-up call."

Dr. Rhodes went into professor mode, giving Gary a mini-lecture about the risks of heart attack, stroke, and kidney failure associated with hypertension. "I can't tell you how many people I've seen on dialysis who were like you at one point. They wish they'd taken their meds."

Gary hesitated. "Just give me a month. Two at the most. If I can't get it down on my own, I promise I'll come back and start whatever you recommend. I understand that this is serious."

"Okay," said Dr. Rhodes, as he turned to Carl. "He understands the risks involved."

Carl finished the conversation, explaining the need to wait for the third cardiac blood test result. Assuming it was normal, the plan was to have Gary go home and come back in a few days for a stress test. In the meantime, he would begin the medications he agreed to start taking.

Dr. Rhodes extended his hand to Gary's. "It was nice meeting you. Good luck to you."

As we left his bedside and headed back toward our workroom, Dr. Rhodes smiled as he looked over at Carl. "What disorder do you think he has?"

I presumed he was referring to medical conditions. Given his age, hypertension, smoking, and the onset of the pain while under physical strain at work, heart disease seemed most likely. The forthcoming stress test would give us a better answer. Another possibility was something coming from his gastrointestinal tract—perhaps bad reflux or an ulcer, but our information really didn't support that. Nor did his symptoms fit the classic picture of a panic attack. Gary did not relate any psychiatric history or acutely stressful events in his life. We'd already been through this discussion after Bruce presented Gary's case in our conference room. Evidently, after talking with Gary, something had changed. But what? I was jarred by Carl's answer.

"Probably obsessive-compulsive disorder," he said.

"It seems more like obsessive-compulsive personality to me," Dr. Rhodes said.

"What's the difference?" Bruce asked.

"Something silly about whether the obsession bothers them or not," Carl said, shaking his head. With many doctors, psychiatry ranked near the very bottom of the medical pecking order. An old aphorism in medicine was that while surgeons "do everything but know nothing" and internists (my field at the time) "know everything but do nothing," both were in agreement that psychiatrists "know nothing and do nothing."

"Maybe we should get a psych consult to let them sort it out,"

Bruce said, smiling. "Maybe if he takes one of their pills, it will convince him to take ours."

The three of them broke out in laughter. The medical student on their team frowned at first before forcing a smile to fit in with her supervisors. I stared at my clipboard and pager, pretending to be preoccupied with issues on my roster of patients. None of them seemed to notice my silence.

Inside, I was quickly moving from disbelief to fury. Gary's decision seemed reasonable. It was not as if he had a textbook case of bacterial pneumonia and had refused antibiotics. Even on the spectrum of high blood pressure, his readings of 150/100 were relatively mild; various studies had demonstrated average reductions of 5 to 10 points (or more) with diet and exercise. Had his pressure been 190/120, it would have been another story. Further, he had agreed to take aspirin, nitroglycerin as needed, and the nicotine patches.

Given this data, why did they assume that he had a psychiatric illness because he wanted to eat better and drop some pounds before resorting to blood pressure pills? Because he was black? Because he was a patient in a public hospital? Because he worked at a hardware store? Or was it because he challenged their knowledge and authority in some fundamental way? Perhaps it was a combination of all these factors. It was as if Gary had shown himself to be "too smart" to be a patient in this hospital and therefore had to be mentally ill.

I was probably more sympathetic with Gary's decision because when I'd received my own diagnosis of hypertension years before, I, like Gary, didn't see taking medication as the first option. For me, the goal of avoiding blood pressure drugs provided motivation as strong as the longer-term fears of stroke and dialysis. Why take a pill, with all of its potential side effects, I wondered, when I could achieve the same result by changing how I ate and exercised?

My doctor agreed. He urged me to complement basketball with other aerobic and strength training exercises. He talked to me about expanding my range of fruits and vegetables, limiting fast food, and drinking water rather than soft drinks. Like me, he considered it important that I exhaust the basics before starting medication. And it worked. Within a few months, my blood pressure was consistently normal.

During my third year of medical school, I learned about the DASH diet, targeted exercise programs, and the benefits that both had on patients. Data from a subset of the DASH study suggested that black patients responded even better to the diet with greater reductions in blood pressure than white patients did—a finding validated in a subsequent study. If anything, Gary's doctors should have eagerly supported his lifestyle goals rather than mock them.

Perhaps they were more influenced by studies that suggested that black people were less likely than whites to adhere to lifestyle changes. And Gary's hypertension was not an isolated problem. He'd come to the hospital with chest pain. Further, he smoked cigarettes. And he was in his mid-fifties, prime age for early heart attacks.

Most doctors would have made similar recommendations and urged Gary to take a blood pressure pill. But the way Carl and the other doctors responded still felt wrong. Why had they treated Gary's responses and vows to change with what seemed like complete disdain? Even if he wasn't making the best medical decision, he'd neither done nor said anything that qualified as a prima facie case for a psychiatric disorder. If questioning a doctor's advice meant getting tagged with a psychiatric label, then virtually everyone I knew was mentally ill. I couldn't escape the sense that racial bias, likely unconscious, had shaped their response.

I didn't have time to think about Gary for the next several hours. When we got back to the workroom, a nurse paged me about one of my patients, a frail man in his early eighties with terminal cancer who was in the hospital for pneumonia. The antibiotics we had given him had worked. But he'd started having diarrhea the day before, and now his stools had become bloody. He'd traded one problem for something equally serious. He wasn't going to live much longer, and his wife and son, whom I had met the day before, knew it. Our goal had been to get him through this crisis and arrange hospice so he could die at home. I hoped that was still possible.

I paged my supervising resident, who talked me through how to manage the situation. After doing so, he told me that we'd gotten a new admission from the emergency room, another elderly man, this one with fever and confusion from rancid bedsores. Meanwhile, my pager started beeping, another patient urgently needing something. I wanted to hurl the chirping device across the room. How was I supposed to handle all of this sickness?

The frenetic pace had slowed by the time I received the page from the nurse asking me to enter the discharge order for Gary. His hospital summary listed two diagnoses. The first was chest pain. Underneath, Carl discussed the possible causes, with coronary heart disease being most likely. The second diagnosis, right there for everyone to see: obsessive compulsive personality disorder. *What?!* I was confused, then shocked. The fact that Carl, Bruce, and Dr. Rhodes had joked about this was bad enough, but they had gone further and made it part of his medical record. How could they have entered this so cavalierly? Had they consulted psychiatry for a second opinion? The chart gave no indication that they had. Carl, who'd been so disdainful of psychiatrists, nevertheless took it upon himself to dole out one of their diagnoses.

I prodded my memory for what I'd learned in medical school about this disorder, usually referred to by its abbreviation, OCPD. Patients with this condition are perfectionist, inflexible, and controlling. While patients with the better-known obsessive-compulsive disorder (OCD) are distressed by their obsessive thoughts and compulsive behaviors, those with OCPD often perceive themselves as being just fine. They are more inclined to believe that other people, who don't measure up to their lofty standards, are the ones with problems. A joke in medical school is that if you want to see someone with OCPD, just look in the mirror or at a classmate.

Although I could have entered the discharge order and let the nurses handle the rest, I couldn't leave it there. I wanted to talk with Gary, to see for myself whether Carl and Dr. Rhodes had picked up on something I'd overlooked. I found Gary sitting up in bed, reading a science fiction book. The cardiac monitor had been removed. He had on his own clothes—a red polo shirt and a pair of blue jeans. He looked like a dad from my old neighborhood.

I introduced myself and explained that we were about to discharge him, but first, I was just checking on what had taken place after we'd left his room that morning. "Did any of the doctors come back and talk with you?" I asked.

He nodded. "They told me that my third blood test was negative and gave me an appointment card for the stress test later this week. They advised me to take off from work until then."

"Did they talk with you about seeing anyone else?"

"They got me a primary care appointment next month. I want to start coming here."

"Did they mention anyone else, for any other reason?" I asked.

He shook his head. "Is something wrong?"

I was pressing too hard. It wasn't my job to get Gary upset over something that didn't seem to have bothered him as far as I could tell.

Nonetheless, I was dismayed that Carl and Dr. Rhodes had labeled Gary with a psychiatric diagnosis without discussing with him the "symptoms" they thought they perceived. They had not offered any means to address this "problem," such as a stress management class or other counseling. From what I could tell, their sole basis was a ten-minute interview where he'd agreed with everything they suggested, except when he gave valid and coherent reasons for wanting to delay taking a blood pressure medicine.

All these thoughts competed for my attention, but all I said was, "No, no problem. I just want to make sure everything is covered. It looks like everything is set until you come back."

I wanted to say much more. I wished he'd been in that hallway with me earlier in the day, to see how the doctors had ridiculed him for having ideas about his own health. I wanted him to know what was in his chart, to see what I believed—that his race and class had led doctors to label him as having a mental illness. I was tempted to tell him that I could personally relate to his desire to lower his blood pressure without medications because I'd made the same decision myself. I wanted to tell him that he was just the kind of patient I'd want to treat, the kind who's thoughtful and knowledgeable about his health. I had an outpatient clinic at the hospital; maybe he'd like to come there and we could work out a plan together.

I didn't say any of those things. I felt like doing so would have been opening up a Pandora's box that I couldn't close. As a young doctor with no power, I signed the discharge order and wished Gary well.

"Thanks," Gary said, as we shook hands. "Good luck in your training."

A psychiatric diagnosis is not a harmless label. Several studies have explored the ways that people with mental illness receive worse medical care. When psychiatric patients report medical concerns, such as chest pain, doctors take them less seriously. Doctors often review the charts of patients before meeting them and form preconceived ideas based on the information written by other doctors. A person with OCPD may be seen as a potential problem. "He's going to do whatever he wants anyway, so why bother?" I've heard doctors say. While obsessive-compulsive traits might be expected, or even welcomed, in a medical or psychiatric private practice that caters to rich clientele, in a lower-income community clinic where people are stacked one appointment after the next, such a person would more likely be viewed as a "difficult" patient, someone you'd want to get out of your office as soon as possible.

In this case, Gary's diagnosis wouldn't be something that he could easily fix. In contrast, a person recovering from alcohol or drug abuse, while likely to face significant discrimination and distrust, has the

ability to establish a clear pattern of clean time documented by laboratory testing. Personality disorder diagnoses are far more subjective.
The medical doctor is unlikely to ask, "What progress are you making
with your personality disorder?" Rather, depending on their view of
psychiatry, treating doctors would view Gary's labeling as useless at
best, or, more likely, as a sign that he is a "problem" patient.

The following morning during attending rounds, I thought about
confronting the doctors who had labeled Gary to make them aware
of the role that I felt racial bias had played. But I kept quiet. I'd gotten just about an hour of sleep overnight and simply wanted to get
home in time for a nap before Kerrie and I met with the wedding
planner that evening. In addition to the typical intern's fear of challenging supervisors and becoming a "difficult" person myself, I already knew how they'd respond. They would have told me that I had
misinterpreted the situation, that race had nothing to do with their
psychiatric diagnosis of Gary. They would have cited legitimate medical evidence for their blood pressure medicine recommendation and
reminded me of how hard people find changing their behaviors. Perhaps they would have suggested that the stress of internship was af-
fecting me, and that maybe I should talk with someone about that?

Surely, I had no reason to think of these doctors as racist in any
classic sense. I'd had lunch with Bruce and we'd discussed in depth
our internship experiences and future ambitions; he'd given me advice prior to one of my rotations that proved helpful. I'd talked
about pro football and college basketball with Carl, who'd gone to
a Big Ten school, and he'd invited me for drinks with some of his
friends. Dr. Rhodes had mentored a few black students and residents in the past and was always friendly with me. As far as I could
tell, all three doctors regarded me as a genuine peer, as one of them,
in contrast to the way it seemed they saw Gary.

But at that moment, I didn't feel like I was really one of them. Nor
was I like Gary, who reminded me of a past that I could never reclaim.
I had a foot in both worlds, but didn't have two feet in either.

My suspicion that, if confronted, these doctors would have vociferously denied that Gary's race influenced their psychiatric diagnosis is supported by the Kaiser Family Foundation's 2002 national survey of physicians, published not long before our encounter with Gary. It found that an overwhelming 75 percent of white physicians said race and ethnicity do not affect the treatment of patients, while 77 percent of black doctors said that race and ethnicity do impact how patients are treated. Smart people from two groups were seeing entirely different realities.

It was clear that my colleagues did not see their actions toward Gary as racially biased, or else they would not have been so brazen in my presence. But I avoided approaching them about what they had done. Once again, personal ambition and comfort trumped racial solidarity. Learning to be a doctor was hard enough without my trying to change the whole system too. Further, I didn't want to deal with possibly being mislabeled as racially paranoid, especially considering how deeply most educated white people take offense to being accused of racial bias. But was I selling myself, and my race, short in the process?

In the end, I pretended that nothing had happened. We went about our usual business. Life went on. Gary probably never learned how his doctors had callously mislabeled him.

Several years later, I had an experience similar to Gary's. In my mid-thirties, my knees were paying the price for many years of playing basketball. I'd grown up spending hours upon hours running, jumping, and cutting on unforgiving blacktop. I practiced and competed on just-slightly more merciful hardwood floors throughout high school and college. After my formal playing days were over, the urge to compete remained strong, so I participated in campus intramural games, joined local recreational leagues, and found pickup games whenever I could.

The cumulative effect was gimpy knees. I had torn my right ACL many years before, but I'd recovered fairly well with surgery and physical therapy. Now my left knee was the one bothering me. Recently when I had played tennis, it had buckled slightly as I rushed to the net to retrieve a drop shot. When the swelling didn't go down after several days, I decided to get it checked out. It didn't seem serious enough to justify a visit to the emergency room, but I didn't want to wait another week to see my primary care physician or several weeks to see an orthopedic surgeon. An urgent care clinic, part of the same health care system where my primary doctor worked, had recently opened. This seemed the best option.

Within a few minutes of arriving, an energetic nurse called my name. She gave a warm, friendly smile. "Good morning," she said. We shook hands. "Follow me."

I limped behind her down the hall into an exam room. Once inside, I gave her a brief history of my knee pain. She typed this information onto a computer screen. She then checked my vital signs. My blood pressure was in the gray area between normal and high. I wasn't too worried as I'd checked it at work recently, and it had been fine.

"Dr. Parker should be in shortly," she said. "It's pretty slow here today."

True to her words, the doctor opened the door moments later. He gave me a weak handshake as his eyes scanned me from head to toe. It was only then that I realized how casually I was dressed. In contrast to the usual shirt, tie, and slacks I wore to work, I had on a fleece pullover and sweatpants. In haste, I'd put on white socks that were slightly mismatched. I didn't look homeless, but I didn't look like I had taken much care with my appearance.

With virtually no eye contact, his eyes fixed on the computer, Dr. Parker verified the information the nurse had obtained. He then had me pull up my sweatpants so he could look at both my knees. Next, he asked me to stand. My knees creaked, like a door hinge in need of lubricant. The pain made me grimace.

"You're fine," he said. "Probably just a bruise or sprain. Just take it easy for a while."

That's it? All he had done was look at my leg. He had not touched it to feel if my knee was unusually warm or cold, or whether it had accumulated excess fluid. Nor had he moved my knee through the various ranges of motion. He'd offered no explanation of what part of the knee was bruised or sprained. There'd been no mention of pain meds, ointments, or other analgesia. He did not offer nor suggest any type of knee bracing, just rest. But what if I had a job that required me to move around? He was all set to leave. I knew I had to say something.

"I really just want to make sure there's nothing serious," I said, hurrying to stop him from walking out the door. "Last summer I walked around with a sore hand for three days before I got an X-ray that showed a left third metacarpal fracture."

He looked up and established eye contact for the first time. "Are you a medical person?"

"Yes," I said.

"Are you an X-ray tech?"

"No, I'm a physician."

His eyes widened with surprise and what seemed to me admiration, as if the last thing he had expected was for us to be in the same profession. We traded a few words about the challenges of internship and residency training and the adjustment to life afterward. "Let me take a closer look at your knee," he said.

He went through a detailed physical exam—the kind I had expected from the beginning.

"Everything seems okay," he said. "But I think it would be good to get an X-ray too."

The nurse returned and escorted me to the basement for X-rays. Dr. Parker then came down and reviewed the film with me. It showed some early knee arthritis, but no other problems. He assured me that when the radiologist gave the official reading, he would call me himself. In the meantime, he recommended a brace, and offered me crutches just to have on hand. He also offered me a prescription for pain medication. Based on the X-ray, I told him that the brace would suffice; I didn't need crutches and would take over-the-counter ibuprofen.

As promised, Dr. Parker called me the next day. The radiologist's report had confirmed his preliminary review. He told me that he'd gone over to the nearby orthopedic surgery office and gotten me a better brace than the one they had in the urgent care clinic, free of charge. In the end, Dr. Parker's initial impression was correct; I had a mild-moderate knee sprain. With a few more weeks away from the basketball and tennis courts, the pain and swelling receded.

But I couldn't get out of my mind how I'd been treated as two entirely different patients. Damon Tweedy, the unknown black man, dressed like he was about to mow the lawn, couldn't get the doctor to look him in the eye or touch him; Damon Tweedy, M.D., was worthy of personal, first-class service. While it's widely known that doctors get special treatment from their colleagues, this went far beyond the usual professional courtesy of an earlier or more convenient appointment. Receiving a physical exam, an X-ray, medication, and a brace, when you otherwise would not, wasn't just better service: it was different medical care altogether.

Was Dr. Parker aware that his initial lack of attention had been unfair and insulting, leading him to overcompensate with his subsequent actions? Perhaps, but I was more interested in the reasons for his initial approach to me. He evidently saw me through a mental filter, and his assumptions were not positive. Several authors have written about the negative stereotypes that many doctors associate with black patients: poorly educated, drug abusing, not likely to comply with treatments; in short, the kind of person most doctors don't want to treat.

Granted, the urgent care setting where I saw him, and the emergency room in particular, often bring out the worst in both doctor and patient. From the doctor's lens, the goal of care in an emergency department or urgent care clinic is different from a family practice office. As one doctor told me during my ER rotation at Grady, "We are not here to make friends with patients, but to make sure they end up in the right place." In other words, the goal of the physician in this setting is to move the patient along the assembly line, not to establish a meaningful relationship. Yet the patient probably sees it differently. For far too many in our country, black people especially, urgent care and emergency rooms are the portals to the health care system.

Recognizing that time and urgency constraints might interfere with a good bedside manner did not excuse Dr. Parker's initial actions. At the very least, he should have done a physical exam. While his initial impression proved correct, without an exam or X-ray, a tiny fracture could have been missed and later morphed into something far worse. Had I not had the medical knowledge or sophistication to garner his attention, he would have sent me out of the urgent care—limping, vaguely diagnosed, without brace or crutch, without medicine, and without a follow-up visit. That's bad medicine. Why did I have to prove that I "deserved" the far better care he later showed he was capable of delivering?

Appearance and dress matter for everyone in how they're perceived, but the prevailing wisdom among black people is that it's much more important for us than it is for others. Even if the impact can't be studied or measured objectively, many black people will tell you that they have to dress better than a nonblack person to be taken as seriously. I certainly learned my lesson. Since that day, whenever I have an appointment or tag along with a family member to a doctor who doesn't already know me, I put on a sport coat. Sometimes I'll wear a tie too. At the very least, I'm certain to wear a collared shirt and slacks, and a pair of nice matching socks.

Doctors, like all other people, are capable of prejudice and discrimination. While bias can be a problem in any profession, in medicine, the stakes are much greater. Missing a blood clot in a patient's painful leg because the doctor thinks that black people in a given clinic or hospital are likely to be drug addicts seeking their next fix is a far more dangerous kind of insult than a salesperson assuming that a black customer can't afford a Brooks Brothers suit or Rolex watch. These high stakes make it vitally important for doctors to understand their capacity for prejudice.

The American historical record is full of material about white doctors' abuses and discrimination against black patients, often chillingly described in the words of the doctors themselves. Most of us, including many black people, would like to move beyond the past and accept that this American script has been rewritten. And while many things have improved, studies continue to document the ways that the doctor-patient relationship can undermine the health of black people. My experience with Gary and my own encounter with Dr. Parker are smaller examples of a larger issue.

As doctors, there is ultimately only so much that we can do for our patients, especially for the more disadvantaged in our society. We can't get them good jobs with good health insurance. Nor can we move them into nicer neighborhoods where their children can attend better schools. Despite the knowledge, advice, and treatments we have to offer, we often can't help our patients live healthier lives. But as doctors, we can do one simple thing for them: We can make our very best effort to treat everyone fairly.

7

The Color of HIV/AIDS

I'll be damned," Adam, a medical resident, said, shaking his head. "Our patient in room thirty has been lying."

We were sitting next to each other in a musty workroom filled with the scent of stressed-out residents and stale pizza. It was seven p.m. Our sister team had admitted the first wave of new patients to the medical ward and was frantically trying to wrap up their work so they could get home. Adam and I were the long-call, overnight team, which meant we'd been on duty for twelve hours and faced another eighteen before we would be set free. I was writing the admission note on an elderly woman who'd come to the hospital that afternoon with a blood clot in her leg. Adam was on the computer looking over the most recent lab results for our patients.

The patient in room thirty, George, had come to our hospital two days earlier complaining of fatigue, weakness, and short-term memory problems. He'd been losing weight and his blood counts were low. In his late forties, he worked at a local, predominately black college that he had graduated from twenty-five years earlier.

George told us he had been healthy his entire life until about six months earlier, when he gradually started feeling tired and had trouble focusing at work. His appetite went away and his weight dropped; he lost twenty pounds without trying. His red and white blood cell counts were abnormal, and his family doctor worried that he might have cancer. When further tests did not detect any cancer, however, his doctor suspected that George was depressed. He tried Prozac and Zoloft, but neither helped.

Adam's computer screen had revealed some critical truth about George. "Lying about what?" I asked.

As a medical intern, hearing lies was a daily part of my job. We'd been taught—not in a formal way, but through the offhanded comments of our supervisors—to double whatever amount of alcohol or cigarette use the patient reported, and to accept this higher number as being more accurate. For street drugs, a patient's word meant nothing without a urine test. Aside from drug abuse, people most commonly lied about whether they followed a healthy diet, exercised regularly, or took their medications as prescribed. Lastly, many lied about sex.

"He's HIV-positive," Adam replied.

Of course, I thought, experiencing the same satisfaction I felt when the final twist is revealed in a good movie or detective novel. HIV made sense. We'd been instructed to always include it on our list of usual diagnostic suspects. The risk of missing it was too great, not only for the patient, but for whomever they could go on to infect. In George's case, HIV explained everything: the weight loss, fatigue, poor concentration, abnormal blood counts, everything. Yet, despite my textbook knowledge, I was still surprised. What I was about to see was that George, in many ways, represented the changing face of HIV/AIDS.

The mid-1990s was a time of dramatic developments in the battle against HIV/AIDS. The introduction of a new class of medications, the HIV protease inhibitors, transformed treatment, bringing many people back from death's door. Between 1995 and 1998, AIDS mortality in the United States dropped more than 60 percent. Among white men, this decline was even more pronounced, with reductions in death rates approaching 75 percent.

The same era also brought what social scientists call "shifting demographics" in the evolution of HIV/AIDS in America. Since the first reported cases in 1981, HIV/AIDS, aside from those with hemophilia or intravenous heroin addiction, was widely regarded as a disease of gay white men. In the early years, movie star Rock Hudson and musician Liberace were its most famous victims, and the activists seen in mainstream media were white men. From the outset, however, this was never the full story, as black people accounted for a quarter of HIV cases during the first decade of the epidemic, a proportion nearly double theirs in the general population at the time.

Not surprisingly, with all that is known about poverty, race, and poor health, advances in treatments for HIV had a muted benefit on blacks compared to whites. Not only were HIV medications expensive, but patients had to be tied into quality medical care in order to have access to the drugs and the support systems needed to manage the complicated treatment regimens. Given increasing infection rates and less access to state-of-the-art care, during the early 1990s, the death rate from AIDS among blacks exceeded the rates seen in whites. In 1996, for the first time in the epidemic, more black people in America died of AIDS than whites.

In the years that followed, the color of HIV/AIDS in the United States continued to darken. By 2001, the annual death rate from AIDS for blacks was nearly double that of whites. In 2011, when blacks constituted about 12 percent of the U.S. population, they accounted for 46 percent of new HIV infection cases. Put another way, black people in the U.S. are more than eight times as likely as whites to be diagnosed with HIV. Once diagnosed, they are about nine times more likely to die from AIDS. Hispanics are also afflicted in disproportionate numbers. What had once been seen as a white disease has turned black and brown.

HIV had been on his family doctor's list of possible diagnoses, but George had declined the test, saying that he'd tested negative before and hadn't had sex with anyone other than his wife since. It was not until George was admitted to our hospital that he consented to an HIV test.

"I guess he wasn't completely honest with his family doctor," I said.

"Or with us," Adam replied. "And probably not with his wife either."

I went through what we knew. We'd done the standard HIV risk assessment when he'd been admitted to the hospital. He worked in an office setting. He'd been married for almost twenty years. His wife worked at a prison and had tested negative for HIV ten months earlier. He denied any extramarital affairs, as did she. He told us that he did not use street drugs of any kind, much less ever inject them into his veins. He said he'd never had a blood transfusion. Based on this information, HIV seemed unlikely, and we were all set to undertake a detailed and expensive series of tests to uncover some rare disease.

"You wanna tell him?" Adam asked me.

"Sure," I said. "Let me finish this note, and I'll go do it."

In the half-hour or so it took me to finish the paperwork on the other patient, Adam had changed his mind. "Why don't we go as a team?" he said. "This might be a good learning opportunity for our student. Besides, I know this sounds awful, but I'm dying to know the truth."

This all seemed callous, to be sure. I was looking at George's diagnosis as I would a TV mystery, while Adam was focused on the soap opera element. Our medical student, well into her year of clinical rotations, shared our curiosity. "His wife is going to be pissed," she said. Trapped inside the hospital vortex where disease, disability, and death were constant companions, our reactions passed for normal behavior.

It was only as we stood outside of George's room that I started to fully appreciate the emotional weight of the diagnosis. HIV in 2004 wasn't the universal death sentence it had been two decades earlier; still, other than cancer, organ failure, and a few neurological disorders, it was just about the worst news that a doctor could give.

"Here goes," I said, as I knocked on the door to George's room.

By this point, I'd been a medical intern for nearly nine months. Combined with my years in medical school, I'd been a part of delivering enough bad news for a full season's worth of episodes on a TV medical drama: "Sir, you have cancer"; "Ma'am, your cancer has returned"; "Your husband's stroke has taken away his ability to talk or swallow food"; "Your mother's dementia is progressive, and there are no other treatments left for us to try." Saying and hearing these things for the first time had been heart-wrenching. Now, however, these and other grim pronouncements were stuck in my mind, as accessible to me as the lyrics to my favorite Bob Marley or Marvin Gaye songs. A few days before, I had to tell a woman that her fifty-five-year-old husband had died of a heart attack, and while I truly felt sorry for her, the words had come off my tongue as easily as if I'd been giving directions to the hospital cafeteria.

But I'd never told a patient that he or she had HIV/AIDS—or even watched another doctor do it. All of the HIV-positive patients I'd seen had been diagnosed before I met them. Despite my experiences being part of the worst moments of people's lives, giving George his diagnosis felt different. Cancer, diabetes, and pneumonia were universally seen as diseases of the body, even if the person's lifestyle had in some measure contributed to the illness or made its course worse. HIV, despite its irrefutable biological dimension, was still seen by many as an indictment of one's character or morals. At the time, a part of me agreed. Once universal testing of the blood supply in the mid-1980s virtually eliminated HIV infection through blood transfusions, people came down with HIV in one of two ways: sharing infected needles or, much more commonly, through sex.

When we entered the room, George was propped up in bed, sipping water from a paper cup. A slow-drip intravenous line gave him additional fluids to offset his dehydration. A plastic, handheld urinal hung on his bedrail for easy access; his weakness made the short trip to the bathroom a perilous journey. This was surely not how he had envisioned his life in the weeks before he turned fifty.

"All my young doctors are here," George said to his wife, Janice, who sat upright in a vinyl chair that doubled as a sleeping recliner for overnight stays. Like so many attentive spouses, she'd dragged him to the doctor when, left to his own devices, he would have continued to downplay or ignore his health problems.

"Any updates?" she asked, putting down her book and moving to the edge of the chair.

I wasn't sure how to begin. If George had pancreatitis or an ulcer, it would have been easy to tell him and his wife together. But HIV would affect Janice and their marriage in a way that other medical disorders did not. For all we knew, it already had. I looked over at Adam for guidance. It was time for him to take over. His instinct was to break the news by separating them.

"We'd like to look him over again closely and do some more neurological tests," he said. "With the three of us examining him in here, it will be a little crowded. If it's okay with you, we'd like you to give us a little time alone with him."

Janice seemed confused at first, but she didn't put up a fight. "How much time?"

Adam rubbed his temples. "Give us fifteen minutes."

"I'm going to go down to the cafeteria and get some food," Janice said to George. "Anything you want me to bring you back?"

George shook his head. Janice slung her purse over her shoulder and leaned down to kiss him on his forehead. I couldn't help but wonder how long it would be before she kissed him again, if ever.

After she left, Adam and I took a half-step toward George. Up close, his butterscotch complexion was sallow. Now that we knew he was HIV-positive, we examined him more methodically, looking closely for any signs of the complications that might accompany HIV infection. We felt for enlarged lymph nodes, peered into his mouth for signs of thrush, and searched his skin from head to toe for rashes or other discolorations, however slight. We shined a light into the back of his eyes. We didn't find anything new.

"There's something else we need to tell you," Adam said, retreating a half-step back.

"What is it?" George asked. "Did you find out what is wrong with me?"

"We believe so," Adam said. "Sir, your HIV test came back positive."

George blinked twice and then looked away. After about fifteen seconds of silence, Adam spoke again:

"Did you suspect that this might be possible?"

The question seemed innocent enough, but he was basically asking George about the many not-so-innocent ways that a married man with an HIV-negative wife acquired HIV.

"No, I actually can't believe it," George said, as his eyes briefly met ours. "Are you sure that's what I have? It couldn't be something else?"

Adam told him that the chance for a false-positive test was nearly one in a million. George looked at the overhead television. "So what's next?" he asked.

Adam explained that we would need to check his CD4 count and HIV viral load, both markers for disease progression, and that these numbers would determine how to proceed. A small tear trickled down the bridge of George's nose. "Damn," he said.

"I can imagine how difficult this must be," Adam said. "I'm sorry about this."

George stared out the window. Adam had seemed detached outside of George's room, but he'd turned into a caring doctor inside of it. I could see this skill serving him well in his future career as an oncologist.

Adam stayed quiet for several seconds, giving George space to think. Then he said, "Your wife will be back in a few minutes. How do you want her to learn about this?"

George turned toward us again. "Maybe you should tell her."

Adam nodded. We stepped outside the room to give George a few minutes alone. The nightshift nurses and nurses' aides were on duty now, popping in from one room to the next, administering medications and checking vital signs. I opened George's medical chart while Adam tested our medical student's knowledge about HIV/AIDS. First, I entered orders for the lab to draw blood for a CD4 count and an HIV viral load. Then I wrote a short note to document our conversation informing George of his HIV status. These few words in his medical record—written in clinically detached language—gave no hint of their emotional impact.

By the time I finished writing, Janice had returned. She walked in short, quick strides, her braids flopping back and forth with each step.

"Can we speak to you alone?" Adam asked her. "There's a room down the hall."

"What's going on?" she asked, taking a deep breath.

"He's okay. But there's something important we need to talk about."

We walked off the unit and found an empty conference room. The medical student, Adam, and I—all wearing our white coats— sat side by side at a table directly across from Janice. I sometimes wondered whether patients and their families might take bad news better coming from a single person, but medical care at a university hospital was a team effort.

Adam wasted no time getting to the point: "Your husband tested positive for HIV. I'm sorry to tell you this."

"What!" Janice looked at me, perhaps seeking confirmation. I stared back solemnly. I didn't know what else to say or do. She put her hand over her mouth. "That can't be true."

Adam explained to her how rare it was to have a false-positive HIV test, but Janice was not convinced by the numbers. "I want the test repeated."

Adam said that we would do this, but that we'd also be taking the next steps so as not to delay treatment.

"I just . . . can't believe it," she said. "We have lived a Christian life. I know he would not have done anything to jeopardize that."

Based on what we knew about HIV, George had to have contracted it during the course of their nearly twenty-year marriage. It would have been virtually impossible for him to have been infected before then and never have taken ill. Absent occupational exposure (George worked in a college office), blood or organ transfusion (none), or intravenous drug use (he denied), George had to have done *something* sexual outside their marriage. This was an awful way for her to discover his infidelity; the only thing worse would have been if Janice had learned of his cheating by being diagnosed herself. "What did he have to say for himself?" Janice asked, as a vein bulged on her left temple.

"He seemed just as shocked," Adam replied. "We didn't get into the how or why."

"There's just no way," Janice said, looking down in her lap. "This can't be happening."

Adam advised Janice to get tested herself as soon as possible and then again six months after their last unprotected sexual encounter. He told her that condoms were essential from this point forward. He also mentioned that a social worker would be talking with them the next morning, and that other counseling supports were available to them too. Janice listened silently, her hands firmly gripping the chair armrests. She appeared to be trying to hold herself in place, as if any movement might unleash an emotional torrent.

As we left the conference room, Janice headed toward the elevator instead of rushing to comfort George. Maybe she needed fresh air or time alone to process what we'd told her. We walked back to the ward in silence. Our initial excitement for the case had vanished. What was salacious in the abstract was heartbreaking when seen up close.

Back on the unit we found Laura, the overnight nurse assigned to George. She was in her late thirties, highly organized and detail-oriented yet friendly and calm at the same time. We told her the story and asked her to keep a close eye on them. "Will do," she said. "That poor woman. What an awful situation."

We nodded before moving on to our other work; we had no time to dwell on the cruel twists of life. Adam and the medical student went down to the ED to see a new patient being admitted to our team, while I tended to the usual array of intern duties—managing various medical complaints, reviewing lab tests, and drawing blood samples on feverish people—that kept me up most of the night. The basic tenet of such work is to help people. In the life of an intern, however, practicing medicine felt more like trying to stay afloat without hurting anyone.

The next morning before she left, Laura gave us an update on George. "His wife came back about an hour after my shift started. There was a lot of crying and arguing at first, but nothing that got me or anyone else worried," Laura said. "She stormed out around ten o'clock. We figured maybe it was all too much for her. I went in and talked with him for a while. He said he'd let her down."

According to Laura, he didn't offer other details, but this seemed to be a tacit admission that he'd cheated on Janice.

"She came back again around eleven and stayed the night," Laura said. "I talked with her too. She's mostly in denial right now. I left a message for the social worker to see them first thing. I just hope he didn't give it to her."

Great nurse that she was, Laura had done the emotional heavy lifting that made our jobs easier. When we checked in during our morning rounds, George and Janice were in the same positions that we'd seen them the previous day before breaking the news. They had little to say other than wanting to know if the results from the second HIV test had come in. They hadn't, but we were certain that this test was going to be positive too. We were also awaiting the results of his CD4 count and HIV viral load before starting treatments. Nothing had changed, and yet everything had changed.

Later that morning, I caught up with the social worker assigned to the case. He was in his early forties, balding on top, with freckled skin that looked as if it would sunburn easily. In addition to his work at the hospital, he also had an evening psychotherapy practice in town. He pulled me aside. "You didn't hear this from me, and don't put it on the chart, but I'm pretty certain our guy is gay. The wife doesn't know it. I've seen a fair amount of this in my practice. Besides, as a gay man, I'm pretty good at picking out other gay men who are in the closet."

I wasn't sure what to say or how to respond. George did not appear gay to me, certainly not in the stereotyped manner that gay men were so often depicted in the popular culture. But in the past, I had incorrectly assumed that some men were gay who weren't, and vice versa, so I had no reason to dispute the social worker's assessment. His judgment made sense: It explained how George could have acquired HIV in the absence of any other risk factors. I filed the social worker's theory away as the most likely explanation. We never got a better one.

We could only go so far with our inquiries with George. Now that Janice knew that her husband had HIV, it was up to her to get an HIV test and use condoms if she decided that she could move beyond George's secrets, whatever those turned out to be. As his physicians, the way he had acquired HIV would have no effect on how we treated him now that he had been diagnosed. Yet as we prepared to hand over the case to the infectious disease specialists, George stood out in my mind. His story pointed to something I'd read and heard so much about—black men leading a "down-low" lifestyle— but had yet to see up close.

When I began medical school in 1996, I expected HIV/AIDS to be a centerpiece of my education. AIDS first became known to the medical community in June 1981 when the Centers for Disease Control published a case report of five gay men in Los Angeles who developed the rare infection *Pneumocystis carinii* pneumonia. The following month, the *New York Times* printed an article about forty-one gay men in New York and California diagnosed with the previously uncommon cancer Kaposi's sarcoma. Initially called gay-related immune deficiency, in late 1982 the underlying condition that led to these unusual infections and cancers was renamed acquired immune deficiency syndrome (AIDS). By the spring of 1984, it had an identified cause: infection with the human immunodeficiency virus (HIV).

These developments took place when I was between the ages of seven and ten years old, and were unknown to me. It was not until movie icon Rock Hudson's 1985 announcement that he had AIDS that I became aware of the disease. My mom was a fan of his 1950s and 1960s films, and throughout my early years, I'd caught glimpses of Hudson starring opposite Elizabeth Taylor and Doris Day. My mother was shocked to learn that the movie idol she adored was gay. It was my first exposure to the idea of someone leading a closeted sexual life.

Not long after this, a family friend in his thirties, one long rumored to be gay by people in our family, took ill and died within a few months. To my knowledge, his parents never confirmed that he had AIDS, but given the circumstances, this was the conclusion that everyone reached. These two deaths formed my initial impression of AIDS as a gay disease, even though I didn't understand at the time how being gay increased one's risk of contracting HIV.

When I was in middle school in the mid-1980s, AIDS took on new dimensions with the case of Ryan White. A thirteen-year-old Indiana boy with hemophilia who contracted AIDS through a blood transfusion, White, along with his mother, became a cause célèbre while facing virulent ostracism in his fight to attend public school. A year after White's death in 1990, basketball legend Magic Johnson revealed, in a now-famous 1991 press conference, that he had HIV and was retiring from the Los Angeles Lakers. I was a high school senior at the time, getting ready to start the basketball season as our team's captain and top returning player. Given his fame and incredible talents, Magic's announcement resonated throughout the country, but it carried added meaning in the black community, where, until then, many people had viewed HIV as a disease of urban, gay white men. No one had considered that a world-class athlete such as Johnson could contract the disease.

A few months earlier, I had attended a basketball camp filled with Division I basketball coaches who were scouting our games. One day during a break between games, an ex-player who'd had a brief stint in the NBA spoke to us about the pitfalls of life in major college and professional basketball. He started off talking about drugs. Then he turned to sex:

"If you're having sex, you need to use condoms each time. First off, you don't want any babies before you can afford to take care of them. But there's also AIDS, man. It will kill you."

That evening, I sat in the campus dining hall with a small group of other campers. The conversation eventually got around to our guest speaker. Cedric, a six-foot-four guard from Delaware who had his sights set on playing in the Big East or ACC, offered his opinion about safe sex: "Man, he was bullshitting us. You can't get AIDS from a girl. That's a fag disease."

We all giggled in ignorance. In the macho culture of competitive sports back then, being gay was like having leprosy. Never mind the statistical odds that in a camp of two hundred teenage boys, at least a few were probably gay or would come out as adults. No one believed that reality.

One of the camp counselors, a burly guy with a shaved head and thick goatee who'd played at a small college, had overheard our conversation. "Who told you that?" he asked. We sat up straight, self-conscious like a group of kids caught looking at a porn video. Cedric was tongue-tied. "That's stupid," the counselor said. "Whoever told you that is the same idiot who says you can't get a girl pregnant the first time you bang her. Stupidity can ruin your life."

However accurate the counselor's statements, they had little meaning to me personally. As I finished high school and began college, I hadn't come close to having sex, and given my awkwardness around women, it didn't seem to be something on my horizon. My interest in HIV took a scientific turn in college, where I became a biology major. I learned how the virus infected the body and, over time, progressively destroyed it. My education coincided with rapid changes in the field, most notably the introduction of protease inhibitor medication, the first of which came out during my senior year. Two more protease inhibitors hit the market during my first year of medical school, where my various coursework covered the latest updates in the field.

Starting my clinical rotations as a second-year student, I'd hoped to see this scientific knowledge in medical practice. But in a succession of multiweek stints through surgery, general medicine, pediatrics, and obstetrics-gynecology, I didn't see a single patient with HIV. Some of this was mere chance, as each medical team saw only a sampling of patients admitted to the hospital, and medical students interacted with fewer still. My experience might have been different had I gone to medical school in New York, Washington, D.C., or San Francisco, where HIV was more prevalent. Yet the adoption of protease inhibitors as treatment for HIV infection spoke to a broader trend. Thanks to their introduction, the illness that brought people to emergency rooms, general medicine floors, and intensive care units a decade earlier had become a chronic disease largely managed in outpatient clinics.

I decided during my third year to spend several weeks shadowing doctors in their outpatient HIV/AIDS clinic. I didn't want medical school to pass by without getting to see up close the clinical view of an illness that had such wide-ranging societal implications. The few dozen patients I saw in the HIV/AIDS clinic fit the profile of AIDS that I'd grown up with: They were all openly gay men; most of them white.

During the first eight months of my medical internship, I'd come across only a handful of people with HIV or full-blown AIDS, and even then only in passing. Once, I'd been called to draw blood overnight from a HIV-positive patient who developed a fever, and on two occasions, I'd rushed to the bedside with other doctors to try and revive men with end-stage AIDS who'd gone into cardiac arrest. George was the first patient whose case allowed me to slowly digest the social impact of the disease from its diagnosis. If the social worker's theory was correct about George's sexual orientation, then he fit the profile of gay black men living in secret. A few weeks later, I would see a similar case, but from a different perspective.

Monica was a twenty-eight-year-old woman from a small town about an hour north of Durham. She'd grown up the way far too many black kids do, raised by a single mom after her dad abandoned the family when she was a toddler. For as long as Monica could recall, her mom spent her days on the cleaning crew at a local hospital. With no support from her ex-husband, she also took on part-time evening and weekend jobs whenever she could. Many of the families in their neighborhood had similar stories.

Monica exceeded the expectations most people had for someone with her background. While her brother dropped out of high school and did a short stint in prison, Monica graduated with honors and never got into trouble. She avoided the teenage pregnancy trap that had befallen her mother and aunts. She went to community college and found a job doing billing at a local medical practice. A few years later, while working full-time, she went back to school at nights and on weekends and completed a bachelor's degree. She wanted to become the office manager of a medical practice, or maybe a hospital administrator. She'd set her sights on helping her mother move out of a small two-bedroom apartment into a comfortable two-story house.

Then disaster struck. During a routine gynecological checkup, her doctor discovered a slightly abnormal Pap smear. She was infected with human papilloma virus, a sexually transmitted infection (STI) identified as the main cause of cervical cancer. Based on this finding, he suggested testing for other STIs, including HIV. Monica scoffed at first. She'd had sex with two men in her life. With the first, a boy-friend in college, they'd always used condoms. She'd been careful with the second boyfriend too, but switched to birth control pills after dating for over a year. That turned out to be a life-altering de-cision: Monica's test came back HIV-positive.

Looking back, she remembered getting sick the year before and coming down with what she thought was a bad case of the flu. Working in a medical office, she figured that she'd caught the virus from one of the patients. But the symptoms she'd experienced were probably not from the flu; they were most likely from acute HIV infection.

After absorbing the initial shock, Monica responded with the re-solve that had gotten her out of the ghetto. She was fully compliant with her HIV medicines, taking more than a dozen pills each day spaced out over morning, afternoon, and evening. She did well for three years. She'd just applied for an administrative job at the local hospital and been invited for an interview when she got sick again. Over the course of a few weeks, a nagging cough wouldn't go away and she lost almost ten pounds. Then one day she started coughing up blood. A chest X-ray at her local emergency room showed a large spot on her lung. She was transferred to Duke, where she was ad-mitted to my team.

I combed through Monica's computerized chart to learn her his-tory before meeting her. Most of the notes were from her hospital admission three years earlier and subsequent appointments in the infectious disease clinic she visited every three months. I caught my-self looking for the entry that explained how she'd contracted HIV. Why was I doing that? After this long, it was doubtful that I could tell her anything she didn't already know about how to avoid trans-mitting HIV to other people. Knowing the source of her infection certainly wasn't going to change anything that we did for her med-ically. I had to wonder if I was looking for information that would allow me to pass judgment, the same way so many did back in the earliest days of HIV/AIDS, to determine whether an infected person was an innocent victim (someone with hemophilia, for example) or had made poor choices (an IV drug abuser or someone who engaged in high-risk, unprotected sex).

On her initial outpatient clinic note, I found what I'd been searching for. There, an entry stated Monica had gotten HIV from a boyfriend. In my moral calculus, this put her somewhere between blameless and careless. As I approached her room, I felt that I had pried too deeply. There was nothing wrong with knowing how she got HIV, but why attach moral judgments to it? I wondered why this habit was so hard to avoid.

I tapped on the door of her room and entered before she could reply. Anywhere else in life, I would have been appropriately shunned for my rudeness, but among doctors in hospitals and clinics, this was standard practice. The patients, dependent on our services, rarely offered any protest. Still, I felt embarrassed as I saw her reach to close her hospital gown, which was open in the back. I apologized for rushing in as I introduced myself. Her face relaxed.

"Nice to meet you," she said, her almond-shaped eyes staring up at me.

Her skin had a few dark spots across her forehead, a remnant of teenage acne. She wore braces, like I had a few years before. This tiny detail connected us. We were nearly the same age. In another life, she could have been someone I'd grown up with or someone I worked alongside. Instead, she was a sick woman who might not live to see thirty.

She'd tested negative for tuberculosis at the other hospital. But she kept coughing up blood, although a medicine she'd been given had slowed this down. Our plan was to schedule a lung biopsy to determine whether she might have cancer.

"If I have cancer," she began, "could that be from having HIV?"

I nodded. Some cancers, such as Kaposi's sarcoma and non-Hodgkin lymphoma, develop as the immune system progressively breaks down. They are among several "AIDS-defining illnesses," whose presence indicates that a patient has gone from HIV infection to active AIDS. Since the advent of highly active antiretroviral therapy (HAART) in the mid-1990s, the incidence of these AIDS-defining cancers has decreased greatly. Lung cancer is also more common in patients with HIV/AIDS—for reasons that are not fully understood—but its rates have not declined much despite HAART.

Monica started to cry softly. "I just can't believe that I'm going through all of this."

She told me her story. Her second boyfriend, Larry, had been a drug company representative who'd come to her office marketing a new blood pressure medicine. He had impressed her with his intelligence, charisma, and ambition—he was applying to pharmacy school and eventually wanted to start a chain of pharmacies. Unlike the people she'd grown up around, Larry was a black man who was doing something with his life.

"I thought I knew him," she said, wiping at her tears.

Standing there in her room, fresh off hunting through her chart for the source of her infection, I could easily have condemned her choices. But I wasn't perfect. While I went through high school, college, and half of medical school without putting myself at any risk, during my third year of medical school I had unprotected sex with a woman that I didn't know very well. I accepted without a thought her claim that she was HIV-negative and took birth control pills. That I came out of the situation unscathed didn't change the fact that I'd been more reckless than Monica had. Clearly, HIV was not simply a matter of morality or assigning blame.

Later that day, I met Monica's mother, Geraldine. I had stopped to collect a blood sample only to find Geraldine, as Monica had gone down to the radiology suite for a CT scan. I tried to slip out, but Geraldine would have none of it. After a brief introduction, she wasted no time grilling me on Monica's care.

"So what's this test for, exactly?" she asked.

I explained to her that the CT scan had been ordered to get a better look at the spot found on the X-ray at the other hospital, and also to see if there were any other spots elsewhere.

We talked about Monica's care for several minutes before the conversation turned personal. "How long have you been married?" she asked, pointing to my wedding band.

"Three months," I said, smiling as I thought about my recent honeymoon in Jamaica.

"That's great," she said. "You know, I wish Monica could have met someone like you."

I had heard this from black mothers before. Usually they were referring to the fact that I was college-educated, a professional-to-be, "someone who had his life together," in contrast to the familiar narrative of black men "not doing right," as my mom and grandma liked to say. But Geraldine was speaking on a different, more visceral level: "Monica wouldn't have ended up like this if she'd found a real man."

I felt a skittish sensation envelop me. "What do you mean?"

Geraldine looked away and stared out the window, frowning in disgust: "Her so-called boyfriend. The one that gave her this . . . disease. He was a fairy. A faggot."

I cringed. Words I had once used now sounded like instruments of ignorance and hate. Monica had not given any details about how Larry acquired HIV. Nor did I think it was my place to ask her.

I told Geraldine that I was sorry about what had happened to Monica. There wasn't much else to say. Two days later, the news got even worse: Monica was diagnosed with lung cancer.

Monica was the first woman I took care of with HIV. In the ensuing years, I've seen many more. Women now account for nearly a quarter of all people infected with HIV. The CDC documented the first two cases of AIDS in women in 1983, two years after initial reports of the disease. Both women had acquired HIV through heterosexual sex with intravenous drug users. Foreshadowing the color of the epidemic to come, one of these two women was black and the other was Hispanic. By the late 1980s, blacks accounted for half of all HIV cases in women; most recent estimates place that number at more than 60 percent. In 2010, the rate of new HIV infections for black women was twenty times higher than the rate for white women, and black women accounted for nearly 65 percent of all deaths among women due to HIV/AIDS. Not surprisingly, black children remain far more likely than white children to be diagnosed with HIV.

Many elements account for the higher rates of HIV/AIDS in the black community: poverty and low education, less access to health care, and higher rates of other sexually transmitted diseases. But I left the general medicine service struck by the impact of another factor, sexual dishonesty. Not only had George and Larry been unfaithful to their female partners, but, perhaps, they hadn't been truthful to themselves either. As I grappled with their stories, I reflected on the role that homophobia, particularly within the black community, may have played in their actions.

One morning when I was six years old, I was waiting at my neighborhood bus stop when a boy my age who lived at the other end of the street came up to me. "Are you a fag?" he asked. At that age, I had no idea what that meant. Judging from the smile on his face, however, and the teasing stares of some of the older kids around us, I sensed it was something bad.

"No," I said, praying this was the right answer.

"Good," he said, "'Cause I don't play with fags."

From then on, I was determined never to do anything that might make that label apply to me. During recess in elementary school, we sometimes played a game called "smear the queer," where the person who held the football was "the queer." I doubt the kids knew what *queer* meant, at least not in the adult sense. I certainly did not. But I made sure to never be "the queer."

By the time I became a teenager and began to understand the basics of sex, words like *queer* and *fag* had been so equated with weakness and inferiority that it seemed only natural for me to look down on gays and want to separate myself from them—especially from gay men. My parents, conservative in all matters sexual, did not approve of gay relationships, but they never had much to say on the subject, in contrast to the special condemnation gay people received at the hands of preachers I saw on television or read about in newspapers. Rather, they simply dumped homosexual behavior into the cauldron with all other sexual acts that took place outside the confines of traditional marriage and was thus to be avoided. Looking back, even if they had been openly supportive of same-sex relationships, I'm not sure that they could have counteracted the vicious antigay message I was hearing all around me.

During basketball practices and games, whenever we played poorly, some coaches and older players would say that we were acting like fags or sissies, as motivation to make us work harder and perform better. We, in turn, used that same language to taunt our teammates and opponents. Back then I used those words more times than I can count. I never openly ridiculed anyone or harbored any violent impulses toward kids I thought might actually be gay. I simply avoided them.

My homophobia persisted in college. One day after a game or practice, a black teammate, talking about a gay singer or actor he'd seen on television, proclaimed that if his son ever started to act effeminate, he would "beat it out of him." With his quick temper, there was every reason to believe that he was serious. Two or three teammates chimed in, agreeing with him. A few others laughed or smiled. I shrugged in tacit acceptance, as if trying to beat homosexuality out of your own child made as much sense as attacking someone who'd harmed your family. Or maybe I shrugged because we'd all heard so many statements like this before that it hardly seemed remarkable. No one objected or seemed troubled by his ignorant rant.

That same year, I was having lunch with a group of classmates, all black men, when we had a similar discussion. "There is no way I could have a gay son," Allan said.

"Maybe it's not in your control," his roommate said. "Maybe people are born like that."

"That's crap," Allan replied. "It ain't natural. It's all about how you raise your kids. Dudes turn out that way when they don't have a strong male influence."

The notion that being raised by a woman would make a man desire another man doesn't make sense, especially given how many black boys are raised by single moms, but we all accepted his flawed logic. He won the argument with a stupid answer.

My attitude finally began to change during medical school where I worked with a few gay doctors and medical students, the first people I'd known well who were openly gay. I realized that in our shared experience in the medical field, our lives had a lot more similarities than differences. Further, my medical education revealed a certain commonality shared by all people. Even if one sexual, racial, or gender group got a given disease more frequently than another, all of us were vulnerable to sickness, injury, and, ultimately, death. From all I could tell, gay people, like everyone else, sometimes dealt with these problems well and sometimes did not. Across the span of a person's life, where so many things, both good and bad, could occur, being gay (or not) was just one part of any narrative.

The medical profession has historically suffered from similar homophobia. Until the early 1970s, homosexuality was regarded as an official psychiatric illness. Dr. Mark Schuster, chief of general pediatrics at Boston Children's Hospital, has spoken at length about his experiences as a gay Harvard medical student during the 1980s, when some doctors openly discriminated against gay patients and medical students. Schuster once saw a surgeon refuse to operate on a patient whom he suspected of being a lesbian. Later, when Schuster came out to a professor who'd previously given high praise to his work, the professor revoked his offer to write Schuster a recommendation for pediatrics training. Shuster reflected that he often found himself in the burdensome position of choosing between being a doctor and being openly gay.

Surgeon and writer Pauline Chen recounted a similar version of medical antigay bias in a 2012 *New York Times* article, in which a supervising physician during her training chastised a group of young doctors for prescribing a "homosexual dose" of medication, meaning one too weak to properly treat the patient's problem. During my own surgery rotation in the late 1990s, the senior surgeon, frustrated with his junior colleague's efforts, told him that he was "operating like a fag." In each case, powerful people were using homosexuality as a proxy for weakness and incompetence.

By the time I met George and Monica, I'd grown up enough during medical school to begin moving past this sort of bias, at least enough to recognize it when I saw it and to take care never to perpetuate it through my words or actions. As a black man, hating gay people simply didn't add up. How could I get upset about being discriminated against because of my race while ignoring, or worse yet, being a part of, prejudice that others faced?

But many blacks see it differently. In the era of HIV/AIDS, much has been said and written about homophobia within our community. Black people are often described as the most homophobic racial group in America. There is some data to support this contention. In 2008, black voters supported California's Proposition 8 renouncing marriage rights for gay couples at higher levels than all other racial groups. A 2013 Pew Research Center poll showed that while half of whites supported same-sex marriage, just over a third of black respondents felt similarly.

Based on the comments of public figures, as well as private discussions I've been part of over the years, it's clear that many black people reject a link between the civil rights struggles of the 1950s and 1960s and the contemporary legal efforts on behalf of gay people. Barack Obama framed the issue during a 2008 presidential campaign speech, which took place at Ebenezer Baptist Church in Atlanta, Dr. Martin Luther King Jr.'s church. "If we are honest with ourselves," Obama said, "we'll acknowledge that our own community has not always been as true to King's vision of a beloved community. We have scorned our gay brothers and sisters instead of embracing them." It was fitting that Obama's comments took place where they did, as black churches are widely seen as a main source in shaping the community's antagonistic attitude toward gays. In some of the black churches I've attended, the antigay sentiment has ranged from tacit disapproval to outright denunciation. For every Reverend Calvin Butts in Harlem and Reverend Dennis Wiley in Washington, D.C., both supporters of gay rights and acceptance, there are many more clergy who take the opposite stance.

In recent years, a handful of gay black celebrities have spoken on the issue. In a 2011 interview with the *New York Times*, CNN anchor Don Lemon asserted that being gay is "about the worst thing you can be in black culture. You're taught you have to be a man; you have to be masculine. In the black community, they think you can pray the gay away." Lee Daniels, director of the movies *Precious* and *The Butler* offered a similar perspective, saying: "Black men can't come out. Why? Because you simply can't do it. Your family says it. Your church says it. Your teachers say it. Your parents say it. Your friends say it. Your work says it."

To be sure, certain white churches, public figures, and political organizations can be equally virulent, if not worse, in their condemnation of gays. Hispanic and Asian cultures also possess their own share of homophobia. But when it comes to how these beliefs intersect with health, blacks are the group least able to afford such attitudes. In 2010, the Centers for Disease Control and Prevention reported that gay and bisexual black men, despite being a much smaller group than white gay and bisexual men, accounted for approximately the same number of new HIV infections; in 2011, this black group surpassed their white counterparts. Among the many causes of higher HIV/AIDS rates among black people, homophobia and the resulting sexual secrecy clearly play an important role. The time has come for the black community to confront some of its prejudices toward gay people.

In the final days of my internship, I had a chance to display my ever-increasing acceptance of gay people, but I almost blew it with one harmless-sounding question. On the medical ward one night, I admitted a young man named John. He'd developed sudden-onset chest pain at work, and within an hour, found himself in our emergency department where he was quickly diagnosed with a pulmonary embolus—a blood clot in his lungs. He was being admitted to the hospital to receive intravenous blood thinner and to search for any underlying cause of the clot. Before this, he'd been in great health. I stared at the age listed on his chart. We were both thirty. I wondered how I would have handled such a health scare. Would it have prompted me to quit the grueling life of medicine and find something else to do?

After taking the usual medical history concerning his recent physical symptoms and past health problems, I turned to his social history. As the medical internship year went on, I often found myself more interested in patients' social and emotional backgrounds than in their medical histories. A heart attack or stroke could only manifest itself and be treated in so many ways, but each person had the potential to teach me something about a particular part of the world or way of life that I'd never experienced, allowing me to grow both as a doctor and a person. For this reason, I'd found the field of psychiatry increasingly appealing.

John had grown up an only child in Raleigh and played baseball in high school. His dad was a lawyer and had attended the University of North Carolina at Chapel Hill (UNC) in the early 1970s during the era when black student enrollment there climbed. His mom was a high school history teacher who had also graduated from UNC. John followed his parents' path in going to UNC. After law school at Georgetown, he'd come back to North Carolina and become a junior associate at a law firm in Raleigh.

He drank one or two beers on the weekend. He'd never smoked cigarettes. He tried marijuana once during his freshman year at UNC.

"Do you have a wife or girlfriend?" I asked, as I continued the social history inventory.

He looked at me uncomfortably. He stuttered. "No, I . . ."

I knew I'd made a mistake. During my rotation through another medical service earlier that year, I'd been supervised by an openly gay doctor who corrected another intern during a presentation for addressing the patient and the woman beside her as sisters when in fact they were long-term partners. John rubbed his hands over his knees, his eyes darting away from my stare; he wanted to change the subject. As with George, it hadn't even occurred to me that he might be gay. I tried to take my size-fifteen foot out of my mouth.

"Are you involved with anyone seriously? A partner, a friend, or anything like that?"

Beads of sweat sprang up along John's hairline. "Yes. I have a partner."

Usually that was code for a same-sex companion, but I was done making assumptions. "How long have you two been together?"

"About three years. He should be here any minute. He was in court today."

"Two lawyers," I said. "That's almost as bad as a doctor couple."

He nodded, smiled, and then told me a little more about their history together, which went back to their time as law students. I completed the rest of the medical interview and physical exam, just as I'd done hundreds of times before. We shook hands and I wished John the best. I hope I'd shown him that I was willing to discuss his personal relationships and treat them no differently from any other person. He'd just had a life-threatening episode and wasn't yet in the clear. He deserved to be treated the same way as the next person facing these same fears.

Although far from perfect, I'd come a long way from the teenager and young adult who'd been firmly homophobic. I deeply regretted the times I'd used gay slurs or laughed at demeaning jokes about gay people. As my pager beeped and I headed off to see the next patient, I thought about how society might be different if more people had experienced changes of attitudes the way that I had. Perhaps if George or Larry had been surrounded by acceptance rather than hate, maybe they wouldn't have felt pressured to conceal their sexual identities. Maybe tolerance could have saved Monica's life.

PART III

Perseverance

8

Matching

L onnie, a Durham native a few days shy of forty, decided one
morning that he was going to celebrate this upcoming milestone
by lighting birthday candles. But instead of setting them atop a cake,
he tossed them onto the wooden porch of his neighbor's apartment.
When the police and fire trucks arrived on the scene, Lonnie ran
back to his apartment and began hurling kitchen knives out of a window. Within an hour, he was brought to the Duke emergency department, where, just a few months after finishing my medical
internship, I was now on duty as a psychiatry resident.

"We've got a live one," the charge nurse said to me.

I looked up from the computer screen, where I'd been checking
basketball and football box scores. It had been a quiet Sunday morning in the psychiatric wing of the emergency department. One patient had gone upstairs to our inpatient psychiatric unit about an
hour earlier. Another was calmly awaiting transfer to the state hospital following a serious suicide attempt. Both patients had been seen
and treated overnight by one of my colleagues. I'd been on shift two
hours without having to do much at all.

"What's the story?" I asked the charge nurse.

"Schizophrenic. Tried to set his neighbor's apartment on fire. He's
been rambling about Al Sharpton and Jesse Jackson. Real delusional.
It's probably safe to say that he's off his meds."

"Or maybe he's high on something else?" I countered.

"I don't think there's a drug in the world that can make you this crazy," he said.

We shared a quick laugh. From a detached point of view, psychotic behavior was sometimes quite funny. But when you stopped and considered the person behind these symptoms, it was profoundly sad. And if you acknowledged that such illness could strike a friend or child and ruin his life, it was downright scary. It was easier to laugh than to cry or feel helpless.

I opened the computer database and scanned for records. Lonnie had been here once before, about a year earlier. That time he'd come in believing that the FBI was sending him threatening messages through his cell phone, so he'd coated his phone in flour and cooking oil and set fire to it in the middle of a busy street. He received injections of antipsychotic medication and was shipped to the nearest state psychiatric hospital. As I always did, I checked his chart to see whether he'd had any alcohol or drugs in his system at that time that might have explained his behavior. He had none. The nurse was right; this guy was really sick.

Hearing someone scream, I jogged to the rear area where the psychiatry patients were held. This space, like virtually all hospital psychiatric areas, was a locked wing, this one modernized in requiring a bar-coded ID badge rather than a clunky key to come and go. I pressed my badge against the sensor, turning the light from red to green. This allowed me five seconds to open the heavy wooden door before it automatically locked again.

Inside, there were two small seclusion rooms to the left, where the most ill and dangerous patients were housed while recreational drugs cleared their systems or our tranquilizing ones took effect. To my right, a large open area was divided into several small cubicles, each consisting of a lounge chair bolted to the floor and a television secured to the adjacent wall.

Lonnie was in the first seclusion room, screaming. He paced back and forth in the confined area with the urgency of a drug addict in need of a fix, but if his records were any indication, his problem had nothing to do with drugs. Over his thin frame he wore a T-shirt and sweatpants that had several holes of varying sizes and were blotched with paint stains. His thick hair and scraggly beard both looked uncombed and unwashed.

"This is racist shit," he yelled at the two police officers who stood outside the partially opened metal door. "That motherfucker tries to infect me with Ebola and I get locked up? You gonna let him kill all the niggers in Durham, ain't ya?"

The older police officer, a gray-templed New York transplant with broad shoulders and thick biceps, stared at Lonnie blankly. His younger colleague shook his head in disgust. Everyone Lonnie had encountered thus far, from the police officers who'd brought him in to the nurses and emergency room doctor who'd seen him, was white. Even the on-duty nurse's aide (most of whom were black) that day happened to be white. Like Chester, the racist white patient who encountered one black staff member after another, Lonnie picked the wrong day to get sick.

"I'm gonna sue all you crackers for this," he screamed, as spittle sprayed in several directions. "You just wait. I'm gonna get Johnnie Cochran and Al Sharpton and Jessie Jackson to come down here and put your white asses out of business."

"I can't wait," the older officer said sarcastically. "I need a new job anyway."

Medication is the staple treatment for acutely psychotic behavior. In the emergency room and psychiatric hospital, it often comes in the form of a needle in the rear end. The psych nurse, Suzanne, a brunette in her mid-forties, had already drawn up the tranquilizers— a mixture of Haldol and Ativan—into a syringe. In these settings, this combination was to agitated psychotic patients what insulin was to diabetic patients. Even the proportions were standard. Haldol was given in a dose of 5 milligrams, while Ativan was given in 2-milligram doses. So common was this cocktail at the places I worked that doctors and nurses simply referred to it as "five and two"—shorthand that communicates as quickly in a hospital as "I'll have a Number two" does at the fast-food restaurant drive-thru window when a customer orders a burger and fries.

Unless patients were trying to escape, or presented an active threat to hurt someone (including themselves) or to destroy hospital property, I liked to at least make an attempt to talk to them before they were held down by police and stabbed with a needle. Despite all of his paranoia and aggressive words, my instincts told me that Lonnie understood he had no chance of getting past the burly officers. Whether that meant he would agree to take medications on his own, however, was another story. But I thought it was at least worth a try.

When I came into his line of sight, Lonnie, who'd been cursing at Suzanne about how she was trying to poison him, stopped talking. His eyes lit up. He smiled the ragged smile of someone with several missing teeth. "Michael Jordan," he said.

Lots of people had said that I resembled Jordan through the years. A dollar for every time I heard this comparison would have financed a short trip to Jamaica, dining and hotel included. But maybe Lonnie, with his delusional mind, thought I *was* Michael Jordan.

I stood hesitantly at the entrance to the seclusion room. "My name is actually Damon."

He studied my face closely. I wondered what sort of bizarre and disconnected thoughts were dashing around in his fragmented mind. Should I have just played along?

"But you related to him, right, man?" he asked.

"Not that I know. But a lot of people have said that I favor him."

"You play ball too," he said, more a statement than a question, while excitedly mimicking the motion of a jump shot. He stuck out his tongue like Jordan did so many times, only Lonnie's was covered with a scaly, thick white film that looked like part of an ongoing infection.

I would have much preferred people to think that I looked like Jordan on the basketball court rather than in street clothes, but that never happened. Not even once. "I used to play a bit," I said. "But I don't have much time anymore."

Lonnie's jagged smile faded. I had dampened his fantasy. He glanced over at the two police officers who stood behind me.

"So, can you tell me why they brought you here, to the hospital?" I asked.

Lonnie looked at the officers again. I turned around. Both had their arms folded, which accentuated their biceps. Both wore latex gloves, something police often did around psychiatric patients in the emergency room, on the chance that they might have to grab and restrain the patient at a moment's notice. The psychiatrists and nurses usually didn't get their hands dirty.

"Can you give us a little bit of privacy?" I asked.

The older cop gave me an "Are you sure about this?" look. When I nodded, he shrugged and motioned to his partner. Both of them stepped back about twenty feet toward the center of the room. Suzanne went with them. It was more symbolic privacy than anything real.

Lonnie started a loud, rambling story about his neighbor trying to infect him with Ebola. Apparently this neighbor was in cahoots with the property manager to make all of the black people at the apartment complex deathly ill, as if a virus like Ebola could somehow be confined in such a way that it would only make the black residents sick. There had been news reports at the time about poorer blacks in the area getting displaced by affluent whites through urban renewal projects, or gentrification. So there was a kernel of truth to Lonnie's paranoia. However, his schizophrenic brain had distorted that reality into a delusion.

Although I'd been training in psychiatry for just a few months, this was sufficient time for me to know that there was no point in trying to use reason to convince him of what was real. That approach usually made things worse. He couldn't go back home, so I had to figure out how to get him calm while we processed his transfer to the state hospital, where the severely ill and aggressive patients went. The only other option would have been to have the police take him to jail for setting fires and throwing knives at people. But once he got there, from what I'd seen done before, they would simply have sent him back to us. He needed medication.

I glanced back at the police officers and Suzanne, who awaited my direction. I told them that I needed a few more minutes, then turned again to Lonnie. Leaning down slightly to minimize our height difference, I spoke slowly and softly, hoping my voice and mannerisms might help calm him. I tried to put myself in his place and imagine where his mind might be traveling. The first feeling that came to me, surprisingly, was power: "It sounds like these white people around here are a bit scared of you," I ventured.

"Yeah," he said, smiling again. "I want to make them all shit on themselves like babies."

I laughed—because of the absurdity of his words, but also because Lonnie was tapping into a familiar sentiment I'd heard so often. I used that familiarity to dig into what I'd long thought was a source of that attitude: "You also seem a little scared too. I get it, man."

Lonnie broke eye contact, bowing his head so that his chin almost touched his clavicle. His hands quivered slightly. For a second or two, I worried that I might have said the wrong thing, something that could make me the target of his racial delusions. I took a step back. But he had no more fight left. He looked defeated, embarrassed, and ashamed.

"Yeah," he said. "I need to get some sleep, man. I'll take those pills. They ain't so bad. You don't need to give me no shot."

I spun around to see if Suzanne had heard Lonnie, as he'd never lowered his voice enough to keep her and the officers out of earshot. Her jaw dropped ever so slightly. She looked at the capped needle and syringe in her right hand before her eyes darted back up to meet mine. "So, you don't want to give him the shot?"

"It sounds like he'll take the pills," I said, turning back to Lonnie. "Is that right, sir?"

Lonnie nodded. Suzanne scurried toward the locked door and used her ID badge to get back to the nurse's area where the medications were stocked. She returned moments later with two small individually sealed tablets in one hand and a tiny cup of water in the other. She popped the foil and plunked them into his hand. Lonnie swallowed the pills. He even allowed Suzanne to observe him for "cheeking," where patients pretend to take a medication only to spit it out moments later. Lonnie then stretched out on the slab that functioned as a bed. Within half an hour, he had fallen asleep.

"Good work," the senior officer said to me. "The last thing I wanted was to throw my back out wrestling with him."

"Same here," his younger colleague chimed in. "It looks like you're in the right field."

Suzanne smiled. She asked me if I'd thought about working in the psych ED as a career. By meeting Lonnie on his level, I'd saved everyone a lot of trouble. The police and Suzanne didn't have to deal with the inherent risks of an uncapped needle and an agitated psychotic patient. More important, I'd helped Lonnie. The senior doctor—in charge of the entire ED—had already ordered Haldol and Ativan; Lonnie was going to get the "five and two" cocktail regardless of what I did. What I'd done was save him the discomfort and humiliation of being forcibly restrained like an animal.

During medical internship, I'd drawn blood from veins and arteries all over the body, inserted needles into abdominal and chest cavities to drain away excess fluid, placed central catheter lines, and performed CPR. I conducted hundreds and hundreds of physical exams. Rarely did anyone compliment me, even as I became increasingly proficient with these various procedures. With Lonnie, I hadn't raised a hand. Nor had I suggested a drug that worked better than the standard ones any ED doctor could order. All I had done was talk to him. Yet this had made a clear difference in his willingness to accept treatment. Never had I felt like I'd done so little while those around me thought I'd accomplished so much.

"I think it's great for the patients here to see a black male like yourself," Suzanne said. "You know, someone they can look up to. It would have been a mess here otherwise. Thanks."

I wasn't sure if she was thanking me for being black, for being calm, or for both. In the short time I'd worked in the psych ED, two-thirds of the patients who came through had been black. On the inpatient psychiatric unit, about half of the patients were black. During medical school and my internship year, I'd certainly had black patients respond favorably to me, but no scenario had ever been quite this dramatic.

While race had been an important issue for me throughout medical school and my internship year, I wasn't sure what to expect as I began my psychiatric training. I soon discovered that, there too, race was often a factor in the hospital and clinic. Psychiatry, like other areas of medicine, operates on a two-tiered system of public versus private care. In many ways, however, the distinctions are more blatant. Those with private health insurance, or who have the ability to pay out-of-pocket, have access to private facilities and providers, whereas those who don't or can't are relegated to a public system that has come under ever-deepening budget cuts.

As a resident, I worked in both settings and saw the disparities play out on a daily basis. A typical case might involve a young woman who'd come to the emergency room following an overdose on prescription pills. After doing the initial medical and psychiatric evaluation, the next and most important detail was to determine her insurance status. This single factor would determine whether she went to our inpatient unit or one of several private hospitals in the area where there would be other depressed and anxious patients like her and she could get individualized treatment, or whether she was shipped to a state hospital, where she would be surrounded by aggressively psychotic, manic, and antisocial personality disorder patients. Invariably, it seemed, the private patient would be white, the public one black.

The contrast was most overt with substance abuse treatment. Much of our inpatient psychiatry work during the first two years of residency training involved people with alcohol and drug problems. In Durham and its surrounding areas, cocaine and its cheaper derivative, crack, remained the street drug of choice well into the 2000s. In local public settings, the usual protocol was to admit a patient for four to seven days for alcohol detox and two to three days for cocaine withdrawal (if accompanied by suicidal thoughts). The patient would then be discharged to outpatient treatment. Occasionally, a person might be accepted to an off-site residential program (fourteen to twenty-eight days), but that typically required them to have established outpatient care first and to have remained alcohol- and drug-free before they could be enrolled.

All too often, patients struggled under this system. While rotating at the state hospital, I saw Steve, a mechanic in his early forties who'd been abusing cocaine for almost two years, having started shortly after his wife and young daughter were killed in a car accident. His supervisor had recently confronted him about his drug use and threatened to fire him if he didn't seek treatment. Without health insurance to cover the costs of private office care and a three-month wait to be seen at the county clinic, Steve came directly to our hospital. Because the alcohol and drug detox unit was full, he was sent to the general admissions wing, where he was surrounded by patients like Lonnie who had severe mental problems.

Steve had arrived at the hospital on a Friday evening after work. Unbeknownst to him, that was the worst possible time. All hospitals operate with skeleton crews on weekends, but this tradition was more pronounced at the state psychiatric facility. There, one on-call weekend doctor at any given time covered the entire hospital of several hundred patients. Out of necessity, this psychiatrist saw only the patients who were having crises. After meeting one of my harried colleagues for a brief assessment when he first arrived, Steve didn't see a physician or social worker again until Monday.

By the time I met Steve as his assigned doctor, he'd been in the hospital for about sixty hours. With my supervisor beside me, we went through the usual psychiatric interview, asking about mood, anxiety, and psychotic symptoms along with assessing for any suicidal or homicidal thoughts or impulses. Steve's problems were basically limited to his cocaine addiction. We recommended grief counseling to help him cope better with the loss of his wife and daughter, but that was something that would be done on an outpatient basis. "We're planning to discharge you tomorrow," my supervisor said, after we reviewed with Steve his treatment options.

"But I came here for help," he protested. "This is the first time I've seen a doctor or therapist since I've been up on this floor."

Medically speaking, the purpose of detox was to prevent medical complications and monitor for suicidal behavior. Steve had stable vital signs and denied suicidal thoughts, so he technically didn't need any sort of treatment to address these specific criteria. My supervisor and I glanced at each other. She was in her late fifties and had worked at the hospital for many years. She was sympathetic to Steve's plight and his apparent sincerity.

"Before we came and talked to you," she began, "we tried to see if the detox unit would accept you as a transfer, but they declined since you've completed the majority of your detox here without any problems."

"But I think it would have helped to be around other addicts instead of here," Steve said, looking over his shoulder, where a woman paced the hall cursing to herself. "Most of the people here, you know, you can't really talk to them. They got even worse problems than I do. And now you're already telling me I have to leave?"

He told us his boss had given him a month to get treatment. Like many other people with substance abuse problems, he'd come to the hospital seeking a jump start toward a clean life. Spending three days around psychotic patients hadn't been much help. Compared to many of the drug-abusing patients who came to the state and VA hospitals, Steve had several factors in his favor—stable job, no criminal record, no history of failed treatments or misuse of the medical system—that made him a good candidate to succeed in a counseling-based inpatient program. But the next available opening was more than three months away.

The next day Steve was scheduled for discharge. The social worker responsible for arranging aftercare told Steve our plan. "We've gotten you an appointment for next Friday. That was the earliest that we could get you."

"That's ten days away," he said, his dreadlocks flopping as he shook his head. "I mean, I'm not mad at you guys. I know you've done the best you can. It's just not what I expected."

He was right: We had done the best we could with the resources available, but that didn't make us feel better. He genuinely wanted to get better, and we offered little help. Earlier that year, I spent a month at a private inpatient rehab facility not far away and saw the contrast. The patients had the same problems—addiction to alcohol, cocaine, heroin, and prescription pain medications—yet the approach was vastly different. Instead of planning their client's discharges the moment they arrived, this facility saw itself as providing real treatment.

The program consisted of several daily group therapy meetings along with individual sessions at least twice each week. Family involvement was a crucial component of treatment. The patients had a variety of constructive ways to spend their down time. While it's true that some in the public system succeeded in staying off drugs and some in private programs failed, it was hard to imagine that this more comprehensive treatment did not give patients a better chance at success. The private facility claimed that the majority of their clients remained clean after three years; in contrast, at the public facilities, most of the people whom I saw with drug problems never made it more than a year without relapsing.

During my time working at the private facility, over a hundred patients passed through, but just one was black. In contrast, blacks routinely made up more than 50 percent of the people seeking drug treatment at the public facilities where I worked. There was no reason to think that overt racism was behind these numbers. Instead, as is often the case in medicine, the disparities were more socioeconomic than racial. But the economic disparity largely played out along racial lines.

As I had several times earlier in my medical training, I found myself questioning where I fit in this scenario. Certainly I owed it to all the patients I saw to be as competent and compassionate as I could. But as a black doctor, now training to be a psychiatrist, did I owe black patients something more beyond my clinical expertise? Was it my role to try and help fix these disparities?

The more I thought about it, the more discouraged I became. These problems were far beyond the scope of a single doctor. And in some ways, they seemed even worse in psychiatry. I'd found the specialty that seemed the best fit, but race was complicating things once again. Not until an encounter in my final year of training did I begin to see a more hopeful possibility.

I was a few months into the last year of my psychiatry residency when I met Diane, a woman in her mid-twenties who referred herself to our outpatient clinic. She was a graduate student at Duke. Aside from this information, I knew nothing about her as I prepared to greet her. Unlike most patients I saw at the clinic, she had no paper trail of prior visits, nor were there any notes from other physicians in our hospital database; she was a virtual blank slate.

This abruptly changed once I saw her. She was black, her fair complexion and wavy hair suggested perhaps a biracial background. Immediately, I suspected that her presence on my schedule was no coincidence. Recent experiences had sensitized me to believe that someone had manipulated her assignment. Black students were a distinct minority across Duke's schools. So were black psychiatrists. What were the chances that we'd been paired up randomly?

I was always one of two or three black psychiatry residents at Duke, and the only black man in any class during my entire residency. Just 3 percent of all psychiatrists in America at the time were black, so my experience reflected a national reality. In contrast, Durham had a population more than 40 percent black; the percentage of patients who came to the psychiatry resident clinic who were black was at least that high.

As a result, in the months leading up to my final year of training, senior residents or other psychiatrists leaving this clinic often asked me to take over the care of their black clients. Some said it was the patient's request, while others decided that I would fit well with their patients. Initially, I felt obligated to accept these referrals, as these same-identity requests happened to other doctors too: a woman abused in childhood or raped as an adult who wanted a female doctor, for instance, or a Hispanic patient wanting a Spanish-speaking physician. But we had several female staff to share the load, and the number of Hispanic clients in our clinic was small. With nearly half the patients black, and since I was the only black provider for much of that year, the numbers simply didn't add up. Further, I knew that simply being black gave me no special qualification to treat black people. Sometimes a same-race pairing made perfect sense, but other times they were off the mark.

At the beginning of that year, a faculty psychiatrist had assigned me the case of a frustrated black woman trying to cope with life as a single mother, thinking that because the woman and I were both black, I might be able to get further with her care than the previous resident had. The woman worked as a bus driver. She had two children from different relationships. Her daughter was a high school junior on track for college while her son was in danger of failing out of school. We had little in common. I'd been raised in a two-parent home, was married, and had no children. My supervisor, also a mother, connected to the woman on a level that I couldn't and ultimately took over the case herself. Motherhood, not race, had been the crucial link.

Another time, a graduating senior resident sent to me an anxious middle-aged black man who struggled to find a compatible same-sex partner while feeling ostracized by the homophobia from his conservative family. While I'd moved past much of my earlier homophobia, it was still challenging to apply the skills of psychotherapy toward this case, as it involved discussing the intimate details of his sexual life. Although I put more effort into our sessions than with any other patient that year, I sensed that I was never as helpful to him as the previous doctor had been. During that year, the patient, frustrated by his lack of progress toward feeling better, relapsed on alcohol, something that he had managed to abstain from during the two years he saw the other resident.

With these experiences in my head as I led Diane to my office, I cynically wondered whether the clinic's latest effort at racial profiling would be shortsighted too.

"So what brings you here?" I asked after we both sat down.

"I'm feeling overwhelmed," she said, crossing and uncrossing her legs a few times.

She started by telling me that she was a graduate student and that she felt uncertain about her career path. I felt myself relax. So many of the men and women I saw had problems—bitter divorces, partner infidelity, drug abuse, troublemaking children—for which I had no personal frame of reference. Here I was on familiar ground. I assumed we'd explore the pros and cons of her current path and assess what she wanted from her career and her life, something that I had done myself and talked over with colleagues since college.

"I'm not sure if North Carolina is the right place for me either," she continued. She described growing up in a predominately white neighborhood and attending white schools in suburban Massachusetts. She'd attended a liberal arts college in New York and was having a difficult transition to life in what she saw as a more racially segregated South. Although our backgrounds were different, again, I could relate to her perspective. Finally, I thought to myself, here is a clinic patient I might be able to help simply by talking with them through the lens of my own experience.

I asked her the usual inventory of questions about depression, anxiety, and other psychiatric conditions. She described how she isolated herself, slept poorly, felt tired, and enjoyed little. She seemed quite depressed, certainly enough to warrant some form of treatment. "How long have you been feeling this way?" I asked.

"For a while," she said, her eyes drifting to the narrow, rectangular window behind me. "It probably started when Mom got sick almost a year and a half ago. It's just gotten progressively worse."

Diane explained that her mother had been diagnosed with breast cancer and had undergone surgery, chemotherapy, and radiation. Although her mom was currently healthy, I figured that this had probably factored into her ambivalence about living in North Carolina. I was about to inquire about this when Diane abruptly changed the direction of our session.

"My dad is an awful person," she said, her eyes focusing on me.

I sensed that this was what she really came to talk about. I shifted in my seat. "How so?"

"He's a terrible human being. I've never liked him."

Diane went on to talk about how her dad had cheated on her mother and emotionally abused the entire family as far back as she could remember. She said that his parents were disappointed that he'd married a white woman and that while she was growing up, it felt like he was taking out their disapproval on her and her mother.

Diane's racial dilemma came into focus. While she identified with her white mother and hated her black father, to the outside world, Diane's light-brown skin, full lips, and other features signaled that she was black. She could not, like some biracial and other multiracial people, pass for white. I was getting the clear sense that her problems were more complicated than simply not liking graduate school or living in Durham.

"Have you ever had mental health treatment before?" I asked.

"In college, I went through a down period my sophomore year. I saw someone in the student health clinic and he prescribed Paxil. I took it for a few weeks and felt even worse. I don't want to do that again. That's why I didn't go through the student clinic this time around."

I'd entered psychiatry with a biomedical slant; my favorite rotation during residency was the hospital consult service where I evaluated medically complex patients and considered medication actions, side effects, and drug interactions. My first thought was that Diane probably needed to try a different antidepressant medicine, perhaps one less sedating than Paxil. When I hinted at this possibility, she made it clear that she didn't want to take any pills.

That left counseling, or psychotherapy, as the mental health community refers to it. Despite the interchangeable use of these terms by the lay public, I'd picked up on the distinction pretty quickly. Counseling could be done by almost anyone—a pastor, a teacher, a coach, a family doctor—whereas psychotherapy was the domain of psychiatrists, psychologists, and specially trained social workers. In other words, counseling was the cheap watch you bought at Walmart; psychotherapy was the timepiece sold at a jewelry store. A person like Diane—intellectual, cosmopolitan, conflicted—would come to a therapist expecting to develop a better understanding of herself. At that nascent stage of my psychiatric career, I certainly didn't see myself as skilled in that way.

As if my limitations weren't enough, Diane imposed her own upon me. "I don't know if you can help me," she said.

"What do you mean?" I asked, worrying that my inexperience had shone through so soon.

"Please don't take offense," she began, looking away. "But I don't trust black men. They scare me. Especially when they are bigger or darker-skinned like you."

I sat speechless as Diane talked. This seemed like the worst match imaginable.

She said that her father had a dark complexion and stood a broad-shouldered, thick-chested six foot two. Diane had taken after her mother and was five-one and little more than a hundred pounds.

My instinct was to take offense that by virtue of my appearance, she had lumped me with a person whose actions sounded despicable. But another thought entered my mind. This sounded like textbook transference, a psychological term for when patients project feelings and emotions about an important person in their early life (like a parent) onto their therapist. Until then, I had been somewhat dismissive of the psychotherapy glossary, but with Diane, the concept of transference finally made sense to me. I could see why a man who reminded her of her father would make her afraid. But where was I supposed to go with this knowledge?

My inclination was to find a different resident for her to see. In that clinic, I worked alongside two white women and a Hispanic woman in my same year of training. Maybe as a sophisticated Duke graduate student, she would even be better off with a faculty therapist. I told Diane that I would call her after consulting with my supervisor.

After I finished seeing a man with bipolar disorder who needed his prescription medications renewed, I went to Dr. Carpenter's office to discuss Diane's case. Dr. Carpenter was in her mid-fifties and had been on faculty for two decades. She had gone to medical school knowing that she would become a psychiatrist. During our thirty-minute meeting, I tried my best to get Diane assigned to another resident, offering examples of other episodes where well-intentioned but ill-advised race matching had gone bad. How could it get worse than with a black woman afraid of black men?

"You're trying to take the easy way out," she said. "This would be a good case for developing your psychotherapy skills. And if you give up on her now, she will feel abandoned and rejected, which will only feed into her negative feelings about African American men."

I was skeptical. It sounded like something I might have heard on an episode of *Oprah*. But sensing that I had no other choice, and fearing a negative evaluation sent back to my training director indicating that I was obstinate and defensive, I followed Dr. Carpenter's advice. I called Diane later that afternoon and scheduled a visit for the next week, doubting that she would come. A part of me sincerely hoped she would not.

My suspicion at being assigned Diane's case based on a race-matching goal was rooted in a larger history; it reflected the evolving rationale for affirmative action in medicine.

Forty years earlier, with the images of Jim Crow still fresh in America's consciousness, affirmative action programs were started on the notion of redressing historical inequalities in access to education and job opportunities. In medicine, the effect was quickly felt: By the mid-1970s, the proportion of black medical students had nearly tripled. But inevitably, these gains came at the expense of others. The first main challenge to this new order was the 1978 U.S. Supreme Court *Bakke* case, where an applicant brought suit against a California medical school asserting that his rejection stemmed from the school's policy of setting aside slots for minority applicants. The Supreme Court agreed that quotas were unconstitutional but allowed schools to consider race toward the end of creating and maintaining a diverse student body. The Court's decision guided the affirmative action landscape until the mid-1990s, when a second wave of legal protest emerged. Buoyed by a University of California regents ban on race-based preferences and a federal appeals court ruling that struck down race-based affirmative action programs, the diversity argument had also come under assault.

Motivated by these challenges, as well as the persistent problems of health disparities among black patients, several researchers in the mid-1990s began publishing studies that looked at the role black doctors played in the care of minority patients. They found that black doctors served black patients at six times the rate as other physicians; that black physicians were far more likely to treat patients covered by Medicaid; and that the supply of physicians was lowest in areas with higher numbers of black and Hispanic patients.

Over time, a related group of studies reported that black patients tended to have more positive interactions with black physicians. The conclusion from these articles was that increasing the diversity of the physician workforce could help reduce racial inequalities in health care, a position advocated by leading mainstream medical organizations such as the American College of Physicians, the Institute of Medicine, and the Association of American Medical Colleges. This has become the lead argument for affirmative action in medicine.

But this stance too has its limitations. Some of the research in this area has shown no additional benefits to black patients, while critics have argued that several influential studies were either methodologically flawed or overstated their conclusions. There have even been some reports that hint at the possibility that black doctors, for a variety of reasons, might deliver a lower quality of care.

Moreover, the focus on same-race pairings overlooks a larger aspect of U.S. medical care: International medical graduates (IMGs) constitute about 25 percent of American doctors. The vast majority are of Asian and Middle Eastern ethnicity. In many settings where poor patients—black and white—are treated, IMGs make up an even larger percentage of doctors. Unfortunately, much of the medical literature examining same-race pairings specifically excludes these physicians. In a 2005 essay, Alok Khorana, an Indian physician practicing in New York at the time, examined these issues in his description of caring for an elderly black man with cancer. At the end, he questioned the wisdom of moving toward black doctor-patient pairings as a targeted goal, wondering whether this might "close the doors to self-examination and self-improvement" among physicians.

In my own medical experience, I'd seen same-race pairings work both ways. In some cases, a black doctor seemed to make a positive impact on a black patient's health, whether it was the nephrologist persuading a young man to take his blood pressure medications, the obstetrician convincing a young woman to attend prenatal appointments, or in my case, the delusional Lonnie thinking that I was Michael Jordan and being willing to take antipsychotic medication.

On the other side, I'd seen white doctor–black patient unions operate flawlessly and had myself been a part of floundering relationships with black patients.

What all of this would mean for Diane, and my role as her doctor, I wasn't yet sure.

Diane returned for her appointment the following week. She immediately brought up her reluctance to come back to see me.

"I was talking with a friend a few days after I saw you," she began, "about how ironic it was that I got scheduled with, you know, a black man. I seriously thought about canceling this appointment and requesting someone else. But she basically talked me out of it."

I was once again at a loss for words. This felt like the plot of a formulaic movie, the kind where the first date goes poorly, with the man and the woman swearing never to see each other again, only to be strong-armed into giving it a second try by a friend or domineering parent. But this wasn't that kind of relationship. I was the doctor, the one she'd come to seek help from, only I didn't know what to say or do. So there we sat as the session began, fearful patient and frustrated doctor, both uncertain where this clinical venture would lead.

Gradually, we began the business of therapy. I asked more about her family. Diane spent the next half hour talking about her parents' marriage and their attitudes toward raising her and her older brother. She talked about her brother being a serial dater and his proclamations that he'd never marry or have children, and she wondered whether her family had scarred her in the same way. Then she shifted seamlessly into discussing her ambivalence about getting a Ph.D. and becoming an academic, describing how she felt torn by the desire to do something more exciting and immediately accessible with her life. By the end of that session, I felt a little better about my role: maybe things weren't going to be as bad as I'd initially worried.

In subsequent visits, we broadened our scope to issues of class conflict within our race, the portrayal of race in the media, and what these larger issues meant for her growing up and for the life she wanted to live. As someone who grasped these racial concerns on an emotional level, I was a good sounding board. Over the ensuing months, our weekly visits challenged her anger toward black men and, by extension, her negative beliefs about herself.

About two months later, Diane started dating Mark, a black student in a different graduate department at Duke. She said it was the first time in her life that she'd dated a black man. It wasn't that black men never tried, but she always rebuffed their advances, finding them too aggressive, too intimidating, too much like her father. Mark was well on his way to this same fate when Diane decided, after weeks of exploring her feelings about race in our sessions, that she'd give him a chance. At first she was afraid she might repeat her mother's mistake, but so far Mark seemed gentle and caring—vastly different from her dad.

It wasn't my place to encourage her to date a black man. Nor did I have hang-ups about interracial dating. What mattered was the transformation that she was undergoing—from someone who loathed black men and all of our negative stereotypes to someone who was open to the idea of treating each one of us on the basis of our individual merits. Week after week, we talked about the progress in their relationship.

Finally, after several months, she ended one of our sessions: "You know, I feel a lot better. This has been good. Thanks."

It sounded like a good-bye. When I asked her if she wanted to schedule another appointment, she told me that she would get back to me. About two weeks later, she sent me a heartfelt handwritten note, thanking me for all of my help.

The impact on me was profound. I had entered psychiatry with a biomedical slant, dubious toward those who were strident psychotherapy advocates. But I am certain that no medication could have altered Diane's outlook on race the way that our sessions did. And I had now witnessed the unique benefit that racial matching could have in a clinic setting.

Several years later, I contacted Diane in order to get her consent for me to describe her case in an article that I was writing. I'd periodically wondered how she had been doing, whether the gains she made during treatment had been sustained or if she'd reverted to past insecurities and conflicts. We met at a coffee shop not far from campus. She seemed surer of herself than I remembered. No diverted glances, no stuttering, no tapping of her feet or trembling of her hands. We were meeting as peers.

I started off giving her updates on my career. Then we turned to her life. "I've grown so much since the time I saw you. You really did help me."

She told me that she'd married Mark. They'd recently celebrated their third anniversary. He was nothing like her father. We talked about how unlikely her present life seemed when she first walked into my office. In other areas of her life, things were going well too. She was about to finish graduate school, and had taken a job as a professor at a college in California. She was also doing some writing for a women's magazine. She looked happy.

As the rain outside progressed from a few drops to a steady drizzle, I looked at my watch. I had to get back home. Knowing this was likely the last time that we'd see or speak to each other, we shook hands and said good-bye. I couldn't know whether she would have arrived at this place in life with someone else's guidance, or even on her own, but for once, I felt that by being a *black* doctor—rather than simply a doctor—I had truly offered a patient something more.

9

Doing the Right Thing

On an idyllic spring Thursday afternoon, two patients, Adrian and Henry, were among the half dozen on my schedule. Like most people, they had both made decisions that impacted their health. Those choices were diametrically opposed and, not surprisingly, resulted in dramatically different outcomes. These two men raised a question I'd been asking since medical school, one that I'd heard many doctors, in frustrated moments, bring up: How much impact can we really have on patients' lives when their own behavior influences their health to such a large extent?

After finishing my psychiatry training, I stayed in the Raleigh-Durham area where my wife had established a primary care practice. I'd taken a Duke-affiliated job in which, among other duties, I spent two days each week in an outpatient mental health clinic. Staffed by a mix of psychiatrists, psychologists, and social workers, my primary role was to prescribe medications and provide brief counseling to patients. This followed a model common in mental health practice; the sort of in-depth therapy that I'd done with Diane as a psychiatric resident was carried out by the psychologists and social workers.

For three years, Adrian had been coming to see me every three months for treatment of his chronic anxiety and insomnia. He had a history of alcohol and cocaine abuse, but had been clean for more than a decade. Initially, I had referred him to a psychologist for talk therapy, but he didn't like it. He wanted to feel calmer and sleep better at night, but didn't take to the idea that discussing his life in depth would help. Instead, we had tried a handful of medications with varying degrees of success.

On this particular day, I'd spent too much time gossiping with colleagues over lunch, so I didn't review the charts of my afternoon patients for any interim updates. When I walked to the waiting area and saw Adrian, it was obvious something had happened since we last met. Something bad. His body trembled as he turned to me. The right side of his face drooped. A shiny metal rolling walker was parked next to his chair. He'd lost at least thirty pounds.

Maybe he had been in a car accident. Maybe he had a brain tumor. Or, most likely from what I knew of his history, he had suffered a massive stroke.

His eyes locked on mine. He recognized me, but his face struggled to generate a smile. Could he move his arms to shake my hand? Could he still talk? I wasn't sure how to respond, so I tried to act as if his appearance wasn't distressing to me. "Come on back," I said.

Adrian's wife, Ellen, stood first, helping keep Adrian steady as he slowly rose from his chair. She'd come to a handful of visits with him in the past where they'd talked about marital issues, or the problems with their daughter's taste in men. Her focus had now fully shifted to caring for Adrian. She swung the walker so that he could grab hold of it and keep from falling. With Adrian and his walker sandwiched between us, Ellen and I guided him down the narrow hallway to my office. What three months earlier had taken fifteen seconds from start to finish, now took five minutes.

Ellen wasted no time getting to the point: "A.C. had a stroke two months ago."

She called him "A.C.," the initials of his first and middle names. This always made me think of my dad, who many relatives still called "C.D.," as my grandparents had chosen his initials before settling on a name. Adrian's thick graying hair also resembled my dad's. These similarities made me look forward to our visits, even if progress was limited.

"Where did it happen?" I asked.

Adrian tried to answer: "Baa . . . baa . . . baa . . ."

I was thinking as a doctor, trying to decipher what part of the brain had been affected, and in turn, what bodily functions were diminished or lost as a result. I looked over at Ellen, who fought back tears. This was no clinical challenge for her; this was her new, terrifying reality. She took me back to the moment that Adrian's previous life had come to an end: "We was at home. I was fixing dinner when I heard a loud noise in the other room."

She found him at the other end of their new mobile home, collapsed on the bathroom floor. He couldn't move half his body; he couldn't talk. After a week in the hospital, he was transferred to a rehabilitation facility where he'd received the usual services: physical therapy, occupational therapy, and speech therapy. But Adrian hadn't made much progress, nor did the doctors expect him to based on the severity of his stroke.

I thought about what took place a year earlier. Adrian, then sixty-five, had been admitted to a local hospital for a transient ischemic attack (TIA), or "mini-stroke." People who suffer a TIA often present with classic symptoms of stroke, such as sudden weakness, trouble speaking, or loss of vision, but the symptoms resolve within a matter of hours with a return to normal functioning. When he came to see me after that episode, Adrian acknowledged that he had dodged a bullet. But while he'd taken his daily aspirin and blood pressure medication, his diet wasn't much better and he hadn't stopped smoking cigarettes as he'd been advised. Now the second bullet had nearly killed him.

I looked back at Adrian. His efforts to talk had generated a slow trickle of saliva. He'd lost control of the ability to swallow. I winced. For some reason, saliva and mucus had always bothered me a great deal, far more than the sight and smell of blood or urine. I offered a tissue, but Ellen pulled out a white handkerchief that she used to wipe the pooling spit.

Adrian couldn't eat without the risk of choking or aspirating food particles into his lungs. Ellen pulled up his shirt to show me the tube that connected to his gut, through which he'd likely be fed the rest of his life. He also wore a diaper. My mind shifted to my own life. I had a toddler son at home who ate few solid foods and made a lot of babbling sounds. Dirty diapers were a daily chore. The thought of Adrian functioning at this level overwhelmed me, especially once Ellen started crying. What could I possibly say that would make the slightest difference for them?

"I'm really sorry about all of this," I said, offering Ellen a tissue that she used to dab her eyes and blow her nose. "Is there any way that I can help you?"

Quickly composing herself, she went through a list of things that were more appropriate for Adrian's primary care doctor to address, such as renewing orders for his adult diapers and tube feedings. But desperate to feel useful, I obliged. While this surely helped her, I was left feeling that my actions were ultimately pointless. In terms of treating Adrian psychiatrically, there wasn't much to do. I increased the dose of the new antidepressant that had been started in the hospital, but that felt about as useful as giving Tylenol for a severed limb. After they left my office, I went to the break area in search of sugary comfort food.

The next few patients went by in a blur. As they talked about their marital problems and miserable jobs, I thought about Adrian's future of babbling, tube feedings, and diaper changes. I wanted to tell them to just go outside and enjoy the sunny seventy-five-degree weather. To be grateful that they could control all of their bodily functions and stop complaining about things that, in the end, really weren't that important. If they hated their job, they could get a new one. If their husband or wife was a lousy spouse, they could find another one of those too. But Adrian couldn't get a new brain. This was not the day for my patients to see their empathetic shrink. I tuned them out.

Then Henry walked in. He was my last patient of the day. My mind was focused on speeding through his visit and dropping by the store to get an ice cream cone or box of cookies to eat on the drive home. But when I spotted Henry in the waiting room, my heart skipped a beat. His six-foot frame was noticeably thinner than when I'd last seen him a few months before. His polo shirt and slacks were loose and baggy, as if he was a trim teenage boy who'd put on clothes that belonged to his middle-aged dad. Possible causes for his weight loss swirled in my head. Did he have cancer? Had he quit taking his medications and become so manic and psychotic that he'd stopped eating?

I'd seen Henry for about as long as I had treated Adrian, our visits spaced out every few months. He had been diagnosed with schizophrenia in his mid-twenties, but the psychiatric label had changed a few decades later to schizoaffective disorder—a mixture of schizophrenia and bipolar disorder in his case—after he'd been hospitalized with a full-blown manic episode. The doctors in the hospital had started him on a medication that treated his mania and delusions, but it made him tired all the time and made his muscles too stiff to drive a car or work in his garden. His previous clinic psychiatrist tried a few other medications before finding one that treated his mental illness without limiting his daily functioning.

The only problem was that it caused weight gain. A lot if it. In less than five years on the drug, he gained fifty pounds. With this excess weight came diabetes, hypertension, and high cholesterol, all of which required treatment with other drugs. The medicine that calmed his mind was hurting his body. When I saw his weight loss, I wondered if he had decided to stop taking it for this reason. But that would be a quick way to relapse into a psychotic episode.

I ruled out any acute change in his psychiatric condition, however, when Henry greeted me with his usual enthusiastic grin, an amusing cross between comedians Eddie Murphy and Arsenio Hall.

"Heya Dr. Tweedy," he said as always, "it's a pleasure to see you again."

He sat in the same chair where Adrian had been just a few hours earlier. "How have you been feeling recently?" I asked.

"Good. You know, I still hear that voice, but you know, with the medicine, it's not getting any louder or telling me any of that crazy stuff anymore."

For many years, maybe decades, Henry heard the voice of a man that told him that his mom was an ugly bitch and that his dad was a child rapist. With medication, the voice only said his parents' names without the added commentary.

"How about physically?" I asked. "Have you felt sick or weak?"

"No," he replied. "I've been feeling good, man."

"It looks like you've lost some weight," I said.

The toothy grin came back. "Yes sir," he said, rubbing his hands across his smaller belly. "Twenty-five pounds. I can't wait to get on your scale."

"Have you been missing any doses of your medication?"

"No sir. My wife won't let me get in the bed with her until after I take it."

I suppressed a smile. Henry handed me the results of recent blood tests from his family doctor. Nothing abnormal there. If anything, his numbers were better, with lower cholesterol and blood sugar values.

"What have you been doing to lose so much weight?"

Falling back on the usual medical pessimism, I wondered whether he was taking some kind of diet suppressant or other quick fix that might ultimately prove harmful.

"I've been doing the right thing," he said, smiling again. "I'm getting away from eating all that artery-clogging crap. You know, fried stuff, processed stuff. I also started walking a lot."

It finally sank in: Henry had made real, positive health changes. This visit was going to have a happy ending. Given how the afternoon had started, I'd been so focused on finding the bad that I hadn't seen the good when it was staring me in the face.

"I finally started listening to you," Henry said.

I was thrilled. Because he took a medication known to promote weight gain, I checked his weight at every visit. This provided a natural opening for me to ask about his diet and exercise habits. For the hundreds of patients with whom I talked about lifestyle changes over the years, however, my medical advice gradually felt more like a routine than personalized care, as if I was simply going through the motions. The fact that people often ignored my recommendations only heightened my cynicism. However, Henry had taken my words to heart.

I renewed his medication, energized by his gratitude. We then walked down the hall to the scale. Henry had indeed shed twenty-five pounds. Keep it up, I urged, even as part of me feared that he, like so many other people, might soon slip back into unhealthy habits. Nevertheless, seeing Henry was just what I needed. I decided to follow his lead and go play tennis rather than gorge myself on ice cream and sugar cookies.

On this day, one man had made good choices and increased his odds of a healthy future. The other hadn't and, at least partly for that reason, faced a heartbreakingly new life. Driving to the tennis court, I was nagged by the same unsettling thought that had come to mind periodically over the years, one I usually tried hard to keep at bay: Could it be that despite all the years I spent in medical school and residency training acquiring specialized knowledge and practical skills, that this expertise mattered little to my patients' overall health?

People either made healthy decisions or they didn't. Those behaviors in turn would determine, far more than anything a doctor could do, whether they had a heart attack at fifty-five, cancer at sixty, or lived to be seventy-five or eighty before developing any serious problems. Time and again, black people, such as Adrian, suffered the worst outcomes from these bad decisions. As a physician, what influence could I have, if any, in helping them do better?

The choices that we make have a profound impact on our health. Sometimes it's a single, simple decision—wearing a seat belt or a condom at a given moment, for instance—that can have far-reaching consequences. More often, though, it's the daily decisions repeated over time that catch up with us. Smoking cigarettes, abusing alcohol or drugs, eating too much and too many bad foods, and exercising too little all can lead to an array of diseases. Of the ten leading causes of death in America (among them heart disease, cancer, stroke, and diabetes) each is strongly influenced by our actions. Researchers from the Robert Wood Johnson Foundation, a New Jersey–based philanthropic organization devoted to health and health care, estimated that behavioral choices account for at least 900,000 deaths each year and "represent the greatest single domain of influence on the health of the U.S. population."

While all of us make decisions that shape our health, the reasons we make those choices are more complex. A large body of research has shown the important role of culture and environment. Socioeconomic status, both as we begin life and as we traverse it, is paramount. Whether measured by educational level, income, occupation, or some combination, low socioeconomic status is linked to a wide range of health problems and higher mortality rates.

Low-income settings adversely impact individual behaviors, such as smoking, drug abuse, nutrient-poor diets, sedentary lifestyles, and less likelihood of following medical treatments. These negative patterns in poor neighborhoods often become self-perpetuating. Clearly, such factors have a direct effect on health disparities, as black people remain, on average, at the bottom of the socioeconomic scale. But putting all of the blame on socioeconomic status and personal choice didn't feel right. Was it possible that I was making excuses for inattentive medical practice?

Looking back to medical school, I remember little instruction on how to address the role of lifestyle habits on our patients' health. For example, we learned how cigarettes and alcohol damage the body, but not about why people smoked and drank or how we might intervene beyond prescribing a handful of modestly effective medicines. This biomedical focus persisted as we transitioned to the medical wards. Patients on our services were broken in some physical way, and our job was to fix them, or at least make them temporarily better, whether through surgery or intensive medication therapies. A high premium was placed on "doing something," which meant using your hands or your knowledge of pharmaceuticals.

During my general medicine rotation as a second-year student, our team admitted a sixty-year-old black man with chest pain. He had hypertension and high cholesterol, two risk factors for heart disease. He was also about forty pounds overweight. He was the sort of patient we saw dozens of times throughout our training. After all of his tests came back normal, we discharged him with prescriptions for aspirin, a blood pressure medication, and another pill to lower his cholesterol. The doctors told him that he should lose weight, but did not offer any guidance on how to improve his diet or integrate exercise into his life.

A few hours later, I had lunch with the two resident doctors on our team. Angela, the medical intern, was a black woman from South Carolina who planned to become a liver disease specialist. She was about thirty pounds overweight. Mike, our supervising resident, was a sandy-blond ex-football player from Iowa. I asked them their thoughts on counseling patients about nutrition and exercise.

"We should probably do more," Angela said, eyeing her hot dog and French fries with obvious guilt. "But I guess I'm not in much of a position to tell anyone how to be healthy."

Mike, who carried a few extra pounds too, seemed free of Angela's self-consciousness. He swallowed a large bite from his slice of thick-crusted pepperoni pizza: "That's the responsibility of his outpatient primary care doctor," he said. "We're here to deal with the life-and-death stuff."

This focus on biomedical treatment over preventative care is not limited to Duke or similar schools. Indeed, outpatient primary care physicians—the doctors that Mike felt bore the responsibility for counseling patients on diet and exercise—are often no more inclined than other doctors to have this discussion, even for diseases where these interventions are vital. There are many barriers, among them money (dietary counseling is reimbursed poorly compared to medical procedures), time (physician often see patients every ten or fifteen minutes), and the sense that nutrition talk is better left to dieticians, and that doctors should focus on their expertise (prescribing medications, interpreting tests, and performing procedures). In addition, experience has made many doctors cynical about patient behavior and the likelihood for change.

On the drive home from the tennis court, I tried to remember how much I'd talked to Adrian and Henry about these issues in our past visits, and what I'd said to them. When Adrian didn't stop smoking or eat better after his mini-stroke, did I keep encouraging him to do otherwise? Had I told Henry that weight gain on antipsychotic medication was something he simply had to accept? I could only hope that somehow I'd said the right things. But even if I had, why had Henry listened to me and Adrian hadn't? Was the problem in the system, with them, or with me?

Over the course of several visits, I learned Adrian's history. He'd grown up in the civil rights–era South of the 1950s and 1960s; his dad was a plumber and his mom a homemaker. He'd been drafted into the Army shortly after graduating from a segregated small-town high school. After a year in Vietnam, he came home and found himself overwhelmed by anger and grief, so he turned to alcohol and street drugs to dull these emotions. Nonetheless, he lived a functional life, holding steady work as an electrician. After a rocky ten-year marriage to his high school sweetheart, he divorced, and a year later, met his second wife, Ellen. Together, they had a daughter, now in her late twenties.

By the time we met, he'd gotten involved with a church, and had been clean from alcohol and cocaine for over a decade. But shortly after he retired at age sixty-two, the anxiety and insomnia that had plagued him in earlier years slowly returned. At Ellen's urging, Adrian started coming to our clinic. We talked a little at each visit about the possible causes for his symptoms, such as the conflict with his daughter and his tour in Vietnam, but he was more interested in finding a medication cure than a talking one. Medication did help, but various side effects bothered him when he took them daily, so he settled into a pattern of taking a sedating antidepressant medication a few times a week. This seemed to satisfy him for the most part.

We had been in this state of equilibrium for a while when Adrian came to see me after suffering the mini-stroke. He'd been at home watching TV when the right side of his face became numb and he started slurring his words. He spent two days in the hospital, and his symptoms resolved. The neurologists counseled him on the basics of secondary prevention, which included taking aspirin, starting a blood pressure medication, and revamping his dietary and exercise habits. Last but not least, they told him to quit smoking.

Adrian reported taking the aspirin and blood pressure pill. He said that he'd cut back a little on eating fast food but not as much as he was supposed to. "How about smoking?" I asked. Two of my patients in this clinic who had survived serious heart attacks in recent years had quit smoking after their episodes.

"I stopped for a month," he said, looking to Ellen, then back at me, "but our daughter started having problems with her boyfriend again and . . ."

I'd heard some variation of this from patients many times before. In a perfect world, they could stop X or Y behavior, only life kept getting in the way. I prescribed an antidepressant helpful in smoking cessation, but it worsened his anxiety, so he didn't take it long enough to help him quit. At the next visit, I prescribed nicotine patches and referred him to a stop-smoking class. Adrian canceled his initial session and did not reschedule. He said the patches didn't work and caused him to have bad headaches.

I gave up. Looking back at my notes, I could see that I never mentioned the smoking issue again. I never bothered to ask at what age he started, whether he had tried to quit before, why he thought he smoked now, or what might motivate him to quit. I never considered prescribing another smoking-cessation medicine that I had given to a handful of patients with good results. I'm not sure why I avoided all of this—had I become too cynical to even care whether he kept smoking?

Silence on this issue during our visits continued up through the fateful day that Adrian lost his ability to speak. He had finally stopped smoking, but it was clearly too late. He had not been able to change his behavior in time. Could I have done more to help him?

Henry, like Adrian, had grown up in rural North Carolina in a poor family. His dad worked in a factory while his mom cleaned houses in town. Henry went into the Army after high school just as Adrian did; however, being five years younger, he avoided being sent to Vietnam. Nonetheless, he experienced his own mental struggles. About two years into his Army stint, he started hearing voices. He began to act so strangely around his superiors that he could no longer perform his duties; he was soon confined to a hospital and put on high-dose antipsychotics. This marked the end of his time in the military.

Unlike some with psychotic illness, Henry's problems ultimately proved mild enough that he could maintain a job and a marriage. Other than one time in his mid-forties when he briefly stopped his medicines because of severe side effects, he'd never been readmitted into a hospital after his initial episode. He settled in to work as a janitor for a local post office. He'd been married to the same woman for twenty-five years. They had a daughter who had recently finished college.

By the time I met Henry, he had been stabilized on his antipsy-chotic medication for a few years. It was the best he had ever felt on a medication. Some of the previous drugs he'd tried hadn't worked. Others, while effective in calming his psychosis, caused an assortment of side effects—dizziness, tranquilizing sleepiness, muscle stiffness, and a hand tremor, to name a few. With his current treatment, he felt great—except for the fact that he kept gaining weight. I discussed switching him to a newer antipsychotic drug less likely to cause this problem. He resisted. "I don't want to mess with it," he said. "I can't wind up back in a hospital."

He had a point. Compared with the psychotic delusions of schizo-phrenia or bipolar mania, it's better to be overweight. In psychiatry, many doctors have accepted obesity as collateral damage, since some of our best medications can cause substantial weight gain. Estab-lishing sanity and maintaining a healthy waistline can seem like incompatible goals. Removed as we often are from day-to-day general medicine, many of us are tempted to punt responsibility back to the primary care physician for managing the medical problems that our medicines cause or worsen. In Henry's case, that meant pills for di-abetes, high blood pressure, and high cholesterol.

Until his most recent visit, Henry had shown no signs that he was serious about losing weight. But somehow, unlike with Adrian, I hadn't given up. At each visit, if only for a few minutes, we talked about what kinds of foods Henry ate and ways he could become more physically active. For more than a year, it had been a losing battle, as Henry soared above 275 pounds. But then, on the same day I saw Adrian, Henry showed up 25 pounds lighter. When he returned three months later having lost more weight, I knew this was more than a fad diet. As we talked about his progress, he brought up the issue of race, which he'd never done before.

"You know us black folks don't always eat like we should," Henry said. "That's how we grow up. With all that fried food and other bad stuff. Even when we eat greens, we drown 'em in grease and salt. Now I'm trying to eat one big salad every day and lay off the rolls and other bread. I'm drinking water instead of sweet tea. And I'm walking for thirty minutes every day."

These were real accomplishments. Over the years, I'd seen many black patients undermine their health through bad eating and sedentary living. While America as a nation struggles with its waistline, nowhere is this more evident than with black people, who are 50 percent more likely than whites to be obese. Stunningly, black women are nearly twice as likely to be obese as white women. The role of lifestyle in health disparities cannot be overstated.

"What's been your biggest motivator to lose weight?" I asked him.

He started to tear up. "I want to see how my daughter's life turns out."

Henry continued to lose a few pounds between each visit. Three years later, he had dropped fifty pounds and was just a shade over his weight back when he had started his current medication. He no longer needed to take pills for diabetes or high blood pressure. The dose of his cholesterol medicine had been cut in half.

Several months later, however, after missing an appointment, Henry had a setback. My heart sank as the scale showed he'd gained almost ten pounds. Since it is widely known that keeping weight off is harder than losing it, I feared this was the beginning of an inevitable backslide. I reminded Henry of how far he'd come, encouraging him while silently doubting he'd get back on track. Yet when he returned to my office three months later, not only had he shed the weight that he'd recently gained, but he'd lost a few extra pounds too. "Seeing you helps keep me on top of things," he said.

What had made the difference between Henry and Adrian? The secret didn't seem to be in their backgrounds: Both had grown up poor, obtained similar educations, held steady jobs and marriages, and had raised daughters on the cusp of middle-class lives. Both had psychiatric diagnoses correlated with worse physical health. Both struggled with lifestyle behaviors that were notoriously difficult to change.

Maybe, I thought, at least part of the difference lay with me. I began examining my own attitudes. Had I treated them the same? I'd never smoked cigarettes or used street drugs, nor had I ever gotten much out of drinking, so I struggled to understand the psychology of Adrian's addiction. On the other hand, I could fully connect to Henry's dietary and fitness problems, being intimately familiar with the feelings of making poor food decisions and eating to excess. Maybe these factors made me more invested in helping Henry. Given the impact that physician advice can have on patient behavior, I was left wondering if I'd somehow sold Adrian short.

Of course, it's possible that nothing could have helped Adrian quit smoking or make other health changes after his mini-stroke. But perhaps if I had tried more, at least I could see him now in his diminished state certain that I had done the best that I could for him.

Treating Henry and Adrian made me reflect on my own health. After being diagnosed with hypertension and signs of early kidney disease in my first year of medical school, I had spent more than a decade engaged in a health battle of my own. Armed with medical knowledge and motivated by fear, I radically altered my diet and exercised every day. By the time I began seeing patients struggling with obesity and hypertension, my own blood pressure was under control. My health problems seemed to have been solved.

During my last year of medical school, however, I slowly slipped back into old habits. This occurred in such a subtle fashion that I didn't really notice at first. It started off with me treating myself to a few cookies or a small bag of potato chips after some days in the hospital. On weekends, I'd go out with classmates and pay little attention to what I consumed—eating large amounts of food that were salty and sweet. Overall, I still ate healthier than I had before medical school, and near-daily exercise kept my weight down. I was seduced yet again into the notion that I was healthy simply because I looked that way to the outside world. And when I checked my blood pressure—which I did less frequently—it was higher than the ideal 120/80, but still within the normal range. So I didn't worry.

But that all changed during my grueling year of medical internship. Borrowing from the language of substance abuse treatment, I relapsed. The hectic pace of work allowed for only quick meals. Our nomadic existence within the hospital discouraged a routine of packing sensible lunches. That left the cafeteria—and whatever free lunches around the hospital we could get our hands on—as the default choices. A typical breakfast might offer a choice between French toast and pancakes, a lunch of fried chicken or a cheeseburger, and dinner some variation on the lunch menu. For overnight shifts, midnight pizzas accompanied by high-sodium breadsticks were a mainstay; a high-salt deli sandwich was the "healthy" alternative. It almost seemed as if the hospitals, with their robust cardiology and oncology divisions, were ensuring a steady supply of future patients.

Under the stress of sleep deprivation and what often felt like unmanageable responsibilities, I lost control of what I ate. Eating became more than simply nourishment; it was soothing my emotions. Being a new doctor who treated patients with heart attacks, strokes, and limb amputations was no buffer. I was like the health-food store owner who, under the strain of a failing business or marriage, reverts to his old ways and starts smoking again. I *knew* better but simply couldn't *do* better.

Despite a conscious awareness, on some level, that I was hurting my body, I didn't go for a medical checkup that entire year. The fact that my weight held steady—if anything, I lost a few pounds under the intense strain—allowed me to delude myself into believing I was still relatively healthy. Even after I started psychiatry, sixty-five-hour work weeks, coupled with the challenge of learning new terminology and treatments, kept me busy enough that attending to my lifestyle remained a low priority.

Not until eight months into my first year of psychiatry did I finally make a doctor's appointment. Once there, a nurse quickly ushered me into an exam room and checked my blood pressure. "It's 155 over 95," she said after the cuff had fully deflated.

I asked her to check it again after I had a few minutes to settle, but my blood pressure stayed high. The doctor came in and commiserated with me about the stress of residency and asked me to come back in a month. Over the next few weeks, I began eating better and working out at the gym. And while my blood pressure came down a little, it was still elevated, high enough to require medication. After a long discussion, the doctor prescribed a diuretic drug. I took it daily without any problems, and after a few months, my blood pressure approached normal levels. But as a doctor, I'd seen some of the long-term side effects of blood pressure pills. I was only thirty. Was I ready to start taking a medication every day for the rest of my life?

I decided I wasn't, and weaned myself off the drug over the next several weeks. I intensified my workouts and made my diet more restrictive. Within a few months, I was back to a baseline blood pressure of 120/80. However, my blood pressure eventually climbed yet again, as six months turned into a year and I gradually resumed my previous behaviors. For the next three or four years, I went back and forth in this way. I'd become a close cousin to the yo-yo dieter who loses twenty or thirty pounds only to gain it all back each time. As time passed, I knew that each "diet" would become more difficult. If this kept up, I was going to need medication, perhaps more than one, for good.

Why was making a long-term healthy change so difficult?

For one thing, it's hard to change patterns formed in childhood, perhaps even more so among blacks. Researchers have speculated that strong cultural influences on food preferences, food preparation, and perceptions about eating practices, passed down from one generation to the next, might make it more difficult for black patients to follow a healthy diet. "Soul food," especially popular in the South where the largest numbers of black people reside, tends to contain large amounts of red meat, added fats and salt, and is often deep fried. A 2012 study found that a relatively affluent group of black participants were less likely than whites to adhere to the guidelines of the DASH diet—widely accepted as the diet of choice for preventing and treating high blood pressure—even when controlling for socioeconomic factors. I could relate. On the cusp of being comfortably middle class, I still couldn't get my act together.

I believe the problem runs deeper than simply the food choices themselves. As a general rule, surveys have indicated that black people are more accepting of—and in some cases indicate a preference for—heavier body types. Skinniness is more likely to be seen as a sign of illness—cancer, AIDS, crack addiction, starving African children—and as a result, lifestyle changes aimed at becoming slender are more likely to be viewed with skepticism than enthusiasm.

I had embraced some of these ideas. Despite being a physician, I still viewed some aspects of healthy living—eating salads, drinking water, going to a yoga class, or jogging on a treadmill—with disdain. Employing my own brand of racial bias, I had internalized such behavior as the domain of perfectionist white women who struggled with self-esteem. White men who ate organic food and ran five miles a day in the woods seemed to be practicing some back-to-nature philosophy that didn't interest me. Given my struggles with assimilation since high school, but particularly so since starting medical school, adopting these habits to any extent over the long haul meant selling out some essential aspect of both my masculine and racial identity—even if my rational mind knew such a belief was self-destructive. It was not so much the differences in the food or exercises themselves as what lifestyle change represented.

Henry's progress caused me to rethink my distorted logic. He was a middle-aged, working-class black man with significant mental illness who required long-term use of a fat-promoting antipsychotic medication. In short, he was not the sort of person I would expect to succeed in revamping his lifestyle. Yet he had been able to do just that. Unlike me, he'd been able to see beyond the limitations of race and culture and focus on what was healthy. Inspired by Henry's progress, I took a closer look at my own beliefs and set about finding ways to incorporate what was nutritious from my upbringing—sweet potatoes, leafy green vegetables, and almonds for example—with healthier foods I'd never eaten (tofu and avocados) or, in some instances, even heard of (pomegranate and green tea) growing up. The result has been a truly sustained period of normal blood pressure.

My experience is not unique among black doctors. Over the years, I've seen a far greater proportion of overweight and obese black doctors in comparison to physicians from other racial and ethnic groups. In private conversations, we've talked about our challenges with living healthy. Many agree with me that cultural factors ingrained in childhood are a major factor.

The Meharry-Hopkins Cohort study explored our health dilemma on a larger scale. This project used health data collected on black male medical students from Meharry Medical College in Nashville, Tennessee, from the late 1950s to the mid-1960s, and compared the results to those from white male medical students from Johns Hopkins taken during the same timeframe. Both groups were then followed over a period of several decades. At baseline, the black physicians were heavier, more likely to smoke, and had higher blood pressures. Over time, they were more likely to have hypertension, diabetes, coronary artery disease, and to die at a younger age. As the authors state: "The very physicians who historically have provided most of the medical care for the African-American community fall victim to the same diseases that strike down their patients." Like the demographic data that I heard so often as a first-year medical student, the study's chorus bellowed the same note: being black can be bad for your health.

But as black physicians, the path to a healthier life is within our grasp. We have the knowledge and the economic resources to do better. Maybe this, in turn, can help all the patients we see, but especially the black patients who are often in greatest need of change. As the Meharry-Hopkins authors wrote, black physicians are "role models for the rest of the community. Such positioning carries with it the need for accountability. African-American health profession-als must modify alterable risk factors for disease and adopt healthy lifestyles. We owe it to ourselves, our families, and our communities."

Henry had helped me see past the thicket of race and culture to focus on what I needed. Now my turn had come to do the same for others.

About two years ago, I met Cedric, a man in his early sixties who reminded me of Adrian in several ways. Not long after his first ap-pointment with me, he developed chest pain that led to his hospi-talization. He suffered a mild heart attack, not that much different from Adrian's mini-stroke. He too smoked about a pack of cigarettes each day. He was also overweight. While prescribing medication for his chronic insomnia, I homed in on his smoking and dietary choices. We discussed how, although economic and social backgrounds shape our behaviors, with the right motivation, we can change them. With repeated inquiries at every visit and engaging his wife and children in the process, I never let up. Not much seemed to change at first, but then one day after several months had passed, he came back to tell me that he'd cut back to one cigarette each day and hoped to stop altogether soon. He'd lost fifteen pounds by cutting out fried foods and walking a mile per day.

"You've been a big help," he said to me.

After the last patient had left that day, I went to the break room area to grab a snack before sitting down at the computer to type my notes. A tempting cheesecake was in plain sight. Just as I prepared to help myself, a nurse walked in and told me that I needed to write a prescription for another doctor's patient, as that doctor was on va-cation. The path to her office brought me past the clinic scale as well as the automated blood pressure device. While I now made healthier dietary choices than I had in childhood and throughout much of my twenties and early thirties, the birth of my children had caused me to cut corners again. For lunch that day I'd bought fast food.

I also had drastically less time for exercise and hadn't done much in weeks.

When I got on the scale, it showed that I'd put on more pounds than I had realized. My blood pressure had also crept up some since the last time I had checked it months earlier. I'd been down this road many times before and knew what had to be done.

I took a pass on the cheesecake and went home and pushed my sons on the stroller for an hour at a speed-walking pace. In order to credibly persist in my fight for patients to adopt healthy behaviors, I needed to continue my daily quest to conquer my own struggles.

10

Beyond Race

Nearly seventeen years to the day after I committed to Duke, I attended a reunion celebration that honored the medical school's black alumni. Back in 1996, I had been racially and culturally insecure, afraid that Duke would be too much for me and that I would fail; by 2013, I was a faculty member who comfortably supervised and counseled medical students and residents of all racial and cultural backgrounds. How did I get from point A to point B? As I mingled with classmates and faculty from my earlier years at Duke, I found myself thinking about this transformation more intently than ever. I'd come to the ceremony with the goal of reconnecting with former friends, but the banquet turned out to offer much more; it was the perfect opportunity for me to revisit and reflect upon my past, and to inspire me for the future. My racial journey was part of Duke's larger story.

The formal festivities began with a video tribute to Delano Meriwether, the first black student to attend medical school at Duke. Meriwether grew up in segregated South Carolina before traveling north in 1960 to attend college at Michigan State. Although he was accepted at many northern universities when he applied to medical school, his father urged him to consider Duke. His introduction could not have been more inauspicious as he arrived in Durham the evening before his interview. With the school cafeteria closed, Meriwether, dressed in suit and tie, walked to a nearby restaurant in search of dinner. He was promptly informed by a waitress that he couldn't be served there; moments later the owner told him that if he didn't leave immediately, he would "live to regret his actions." A furious Meriwether left. The next day at Duke, he walked through the hospital where he saw racially segregated bathrooms. He thought of leaving, but decided: "If I make it through this school, can I possibly help someone besides myself?"

Meriwether ultimately thrived at Duke before enjoying a diverse career as a physician that included stints as a cancer researcher, White House fellow, U.S. Public Health Service administrator, and emergency room doctor. The tribute briefly covered his remarkable athletic career too. In 1970, three years after he graduated from Duke, Meriwether began running competitively; several months later, he began winning races. In 1971, he won the 100-yard dash at the national outdoor championships and graced the cover of *Sports Illustrated*, the dream of any athlete. He was a favorite to compete in the 1972 Munich Olympics before an injury derailed his quest. At the end of the video highlighting his remarkable life, he rose from his chair to a standing ovation.

The program then honored several other black pioneers in Duke's medical world, among them Jean Spaulding (the first black woman to attend Duke Medical School), Charles Johnson (the first black faculty member at Duke Hospital), Joanne Wilson (the second woman of any race to become a full professor in Duke's Department of Medicine), and Brenda Armstrong (one of Duke's early undergraduates in the 1960s and later dean of admissions in the medical school). While I'd spoken with each of them several times during my years at Duke, seeing their interwoven stories in one narrative felt like I was experiencing true living history.

Next, the video highlighted that in 2002, two years after my graduation, Haywood Brown was named chair of the Department of Obstetrics and Gynecology, and Danny Jacobs was appointed chair of the Department of Surgery. Black men had secured two of the top positions within Duke's medical school (their tenures helped lay the foundation for the January 2015 selection of A. Eugene Washington, a leading black physician, as the chancellor for health affairs and CEO of Duke University Health System). Toward the end of dinner, a final video profiled a handful of under-forty black alumni, and concluded by telling the inspiring stories of some of Duke's current black medical students, with an eye toward a future so much more promising than the situation Meriwether and others experienced fifty years earlier.

My thoughts turned to my family. What would Grandma Flossie, a housekeeper, and my dad's deceased siblings—farmers and factory workers—have made of my place in this world all these years later? I thought about my old neighborhood, where, absent athletic talent, college for males was truly the exception rather than the rule. I was thankful that my parents had been strict and protective. I was grateful that my brother—a family trailblazer—had shown me that college could be a real option.

Despite my professional success relative to my family and those from my neighborhood, here, among Duke's black medical elite, I was just another face in the crowd. And that suited me just fine. It meant that I was not alone on my nearly two-decade journey with race and medicine. Furthermore, Duke's story was just one of many throughout the country; most medical schools could tell their own narrative of racial resistance and progress. Meriwether, Armstrong, Spaulding, and other racial pioneers had enabled "people like us" to flourish.

As the evening drew to a close, I migrated toward the front where the distinguished guests had been seated. This was my first time seeing Dr. Meriwether. I wanted to walk up to him and introduce myself, to tell him how inspirational his story was to me. I wanted to tell him that as a former athlete of much less distinction, I admired his achievements in track and field. But he was surrounded by so many people, and as I've always been nervous in such settings, all I was able to do was walk past him, smile, and say "thank you." He smiled back. I hope that he understood the significance of his story to my own and so many others like me.

In the months following this ceremony, I revisited some of the places that had served as formative experiences in my medical education.

My first stop was the rural charity clinic where I'd met Tina and Pearl so many years earlier and seen firsthand how not having health insurance can be dangerous to one's health. The clinic still operated on the same schedule, with Duke students from the first- and third-year classes making the ninety-minute commute one Saturday each month.

I arrived on a fall morning not long before the Affordable Care Act took full effect. Since my last visit, the clinic had moved into a 1,000-square-foot double-wide trailer, about twice the size of the previous space. It had come by way of the Federal Emergency Management Agency (FEMA), after flooding caused by Hurricane Floyd in 1999. Despite the upgrade, the new accommodations were still no one's idea of a modern medical clinic.

Inside the patients sat along rows of wooden pews like those you'd see in an old church. By mid-morning, more than a dozen people had arrived. As had been true fifteen years earlier, every patient was black. They didn't have appointments; instead they added their names to a list when they arrived. Rather than a fifteen- or thirty-minute wait to see a doctor for a blood pressure checkup or to get diabetes pills renewed, here a person might have to stay two hours for the same service.

Aside from me, the medical volunteers (a half-dozen students and a supervising doctor) were all white. The patients seemed to eye me as Pearl had done during my first trip there when she'd said: "It's so good to see a young brother in a white coat," even if I wasn't so young anymore. For the first portion of the day, I settled in the rear of the trailer where Dr. Morgan, the physician volunteer, had set up a makeshift office. Pushed up against the nearby wall were a drum set, a keyboard, and several hymnal books used for a weekly choir practice, clear reminders that we were far away from the usual sphere of medical practice. We sat across from each other at a flimsy rectangular-shaped folding table where Dr. Morgan had stacked a few medical journals to peruse if time allowed.

"Are we ready for another exciting Saturday?" Dr. Morgan asked the group of students, as he sipped a cup of coffee.

Despite nearing retirement age, Dr. Morgan was just as enthusiastic as his students, showing no signs of slowing down. He worked full-time during the week in a busy community health practice a half-hour away. He had no connection to Duke or any other medical school aside from this once-a-month clinic, and relished this opportunity to teach students.

More importantly, he saw volunteering in this setting as part of his mission as a doctor. He knew the economic facts about the individual patients and the broader region: "Over twenty percent of the people who live here are below the federal poverty level. Among people who come to this clinic, the number is probably double that," he commented. "As a result, we're the entry point for many of them into the health care system. We're delivering a vital service."

Providers usually saw about fifteen patients on a typical Saturday, but on this cool, sunny day, nearly twice that many people came seeking care. Students saw them in two exam rooms, but so many people had arrived that the team needed to work faster to avoid extra hours in the clinic for everyone—patients, students, and doctor alike. So the students set up a third station at the corner of an open area, next to a water fountain and a bathroom, where they talked to patients in muted tones.

One by one, the students came in to discuss with Dr. Morgan the cases they had seen. Their stories were ones I'd heard countless times. Mr. A had diabetes and high cholesterol and struggled more with his weight since he'd been switched to third-shift. Ms. B had high blood pressure that required the use of three medications.

Mr. C had diabetes, hypertension, and early-stage kidney failure. None of them had health insurance. All were the faces of health disparities.

However, these men and women had better options than the ones I recalled from fifteen years ago. The medications they received were largely available for $4 per month through generic medicine plans operated by Walmart and a few area grocery stores. Dr. Morgan could refer some of them to his community practice, which provided medical services, such as blood tests, X-rays, EKGs, mammograms, and the like, on a sliding-scale fee. Even if patients simply came back here to the free clinic in another month, they would be seeing Dr. Morgan again, rather than meeting a new doctor and starting over as in years past. These seemed like clear steps in the right direction.

But as Dr. Morgan knew, the work that they did in this double-wide was not enough to make a dent in the larger problem. North Carolina had hundreds of small towns like this one, many without the access to outreach programs such as what we offered. For a nearly two-year period after I had worked there as a medical student, this town had been in similar straits, as the clinic, without a faculty leader, had to close its doors until they could find a willing physician to volunteer. During that period, some people scrambled and found their way to doctors and clinics in neighboring towns. Others were left behind and simply went without medical care at all.

In October 2013 when I visited this clinic, the Affordable Care Act was preparing to launch in full, but debate about whether to scrap "Obamacare" still raged. Some critics expressed reasonable concerns—that it might escalate our ever-rising medical costs, have a negative impact on small businesses, or place increasing burdens upon medical practitioners that ultimately interfered with quality medical care. Others, however, attacked the law on a socially divisive level, implying that it was just another government handout to undeserving people. Yet it was clear—as it had been fifteen years earlier—that many of these uninsured patients had jobs, but for them, employment did not guarantee health care coverage.

"I'm really struck by how hard it can be for someone with a steady job to afford health care," one of the students said to Dr. Morgan as we discussed a woman she'd just seen.

I'd experienced the same revelation in medical school. Because health insurance in the United States is most often employer-based, I once thought that most uninsured people simply didn't work. "I just don't think people take the time to understand how diverse the uninsured are," Dr. Morgan replied to her. "Most of them go to work and raise their families just like the rest of us."

"How much impact do you think the Affordable Care Act will have with the people you see here?" I asked Dr. Morgan.

"It has good intentions," he said. "But I'm really not sure if it will do enough."

One big reason, he said, was that North Carolina, like its neighboring southern states, largely opposed Obamacare and rejected the law's provision that would have extended Medicaid coverage to people slightly above the federal poverty level. Analysis from the Kaiser Family Foundation estimated that about 350,000 additional people in North Carolina—including, clearly, many of those who came to this clinic—would have been eligible for coverage if the state had allowed the expansion. Nationally, they estimated that nearly 5 million people in the more than twenty other states that declined the Medicaid expansion would be excluded. Dr. Morgan felt certain that many of his patients would find themselves in the same health care straits as they always had. "It's sad," he said.

While I agreed that having Medicaid was better than having no health insurance, I wasn't entirely convinced that it would fix the health problems of the people we'd seen. I thought about the Medicaid patients—both medical and psychiatric—that I'd treated over the years who were in much worse health than privately insured patients. I recalled the many times I'd heard doctors complain about Medicaid, bemoaning its lower payments and burdensome paperwork. Where would these new Medicaid patients go to seek medical care? But then I remembered the many uninsured patients I'd seen—black and white—who had lost their homes and life savings from an unexpected, and often unpreventable illness, and reminded myself that having health insurance was about more than what took place inside the doctor's office or hospital.

That afternoon, I drifted toward the front of the trailer where the remaining patients calmly waited their turn. Three elder community members who served on the clinic's board had arrived for a scheduled meeting with the student volunteers. They had all been involved with the operation of the clinic since its inception in the late 1980s. When I introduced myself to them as a former medical student who had volunteered there many years earlier, Kathy, affectionately known as the clinic's "matriarch," took off her glasses and smiled.

"I remember you," she said. "I have a picture of you picking cotton next to the clinic."

I laughed in embarrassment, thinking that she had confused me with someone else, but she pointed toward a thumbtack board covered with more than a hundred photographs. There, a twenty-year time capsule came into view. In the photos, I saw classmates and other medical school contemporaries whom I liked and many more whom I hadn't thought about since graduation. Sure enough, near the bottom, I saw the picture of me with two classmates, each of us wearing the short white coats of medical students, our fingertips reaching out to touch the cotton plants all around us. We looked like small children pulling up dandelions in an open field. A second photograph showed me in the clinic sitting next to a classmate while she examined a patient. Memories of the past rose from these images, and I couldn't help but feel nostalgic for those early days of my training.

Kathy and her friends went on to talk about the changes in the town over the years. They told me about how one of the area's main employers had closed down in the 1990s and taken many jobs with it. I learned about the history of segregation in the area and how the civil rights era of their youths had inspired them to persist in their fight for black people to lead better lives. They told me how various family circumstances had made them stay or brought them back to the area, rather than take their chances permanently migrating north as my mother's parents had done. These felt like the stories my dad had told me so often over the years of his family's rural life in southern Virginia. As I had so many years before, I felt an intimate connection between this clinic and my ancestry.

I had one more stop to make before driving home. "Where is the old clinic?" I asked.

"Right down the street," Kathy said. "Go down there and make a left past the church. It'll be the second one on your left."

I followed Kathy's directions, and in less than three minutes, I had arrived. On my own, I would not have recognized the site of the former clinic. The cotton was gone; the fields had been left to the weeds. Across the one-lane road, I saw the old white house where we'd once seen patients. It looked like the small country home it was and gave no clues that it had once doubled as a medical clinic. A family lived there now, but they were not home when I arrived, so my opportunity to peek inside was lost. The surrounding area was filled with the sights of rural poverty I'd grown accustomed to over the years: a single-wide trailer next door, beat-up cars parked in several front yards, a friendly woman and man—perhaps mother and son—with several missing teeth.

Throughout my medical career, black doctors had often asked me to "give back" in two specific ways. One was through community volunteer work, such as at church-based health fairs and urban charity clinics. The other involved reaching out to black college students, medical students, and young physicians in social settings. More often than not, I'd found excuses to avoid both. I'd tell myself that I was too busy being a doctor, one whose clinical work already involved treating the downtrodden on a regular basis. Or that I lived too far away from Duke to drive back to socialize on my own time. Or that my difficulties with public speaking and large social gatherings made others better suited to act as mentors to young and future doctors. Once my sons were born, I shut off even the very limited volunteer engagement that I once had.

But as I left the small town that day, crossing over the railroad tracks and getting back on the highway, I felt that I'd reached a point in my life where I needed to do more on both fronts. On the heels of the banquet celebration, I'd been reminded not only of the impact that the pioneering black doctors of my parent's generation had on later generations of black doctors and students, but also their influence on their surrounding communities of black citizens. Writing this book has been my effort to live up to the standard they set.

A few months later, I ventured to another rural county of North Carolina where I'd rotated during my ob/gyn clerkship as a second-year medical student. There, I'd helped treat many "baby mamas," young black girls with limited education and job prospects facing the reality of raising children as single moms. Back then, I was a sexually naive medical student; I'd since become a full-fledged doctor, married for ten years, with two kids of my own. I was eager to see whether maturity had altered my perspective on these women and their lives.

The Duke-staffed ob/gyn clinic still operated in the same space as it had years before, at the county health department. Two second-year medical students and a second-year ob/gyn resident had taken the identical forty-five-minute drive from Durham that I remembered, one where we had talked about everything from the finer points of examining a pregnant woman to what we would be doing with our lives if we hadn't taken the medical path. But as had been true with the free clinic I'd recently visited, here too I found upgrades from my medical school days. The most obvious was the person who greeted me as I entered the rear hallway.

"You can lose the white coat," Dr. Norris said as he shook my hand. "I like to keep things a little less formal around here." Dressed in a mock turtleneck and slacks, with a graying beard and thinning hair, he looked more like the psychiatrists that I worked alongside than an obstetrician.

Dr. Norris offered some personal background while providing a quick tour of the spartan facility. Born and raised in Virginia, he'd moved to North Carolina for residency training and never left. He was approaching nearly twenty years in practice. He worked at this clinic once each week and at a similar one in a neighboring rural county on another day of the week, a schedule he'd kept for nearly ten years. The rest of his time was devoted to private clinic practice. He'd been drawn to this position supervising Duke trainees because of his dual interests in teaching and providing medical care to people who otherwise couldn't afford it. "This is just as much real medicine as taking care of some rich executive's wife," he said. He sounded a lot like Dr. Morgan.

Dr. Norris's presence had a similar stabilizing effect on this clinic. During my rotation there more than fifteen years earlier, the ob/gyn resident was haphazardly supervised—if at all—meaning that patients were less likely to have consistent medical care. With the reliable presence of Dr. Norris, as with Dr. Morgan at the free clinic, the patients were afforded the luxury of a supervising doctor who knew them. "When you see a different doctor each time," Dr. Norris said, "you're more likely to get impersonal care, and that's often not so good for the patient."

The morning was especially busy—a snowstorm had closed the clinic for part of the previous week, and nearly two dozen women had been rescheduled. Many were pregnant and came for checkups; others came seeking to start, renew, or change contraceptives; a smaller group was scheduled for annual gynecological exams. Most were on Medicaid. Many others were uninsured. The demand for care was immense. The flow of patients was so steady that Dr. Norris and his team staggered fifteen-minute lunch breaks to accommodate the influx.

About mid-morning, one of the medical students came to the staff work area to discuss a case with the ob/gyn resident. An eighteen-year-old woman's impending motherhood was prompting her to abandon plans for college. The student seemed to have difficulty understanding how she had ended up in this situation. I could relate, as I'd felt similarly as a medical student about the pregnant women and young mothers I saw back then.

However, with experience, life had taught me a few lessons. While my wife and I had consciously sought to conceive our first child, our second was not planned. The adjustment to caring for an infant was challenging for me, with the constant sleep deprivation, diaper changes, and other struggles of new parenthood. So the news of a second baby arriving before our first child had turned a year old sent me into near-panic. But it shouldn't have been surprising at all: As a medical doctor, I had a good idea of how babies were made.

Of course, I had several advantages that this young woman and others in the clinic lacked: a steady job with a good income, a marriage partner on even better financial footing, and the invaluable benefits of an advanced education. All these factors made my family's unplanned pregnancy far less life-altering from a social or economic standpoint. But my behavior and the actions of this eighteen-year-old woman—having unprotected sex without thinking through the consequences—had been the same. I understood how this young black woman had wound up with an unintended pregnancy, even as I saw the terrible cost to the black community of having so many single women bearing and raising children without fathers.

Later that morning, a second student presented a case of an uninsured woman in her mid-twenties seeking contraception. She had experienced bad side effects from birth control pills, so her options were limited. Based on a variety of factors, the patient and the doctor decided that an intrauterine device (IUD) would be best. Then came the hard part: Dr. Norris wasn't sure whether she would be able to obtain one at a lower price that she could afford. The clinic received a limited supply that they could dispense at reduced cost. That supply had run out.

I asked whether the Affordable Care Act, with its ambitious goal to expand health insurance to nearly 30 million Americans, might have an impact on these sorts of scenarios. His answer was nearly identical to Dr. Morgan's: "I'm not sure," he said, clearly frustrated. "I think some of my patients will continue to fall through the cracks."

He too mentioned North Carolina's decision to reject Medicaid expansion as a barrier. He offered two real-life casualties, two middle-aged black women whose fibroids caused them to have "basketball-sized uteruses." Along with significant pain, they experienced heavy bleeding during their monthly cycles. With insurance, they would have been eligible for a curative hysterectomy; without it, their clinical situation had to deteriorate into an emergency before they could get such care. He described both women as hardworking and responsible. It sounded eerily similar to Tina's situation that I had encountered as a medical student. It was yet another example of how systematic failures could dictate a person's health and threaten their life in ways beyond their individual control. "It's really a damn shame," he said. "I think the system really needs to be turned upside down and inside out in order to be fixed."

When I started medical school and learned about the adverse health outcomes that afflicted black people, I had assumed these disparities were due chiefly to genetics. To be sure, there are diseases, such as sickle-cell anemia, lupus, and sarcoidosis, which appear to preferentially target black patients at a biological level. But what had become abundantly clear during my years in medical school and as a doctor, however, were the many ways that social and economic factors influence health, and, more than anything else, account for the sickness and suffering that I have seen.

The problems take three forms. First are the system-based disparities that limit black people's access to medical care. Black people are disproportionately uninsured and, if insured, far more likely to have public insurance than private coverage. Further, owing in large part to geographic and residential segregation patterns, blacks are less likely to have access to primary care physicians, and even when available, such care is more likely to involve trainees and other rotating physicians rather than a consistent long-term relationship with one doctor. I'd seen these factors play out in real life with Tina and others at the charity clinic; with dozens of patients who used Atlanta's Grady emergency room for routine care; and with Steve and many others in my psychiatric training who couldn't get the substance abuse treatment or outpatient psychotherapy that they really needed.

Second, the doctor-patient relationship itself serves as a catalyst for differing outcomes. Here, the attitudes and behaviors of both doctors and patients are important. On one hand, some doctors are prone to hold negative views about the ability of black patients to manage their health and therefore might recommend different, and possibly substandard, treatments to them. On the other spectrum, many black people are mistrustful of doctors and medical treatments to their own detriment. I'd seen how Gary's reasonable assertion of medical knowledge and treatment preferences had left him with what I felt was an improper psychiatric diagnosis; how Carla had wanted Leslie sterilized after her stillbirth, and how I'd been disregarded by Dr. Parker until he learned that I was a physician. Over the years, I'd also watched numerous black patients ignore the sound clinical recommendations of well-meaning doctors of all races.

Finally, the unhealthy lifestyle behaviors of many black people are also a real factor. Pearl and others at the charity clinic ate an insalubrious soul-food diet; Leslie's drug use had likely caused her son's stillbirth; Lucy had died before our eyes in the Grady hospital emergency room from a potent mix of hypertension, diabetes, and family dysfunction; Adrian had smoked his way to a second, crippling stroke; and Monica had likely contracted HIV from the clandestine sexual life of her ex-boyfriend.

These heartbreaking stories were each in their own way complex, and illustrate how lasting improvement will only come through an array of changes employed simultaneously. Some of this responsibility rests with government and other large institutions, but much of it must occur at the individual and community level. When it comes to expanding access to quality health care, both government (federal and state) and large private insurers clearly have a major role to play. And it is here that the Affordable Care Act, with its expansion of Medicaid and creation of state-based insurance exchanges, has generated the most attention. The law certainly has some good features: placing millions more under the health insurance umbrella, prohibiting exclusions based on preexisting medical conditions, eliminating co-pays for preventive care, and ending annual or lifetime payout caps. But whether these and other changes will prove to be fiscally viable over the long term, in the face of ever-rising health care costs, remains to be seen.

On the doctor-patient level, efforts to improve the care of black patients have come from two directions. One side has taken a race-focused approach, advocating for widespread collection of race/ethnicity data to monitor for disparities, expanded cultural competency training, and increased numbers of minority physicians. The other method is more race-neutral, focusing on universal quality improvement initiatives to elevate the standard of medical care for everyone; its proponents argue that black people will benefit considerably because they often have worse health and have historically received a lower quality of medical care. For largely ideological reasons, there is a tendency to make these strategies an either/or proposition, but I don't agree. By and large, both methods can be employed simultaneously, and wherever they might conflict, the two sides should be rigorously researched against each other. If the goal is to improve the health of black people, who remain at the bottom of most health indexes, it shouldn't matter whether the means to achieving this follows a liberal strategy, a conservative approach, or something in between.

On the individual level, Henry's lifestyle transformation, along with my own, are just two instances of black people seizing control and deciding to live healthier through better choices about diet, exercise, and self-destructive habits. My parents too, thanks to good relationships with doctors and a willingness to reassess their earlier behaviors, have made major strides; they eat predominately fresh foods, go out walking most days, and take their medications as prescribed. Over the last several years, I've been comforted to see more and more black people at the grocery store buying fresh fish and bags full of fruits and vegetables. I've been equally heartened to see greater numbers of blacks exercising at the gym and at local parks. While there are certainly no guarantees, these habits form the foundation for good health. Ongoing public and private efforts to encourage healthier lifestyles can potentially benefit everyone, but black people especially, given that we are more likely to have an insalubrious foundation.

Despite the tragic stories I've written about in this book, there are clear signs of progress. Nationwide, teen pregnancy, infant mortality, and violent crime among black people are all down from where they were when I entered medical school in 1996. Between 1996 and 2010, the life expectancy of black males increased by more than five years, far exceeding the gains made by any other group during that period. Recent estimates put the narrowing black-white life expectancy gap at less than four years, when it was twice that a half-century earlier. Black people still are not as healthy as whites, Asians, or Hispanics in America, but the foundation has been laid for continued improvement.

While public health and other research studies teach us many things about medicine, I feel nonetheless that the greatest lessons still come from the stories of doctor-patient encounters. Medicine, no matter the many changes it has undergone in recent decades, remains at its essence a face-to-face, human-to-human endeavor. When it comes to race, this human aspect of medicine has certainly caused injury to many black people over our history. But things have gotten better, even during my short time in medicine, and my experiences as a young doctor point toward ways for even further progress. As a black physician, my interactions with white patients pose the same potential cross-cultural challenges that white doctors face in caring for black patients. I've learned a lot about myself in these interactions, and found ways to break through boundaries imposed by racial tension and prejudice.

About six years ago, I met a young man named Keith while working at the same outpatient clinic where I treated Adrian and Henry. Keith was in his late twenties at the time, about five years younger than me, but he'd seen and done things that I couldn't really fathom. Keith had served two tours in Iraq, where he witnessed severely disabled Iraqi children strapped to bombs and sent on suicide missions. One of his closest friends died in a roadside attack. Another friend committed suicide days after his return home. Within six months of leaving the military, Keith found himself plagued by nightmares, severe anxiety, and suicidal thoughts. He was diagnosed with post-traumatic stress disorder (PTSD). By the time we met, he'd been under psychiatric care—seeing a psychiatrist every two months—for more than a year. He took Zoloft. He'd also attended several months of group therapy sessions.

As I skimmed through the note from his initial visit with a clinic therapist, it looked as if Keith's main passions were guns, motorcycles, pickup trucks, and race cars, which suggested that we had no common ground. I'd never held a gun, thought motorcyclists were crazy, hated noisy pickup trucks, and found NASCAR more boring than watching a group of men shaving their faces. In contrast, I liked tennis, drank fruit smoothies, and drove an SUV in which I often listened to classical tunes and rap music. It looked like a classic red state–blue state clash.

These differences were magnified when we met each other. He wore a camouflage jacket and hat with brown sweatpants and brown boots, as if his next stop was to take his pickup truck to some rural outpost to hunt deer. Based on previous patients of similar style and background whom I had encountered, as well as my innate biases, I made several negative assumptions about him. I predicted that he smoked cigarettes (and maybe marijuana), ate a poor diet, was narrow-minded, and probably prone to abusing alcohol and prescription drugs. In short, I looked at him in the same derogatory way that doctors so often unfairly approach black patients.

I suspect he had an equally negative impression of me. I had on a cream-colored dress shirt, camel sweater vest, beige pleated slacks, brown Oxford dress shoes, and a necktie that incorporated all of these earth tones. My watch, bracelet, tie bar, and wedding band all had a striped-gold pattern. I probably looked to him like a vain, wimpy guy who had never gotten his hands dirty. Whatever he thought, his face registered complete surprise when I introduced myself as his new doctor. I'd seen it many times: I wasn't what he was expecting. As so many patients and family members before him had reacted to me, Keith couldn't have looked more shocked if Shaquille O'Neal or Santa Claus had emerged from the doctor's office and greeted him.

I had replaced the psychiatrist who prescribed his Zoloft, so it made sense to start there:

"How have you been doing these last few months?" I asked.

"Good."

"I see that you are prescribed Zoloft 100 milligrams per day."

He nodded. "How often have you been taking it the last few months?" I asked.

It probably sounded like an accusation, but about half the patients I saw didn't take antidepressants as prescribed. Many preferred to take them only when they felt bad or anxious.

"Every day."

"Do you feel that it's helping you?"

"Yes."

"In what way?" I asked.

"I'm calmer."

I waited a good ten seconds to see if he would elaborate. But his poker-faced stare suggested that he was waiting for me to make the next move.

"Are you having any side effects or other problems with the medicine?"

"No."

I glanced at my watch. This terse exchange had only taken two minutes of real time. Patients were scheduled every half hour. My remaining questions about sleep patterns, other psychiatric symptoms, and alcohol and tobacco use weren't going to take more than a few minutes at this rate. Rather than simply proceed in this close-ended way and politely usher him out of my office with more than twenty minutes to spare, as many busy medication-oriented psychiatrists might do, I tried a different approach. When he mentioned that his girlfriend told him he sometimes still thrashed about in his sleep, I used that as an opening to ask more about her, inquiring into whether she worked or not, how they'd met, how long they'd been together, and what he liked and didn't like about her and her family. His one- and two-word answers became complex sentences. Before I knew it, our thirty-minute visit had nearly elapsed, forcing me to move quickly through the remaining symptom-based questions. As he left, I felt that we'd laid the foundation for a cordial doctor-patient relationship.

Two months later, he returned for his next appointment. He started off by telling me that he had gotten engaged. That led us to talking about his parents, who divorced when he was in the sixth grade. He discussed the ways he wanted his marriage to be different from theirs. Unlike many of my patients from separated families, Keith seemed to have a good relationship with both parents. He told me about a recent weekend where he watched a NASCAR race with his mom and played pool with his dad.

"Do you like nine-ball or eight-ball better?" I asked.

He looked at me, seemingly surprised that I knew anything about billiards. "I'll do eight-ball with my girlfriend . . . I mean, fiancée . . . but nine-ball with my friends or my dad, when there's money to be made or lost."

I smiled. As a psychiatrist, I could have followed up with some screening questions to assess whether he had a gambling problem. Instead, I began a conversation. "How long have you been playing?"

"Since I was in the sixth grade. My dad bought a table for my birthday that year."

My dad bought a pool table too when I was around that same age. During the summer, I'd watch the pros on ESPN and spend a few hours afterward imitating their shots. As I got busier with basketball in high school, my mom eventually claimed the space that the pool table took up in our cramped basement as her own, giving the table to my brother for his new place. Still, the joy I got from a game of eight-ball never faded. For many years, well into my twenties, whenever I would visit home, my dad and I would go to a neighborhood pool hall and play a half-dozen games. I'd win some and so would he, but we never even bothered to keep score.

"You ever run the rack in either game?" I asked. A few times, I'd come close to running the rack—playing through the entire succession of balls without missing, keeping my opponent from even getting a turn—but had never actually managed to pull it off.

He smiled. "It's been a while. I'm not good enough to get into any of that high-stakes stuff—I never win or lose more than twenty bucks at a time. But it's just fun."

I'd gotten my answer about gambling without having to ask. The five minutes we spent on pool had nothing to do with Zoloft or anything else ostensibly medical, yet it was important. It helped me see him as more of a person than a stereotype; maybe it did the same for him too.

By the fifth or sixth visit, nearly a year into seeing me, Keith decided he wanted to stop the Zoloft; he didn't like the idea of taking it his entire life. As a medication-based psychiatrist, I could have fallen back on the viewpoint that quitting antidepressant medication was a bad idea. For a subset of psychiatric patients, especially those with schizophrenia and severe forms of bipolar disorder, stopping their medication can be a terrible decision that leads to hospitalization and drug relapse. However, some patients treated for depression and anxiety woes can manage just fine without medicine. You don't know until you give it a try.

So that's what we did. Over the next several months, Keith felt that his mental health remained stable, and from what I could see in our visits, this seemed true. He'd been promoted in his computer information technology job, enjoyed spending time with his fiancée, and had joined a combat veteran's running club that had helped him shed fifteen pounds. Since he was doing well without medication, he could have stopped seeing me, but he continued to keep appointments. We used the time to talk about his engagement, his time in the Army, and anything else that was on his mind. He seemed to look forward to these visits as a way to stay on track—to process in his mind whatever anxiety had built up in the intervening time about the past or present. I looked forward to seeing him as well, as each time he'd tell me some interesting tidbit about hunting, motorcycles, or NASCAR.

Finally, after another year of visits with me, he felt that he could manage on his own. "Thanks. You know the guy I saw before you, he only wanted to talk about medicine and these checklists. I really appreciate your time. Maybe we'll get a chance to shoot some pool one day."

We shook hands. I certainly wasn't a better psychiatrist than the person I had replaced. Some of his patients—a handful of whom were black—never warmed to me as they had to him. With others, busy as I was managing a large caseload while saddled with various administrative responsibilities, I felt content to write prescriptions and talk only superficially about their lives, referring those who needed more to a psychologist or clinical social worker. But something—perhaps a challenge to myself to do better, to overcome some of my biases—made me reach out to Keith.

If Keith and I could find common ground despite the huge differences in our backgrounds and attitudes, then why should it be any harder for other doctors to form strong bonds with patients of another race? Many doctors have done so, of course, and I'll bet they've made the same discovery that I have: A big part of the solution is discarding your assumptions and connecting with each patient as a person. Race, while certainly a powerful influence, by itself doesn't guarantee a human connection any more than any other factor like geography, height, or handedness. It is up to us, as doctors, to find the commonalities and respect the differences between us and our patients. In that way, we can understand what they value, how best to communicate with them, and how to arrive at treatment plans that improve their health while respecting their wishes. This approach is often called cultural competence, but after years of medical practice, it seems to me more like common sense.

I've tried to apply the lessons I learned from my time treating Keith and I think I've succeeded. After nearly seven years in my outpatient clinic, I'd become so overwhelmed with other duties that I decided to step away from this busy practice. For a period of months, I had to say good-bye to my patients. Many were anxious about starting over with a new doctor. Others cried. They all wished me well. In the end, I found that my white, Asian, and Hispanic patients were just as sorry as my black patients to see me go, which, if I'd done my job as a doctor correctly, was exactly as it should be.

Notes

INTRODUCTION

4   *life expectancy nearly nine years less than whites:* See U.S. Census Bureau,
Variations in State Mortality from 1960 to 1990, Population Division Working Paper Series no. 49, May 2003. For example, in Alabama, the state where
King made his professional home, the life expectancy in the years 1959–
1961 for white women was 74.59; for nonwhite women, it was 64.72. The
gap was closer in white men versus nonwhite men (about 7 years).

4   *found virtually anywhere one might choose to look:* For example, see Centers
for Disease Control, CDC Health Disparities and Inequalities Report—
United States, 2013, *Morbidity and Mortality Weekly Report* 2013; 62
(suppl 3); http://www.cdc.gov/mmwr/pdf/other/su6203.pdf. During the
last twenty-five years, health disparities have become an established area of
medical research. See for example National Institutes of Health, Fact
Sheet—Health Disparities, October 2010, available at http://report.nih.gov
/NIHfactsheets/Pdfs/HealthDisparities(NIMHD).pdf.

4   *still significantly lags behind whites:* In 2010, the life expectancy gap between white and black populations was about 3.8 years. This does represent significant progress. See National Vital Statistics Report, *Deaths: Final
Data for 2010* 61, no. 4 (May 2013).

5   *attended a state university with little name recognition:* I attended the
University of Maryland Baltimore County (UMBC) on a Meyerhoff

Scholarship, which was established in the late 1980s under the leadership of Dr. Freeman Hrabowski to steer black students toward science, technology, engineering, and mathematics careers. As of January 2015, alumni from the program had earned 197 Ph.D.s, 39 M.D./Ph.D.s, and 107 M.D.s from such institutions as Harvard, Stanford, Duke, the University of Pennsylvania, MIT, Berkeley, Yale, and Johns Hopkins. http://meyerhoff. umbc.edu/about/results/. See also Freeman Hrabowski, Kenneth Maton, and Geoffrey Greif, *Beating the Odds: Raising Academically Successful African American Males* (New York: Oxford University Press, 1998). In retrospect, the Meyerhoff Program prepared me well to succeed at Duke, but being one of its first students to attend an elite medical school, I entered Duke uncertain about my chances for success.

7   *university's alumni magazine that generated national interest:* See Ron Howell, "Before Their Time," *Yale Alumni Magazine,* May–June 2011. In the article, Howell recounts the sudden death of his closest college friend, using it as the framework for an exposition on the premature deaths of successful black men from his era, as he soberly notes: "while we African Americans were 3 percent of the Class of 1970, we were more than 10 percent of the deaths."

1: People Like Us

11   *race was just part of the story:* Looking back, many of my difficulties adjusting to Duke in the beginning were as much about social class as they were about race. For an interesting article on this issue, read: Stephen Magnus and Stephen Mick, Medical Schools, Affirmative Action, and the Neglected Role of Social Class, *American Journal of Public Health* 2000; 90:1197–1201.

16   *very high proportion compared to their numbers in the U.S. population:* In 2010, Asians represented 20 percent of all entering U.S. medical students while totaling about 5.5 percent of the entire population. See Association of American Medical Colleges, Diversity in Medical Education: Facts and

Figures 2012, *Diversity Policy and Programs*, Fall 2012; www.aamc.org
/publications. See also U.S. Department of Commerce, Economics and
Statistics Bureau, Overview of Race and Hispanic Origin, 2010; http://www
.census.gov/prod/cen2010/briefs/c2010br-02.pd.

17   *Native Americans simply make up a very small percentage:* In 2010, Native
Americans made up less than one-half of a percent (0.3–0.4) of medical
school enrollees. Association of American Medical Colleges, Diversity in
Medical Education: Facts and Figures 2012, *Diversity Policy and Programs*,
Fall 2012; www.aamc.org/publications.

17   *a black cardiac surgeon:* Levi Watkins Jr. grew up in Montomery, Alabama,
during the height of the civil rights movement. His family attended Martin
Luther King's church. In 1966, he became the first black student to attend
Vanderbilt University's medical school. He moved to Johns Hopkins in
1970 for his surgical training where, several years later, he became the first
black surgical chief resident. He would remain at Johns Hopkins until
his retirement in 2013. For brief profiles of his pioneering life, see http://
www.pbs.org/wgbh/amex/partners/legacy/l_colleagues_watkins.html and
http://www.thehistorymakers.com/biography/dr-levi-watkins.

17   *brunch at the estate of Ben Carson:* Dr. Carson has more recently become
known to a wider audience as an outspoken conservative public commen-
tator, highly critical of President Obama's economic and social policies.
From the late 1980s through the early 2000s, however, his narrative of
overcoming childhood poverty was framed as an inspirational success
story, particularly to black students. He described "a self-imposed obligation
to act as a role model for Black youngsters." See Ben Carson, *Gifted Hands*
(Grand Rapids: Zondervan, 1990). During my medical training at Duke
and through my peer network at other elite schools, I observed what I've
called "The Ben Carson Effect," where a disproportionate number of black
students who enter medical school seek to become neurosurgeons like
Carson.

18   *"the best black":* See Stephen L. Carter, *Reflections of an Affirmative Action
Baby* (New York: Basic Books, 1991).

18   *In the mid-1990s, blacks accounted for about 7 percent of medical students:*

Association of American Medical Colleges, Diversity in Medical Education: Facts and Figures 2012.

18   *figure includes three predominately black schools:* Ibid.

18   *less than 2 percent of all U.S. physicians:* See Marybeth Gasman, *The More-house Mystique* (Baltimore: Johns Hopkins University Press, 2012).

18   *The vast majority of these doctors were educated at Howard and Meharry:* In 1970, national data showed that 83 percent of the nation's black doctors had graduated from Howard or Meharry; in 1968, the two schools graduated nearly 75 percent of black doctors. Ibid.

18   *Of the prestigious white schools:* Several writers have provided background on African American enrollment at other elite medical schools. Kate Ledger describes Johns Hopkins in "In a Sea of White Faces," *Hopkins Medical News*, Winter 1998. Fitzhugh Mullan writes about his 1968 alma mater, the University of Chicago, in *White Coat, Clenched Fist* (New York: Macmillan, 1976). John Langone details Harvard's history in The Racial Integration of Harvard Medical School, *Journal of Blacks in Higher Education*, June 30, 1995. In a personal conversation, Keith Brodie, president of Duke University from 1985 to 1993, informed me that there were no black students in his Columbia University College of Physicians and Surgeons Class of 1965.

19   *U.S. Supreme Court upheld a lower court ruling:* For a historical overview of the process by which hospitals were integrated, see Preston Reynolds, Hospitals and Civil Rights, 1945–1963; *The Case of Simkins v Moses H. Cone Memorial Hospital, Annals of Internal Medicine*, 1997; 126: 898–906.

19   *black students were not admitted to Duke until 1963:* For some historical context to Duke's history with race, see Stanley Fish, "Henry Louis Gate: Déjà Vu All Over Again," *New York Times,* July 24, 2009; Robert J. Bliwise, "A Spring of Sorrows," *Duke Magazine,* May–June 2006; Bill Sasser, "Color-Blind or Color-Conscious? Affirmative Action," *Duke Magazine,* March–April 1996; Richard Brodhead, "This Is Not the Time to Rest." Speech to NAACP's 32nd annual Freedom Fund Banquet, November 18, 2006; Emily Rotberg, "A Happy Anniversary: BSA Turns 40," *Towerview Magazine*, February 2007; and Victor Dzau, "Falling Short in America: Increasing

Diversity in the Health Profession." Speech to the Association of Black Cardiologists 30th Anniversary, November 6, 2004.

20 *the medical school decided to offer full-tuition scholarships:* Dan Blazer II, Dean of Medical Education at Duke from 1992 to 1999, was instrumental in establishing these minority scholarships and increasing black student enrollment during his tenure. During an email exchange, he recalled that increasing minority enrollment was one of his top goals as dean. He believed that "developing a critical mass of URMs [underrepresented minorities] could ease the problems socially for those students in our classes," and that the scholarships, because of Duke's racial history, geography, and its aspirations to establish itself as a national leader, were "the only reasonable approach we could take if we wanted the best and brightest black students."

22 *elite schools are widely known to give clear admission preferences to the children of alumni and faculty:* Daniel Golden, *The Price of Admissions* (New York: Crown, 2006). See also Richard Kahlenberg, ed., *Affirmative Action for the Rich* (New York: The Century Foundation, 2010).

23 *famous 1978 U.S. Supreme Court Bakke decision:* See Regents of the University of California v. Bakke, *438 U.S. 265, 1978.* Allan Bakke was a white male applicant in his early thirties at the time of his application to UC-Davis medical school. He had served in Vietnam as a Marine officer and worked as a NASA engineer. He brought suit against the school after being rejected twice, arguing that the school's special admission policy of setting aside a specified number of seats, or quota, for minority applicants was unconstitutional. The case eventually went to the U.S. Supreme Court. In a fractured opinion authored by Justice Lewis Powell, the court struck down the school's use of numerical quotas while continuing to allow schools to use race as a factor in making its admission decisions.

23 *Although they ultimately graduated at similar rates:* Robert Davidson and Ernest Lewis, Affirmative Action and Other Special Consideration at the University of California-Davis, School of Medicine, *Journal of the American Medical Association* 1997; 278:1153–1158. The authors concluded: "an admissions process that allows for ethnicity and other special characteristics to be used heavily in admission decisions yields powerful effects on the

diversity of the student population and shows no evidence of diluting the quality of the graduates."

23   *who oversaw the school's implementation of affirmative action:* Langone, Racial Integration of Harvard Medical School.

24   *mismatch between the student and the school they attend:* See Richard Sander and Stuart Taylor Jr., *Mismatch: How Affirmative Action Hurts Students It's Intended to Help, and Why Universities Won't Admit it* (New York: Basic Books, 2012).

24   *this is one of the costs of affirmative action:* See Shelby Steele, *The Content of Our Character* (New York: St. Martin's Press, 1990). See also John McWhorter, *Losing the Race* (New York: Free Press, 2000). Several black authors have acknowledged the shortcomings of race-based affirmation action while ultimately supporting its use in modified forms. See Randall Kennedy, *Sellout: The Politics of Racial Betrayal* (New York: Pantheon, 2008). See also Eugene Robinson, *Disintegration* (New York: Doubleday, 2010), and Sheryll Cashin, *Place, Not Race* (Boston: Beacon Press, 2014).

25   *Other doctors have traveled this same terrain:* See Keith Black, *Brain Surgeon* (New York: Wellness Central, 2009) and Ben Carson, *Gifted Hands.*

27   *praise felt like another aspect of Stephen Carter's "best black" syndrome:* Stephen L. Carter, *Reflections of an Affirmative Action Baby.*

28   *Affirmative action, despite its flaws:* In addition to concerns about inferiority stigma and academic mismatch, other critics argue that affirmative action is mainly helping middle- and upper-class blacks rather than the working-class and poor groups most in need. They have a point, one acknowledged by some left-leaning writers who suggest a class-based approach to affirmative action. See Richard Kahlenberg, *The Remedy* (New York: Basic Books, 1996) and Sheryll Cashin, *Place, Not Race.* I lean toward this approach. In practice, this means the belief that my working-class background made me a good fit for class-based affirmative action but would not apply to my children.

2: BABY MAMAS

29   *Duke condensed the traditional two-year classroom training into a single year:* For a detailed overview of Duke's curriculum, see Colleen Grochowoski, Edward Halperin, and Edward Buckley, A Curricular Model for the Training of Physician Scientists: The Evolution of the Duke University School of Medicine Curriculum, *Academic Medicine* 2007; 82:375–382.

31   *delusions about pregnancy were not uncommon:* For an interesting series of case reports on the subject from one psychiatric hospital, see Albert Michael, Anil Joseph, and Alphie Pallen, Delusions of Pregnancy, *British Journal of Psychiatry* 1994; 164:244–246.

32   *grown far too comfortable categorizing patients as organ systems or diseases:* There is much thoughtful discussion about the ways that the increased emphasis on medical technology and the business elements of medicine have usurped the traditional focus on the doctor-patient relationship. See Abraham Verghese, Culture Shock—Patient as Icon, Icon as Patient, *New England Journal of Medicine* 2008; 359:2748–2751; Brendan Reilly, *One Doctor* (New York: Atria Books, 2013); Victoria Sweet, *God's Hotel* (New York: Riverhead, 2012); and Barron Lerner, *The Good Doctor* (Boston: Beacon Press, 2014).

Another strain of medical writing highlights that some elements of dehumanization have been a part of medical training for a longer time. See Robin Cook, *The Year of the Intern* (New York: Harcourt, 1972); Melvin Konner, *Becoming a Doctor* (New York: Viking Adult, 1987); and Robert Marion, *Learning to Play God* (New York: Addison-Wesley, 1991). No list of books exploring this subject would be complete without mentioning Samuel Shem's *The House of God* (New York: Richard Marek Publishers, 1978), the highly cynical novel still widely read by those in medical training.

36   *inched closer to experiencing the personal side of death:* For an excellent book about physicians' formative exposures to death, see Pauline Chen, *Final Exam* (New York: Knopf, 2007). See also Sherwin Nuland, *How We Die* (New York: Knopf, 1994), Danielle Ofri, *Singular Intimacies* (Boston: Beacon Press, 2003), and Atul Gawande, *Being Mortal* (New York: Henry Holt and Company, 2014).

37   *We'd been taught that 24 weeks was the cut-off point for a viable pregnancy:* This has improved slightly since the 1990s. For a thorough discussion on the subject, see Jon Tyson et al., Intensive Care for Extreme Prematurity— Moving Beyond Gestational Age, *New England Journal of Medicine* 2008; 358 (16):1672–1681. They found that of children born at 23 weeks, 25 percent were alive at 18 months; for those born at 24 weeks, 56 percent were alive at 18 months. The authors also highlight other factors involved in premature infant survival, such as birth weight and gender (girls do better).

38   *Carla was voicing the fear and anger:* The late 1980s and early 1990s were filled with news stories forecasting a stark future for children born to crack-addicted mothers. In 1989, neoconservative *Washington Post* columnist Charles Krauthammer famously opined that "the inner-city crack epidemic is now giving birth to the newest horror: a bio-underclass, a generation of physically damaged cocaine babies whose biological inferiority is stamped at birth." (Charles Krauthammer, "Children of Cocaine," *Washington Post*, July 30, 1989). While Krauthammer's claims are now often scorned, liberal writers expressed similar concerns about the damage crack-addicted women could cause their children. See Dorothy Gilliam, "The Children of Crack," *Washington Post*, July 31, 1989, and Michele Norris, "Suffering the Sins of the Mothers," *Washington Post*, June 30, 1991.

38   *started paying drug-addicted women:* Cecilia Vega, "Sterilization Offer to Addicts Reopens Ethics Issue," *New York Times*, January 6, 2003.

38   *South Carolina enacted a policy:* George Annas, Testing Poor Pregnant Women for Cocaine—Physicians as Police Investigators, *New England Journal of Medicine* 2001; 344:1729–1732.

39   *Carla's view had once been official policy:* Kim Severson, "Thousands Sterilized, a State Weighs Restitution," *New York Times*, December 9, 2011. See also "Against Their Will, a five-part series. North Carolina's Sterilization Program," *Winston-Salem Journal*, December 2002.

40   *A national survey in the mid-1990s:* Robert Mathias, NIDA Survey Provides First National Data on Drug Use During Pregnancy. *NIDA Notes. Women and Drug Abuse* January/February 1995; 10 (1); http://archives .drugabuse.gov/NIDA_Notes/NNVol10N1/NIDASurvey.html

40   *turned out to be more fiction than fact:* Although cocaine can clearly be harmful to a developing fetus, increasing the risk of premature births, low-birth-weight babies, and stillbirth, the crack-baby epidemic itself never came to pass as once feared. When followed over time, children born to cocaine-abusing mothers are at increased risk for attention deficit problems, but not the severe intellectual disability and antisocial criminality once predicted. See Susan Okie, "The Epidemic That Wasn't," *New York Times,* January 27, 2009, and Theresa Vargas, "Once Written Off, 'Crack Babies' Have Grown into Success Stories," *Washington Post,* April 18, 2010. Research in this area is complicated by the fact that children born to crack-addicted mothers often grow up in harsh environments where they are exposed to poverty, violence, neglect, and abuse, all of which predispose children to behavioral problems. Many experts now believe that cocaine's effects in pregnant women are comparable to cigarettes and less severe than alcohol— two legal drugs used much more commonly among pregnant women. For example, see profile of Emory University researcher Dr. Claire Coles in Mary Loftus, "Just Blowing Smoke," *Emory Magazine,* Autumn 2013.

41   *Leslie had put the worst face of black America:* Pervasive negative stereotypes about black people are as old as our nation. As more black people have ascended into the middle class since the civil rights era, tensions have arisen between middle-class blacks and their poorer counterparts. See Lawrence Otis Graham, *Member of the Club* (New York: Harper Collins, 1995); Eugene Robinson, *Disintegration* (New York: Doubleday, 2010) and Sheryll Cashin, *The Failures of Integration* (New York: Public Affairs, 2004).

44   *as they were at many community clinics back then:* These community clinics historically had served poor black patients. Over the last 15 years, however, North Carolina has seen a rapid influx of Hispanic residents. In 1990, Hispanics made up 1.2 percent of the state's population; in 2000, it had risen to 4.7 percent; by 2010, it had climbed to 8.4 percent. Between 2000 and 2010, North Carolina had the sixth greatest Hispanic population growth in the nation; http://censusscope.org/2010Census/states.php?state=NC&name=North%20Carolina http://ui.uncc.edu/sites/default/files/pdf/NCCensus2010.pdf.

45 *As male medical students, we'd been told to have a female staff member:* For a thorough discussion about the complexity of male physicians examining female patients, see Atul Gawande, *Better* (New York: Henry Holt and Company, 2007).

45 *More than 70 percent of black children are born to unmarried women:* According to 2010 data from the Department of Health and Human Services, 72 percent of black children are born outside marriage, compared with 53 percent of Hispanics and 29 percent of whites. See National Vital Statistics Report, *Births: Final Data for 2010* 61, no.1 (August 2012); http://www.cdc.gov/nchs/data/nvsr/nvsr61/nvsr61_01.pdf.

46 *Many people use these numbers as a statement about the breakdown of black communities:* For what would be considered a traditional African American perspective, see Juan Williams, *Enough* (New York: Crown Publishers, 2006). See also Bill Cosby and Alvin Poussaint, *Come On, People* (Nashville: Thomas Nelson, 2007). For other conservative views on the subject, see Shelby Steele, A *Dream Deferred* (New York: Harper Collins, 1998), and John McWhorter, *Winning the Race* (New York: Gotham Books, 2005). For a more left-leaning analysis, see Eugene Robinson, *Disintegration.*

46 *the rates among black teens remained more than twice that seen among white teens:* National Vital Statistics Report, *Births: Final Data for 2010.*

47 *potentially dangerous sexually transmitted infections:* Untreated gonorrhea and chlamydia in pregnancy are associated with a variety of possible complications, including premature birth and low birth weight. STDs and Pregnancy—CDC Fact Sheet; http://www.cdc.gov/std/pregnancy/STDFact-Pregnancy.htm.

47 *Early births, 60 percent more common in black women:* National Vital Statistics Report, *Births: Final Data for 2010.*

48 *infant mortality rate in the United States among blacks remains twice as high as among whites:* National Vital Statistics Report, *Deaths: Final Data for 2010* 61, no. 4 (May 2013); http://www.cdc.gov/nchs/data/nvsr/nvsr61/nvsr61_04.pdf.

53 *What is known about genetic predispositions:* See Danielle Dick and Arpana Agrawal, The Genetics of Alcohol and Other Drug Dependence, *Alcohol Research and Health* 2008; 31 (2):111–118.

3: CHARITY CARE

58   *body mass index far above what my pocket guide listed as ideal:* Body mass index (BMI) is a number calculated based on a person's height and weight that is used in adults to identify those with weight problems. A BMI above 25 is regarded as overweight; a BMI over 30 is considered obese. Pearl's BMI was 36.

60   *handful have become famous:* Bellevue Hospital Center is the oldest public hospital in the country (founded in 1736) and is probably best known for its psychiatric facilities. Cook County Hospital was featured in the 1993 blockbuster movie *The Fugitive* and was the inspiration for the equally popular 1994–2009 medical drama *ER.* I describe Grady hospital's history in chapter 4.

60   *Public hospitals began to decline:* For a concise overview of the history of public hospitals, see Howard Waitzkin, Commentary—The History and Contradictions of the Health Care Safety Net, *Health Services Research* 2005; 40 (3):941–952.

60   *Combined with other fiscal factors:* In addition to Medicare and Medicaid passage, rising health care costs and local fiscal crises have been implicated in public hospital contractions and closures. Ibid.

61   *Between 1987 and 1998 . . . the number of insured rose from 32 million to 44 million:* See Michael Gusmano, Gerry Fairbrother, and Heidi Park, Exploring the Limits of the Safety Net: Community Health Centers and Care for the Uninsured, *Health Affairs* 2002; 21 (6):188–194.

61   *One national study:* Christopher Forrest and Ellen-Marie Whelan, Primary Care Safety-Net Delivery Sites in the United States: A Comparison of Community Health Centers, Hospital Outpatient Departments, and Physicians' Offices, *Journal of the American Medical Association,* 2000; 284 (16):2077–2083.

61   *Another study in rural Massachusetts:* Sarah Kemble, Charity Care Programs: Part of the Solution or Part of the Problem? *Public Health Reports* 2000; 115 (5):419–429.

61   *In recounting their respective outpatient experiences:* For physician narratives on the disparities observed between public and private clinics, see

David Ansell, *County: Life, Death and Politics at Chicago's Public Hospital* (Chicago: Academy Chicago Publishers, 2011), and Fitzhugh Mullan, *White Coat, Clenched Fist* (New York: Macmillan, 1976).

62   *echoed their sentiments:* Neil Calman, Out of the Shadow: A White Inner-City Doctor Wrestles with Racial Prejudice, *Health Affairs* 2000; 19:170–174.

62   *They were like characters:* See Henry Louis Gates Jr., *Colored People* (New York: Vintage Books, 1994). A similar troubling pattern is observed in Lisa Cooper's case study of a young black man with severe hypertension who states, "I don't eat right. I don't cook. I like McDonald's, Burger King, Wendy's, you name it." See Lisa Cooper, A 41-Year-Old African American Man with Poorly Controlled Hypertension, *Journal of the American Medical Association* 2009; 301 (12):1260–1272.

63   *she was slender in comparison:* Tina's body mass index (BMI) was 22, which fell within the recommended normal range (18.5–24.9). Pearl, in contrast, had a BMI of 36. All of the other women I saw that day also had BMI scores over 30, which would classify them as obese.

66   *Not only are fibroids two to three times more common in black women:* For a recent overview, see Heba Eltoukhi et al., The Health Disparities of Uterine Fibroid Tumors for African-American Women: A Public Health Issue, *American Journal of Obstetrics and Gynecology* 2014; 210 (3):194–199.

67   *covers more than 50 million people:* In 2000, Medicaid covered 46 million people during some portion of that year. These numbers steadily increased throughout the decade to a high point of 68 million in 2009. See https://www.ccwdata.org/web/guest/medicaid-charts.

72   *Hypertension is the prototypical disease:* For an overview of racial disparities with hypertension, see Robin Hertz et al., Racial Disparities in Hypertension Prevalence, Awareness, and Management, *Archives of Internal Medicine* 2005; 165 (18):2098–2104. See also David Martins et al., Hypertensive Chronic Kidney Disease in African Americans: Strategies for Improving Care, *Cleveland Clinic Journal of Medicine* 2012; 79 (10):726–734.

72   *The reasons offered as to why black Americans suffer so severely from hypertension:* For a brief summary of competing theories, see Flavio Fuchs, Why

Do Black Americans Have Higher Prevalence of Hypertension? An Enigma Still Unsolved, *Hypertension* 2011; 57:379–380.

72 *Armed with data from several research studies:* The most influential one at the time was the publication of Dietary Approaches to Stop Hypertension (DASH) in which Laura Svetkey, a Duke professor of medicine, was one of the lead investigators. See Lawrence J. Appel et al., A Clinical Trial of the Effects of Dietary Patterns on Blood Pressure, *New England Journal of Medicine* 1997; 336:1117–1124.

73 *Terms like glomerular filtration rate, thiazide diuretics, and calcium channel blockers:* Glomerular filtration rate is a test used to assess how well the kidneys are working. Thiazide diuretics are a type of diuretic (also known as water pills) that puts more sodium and water into the urine to reduce bodily fluid volume and blood pressure. Calcium channel blockers are another type of medication that lowers blood pressure.

73 *A 2005 New York Times article:* Janny Scott, "Life at the Top in America Isn't Just Better, It's Longer," *New York Times,* May 16, 2005.

74 *A 2002 Institute of Medicine report:* See Institute of Medicine, *Care Without Coverage: Too Little, Too Late* (Washington, D.C.: The National Academies Press, 2002).

74 *A major 2001 study:* David Baker et al., Lack of Health Insurance and Decline In Overall Health in Late Middle Age, *New England Journal of Medicine* 2001; 345:1106–1112.

74 *nearly twice as likely as white Americans to live without health insurance:* Marsha Lillie-Blanton and Catherine Hoffman, The Role of Health Insurance Coverage in Reducing Racial/Ethnic Disparities in Health Care, *Health Affairs* 2005; 24 (2):398–408.

74 *A 2007 study found:* J. Michael McWilliams et al., Health of Previously Uninsured Adults After Acquiring Medicare Coverage, *Journal of the American Medical Association* 2007; 298:2886–2894.

75 *Tina was one of approximately forty million uninsured Americans:* See U.S. Census Bureau, Health Insurance Coverage: 2000; http://www.census .gov/prod/2001pubs/p60-215.pdf. Since 2000, the number of uninsured Americans has consistently remained above 40 million. For data between

the years 2007 and 2012, see the Henry J. Kaiser Family Foundation, Key Facts About the Uninsured Population: http://kff.org/uninsured/fact-sheet /key-facts-about-the-uninsured-population.

75   *failed 1993 Clinton health plan:* For an overview from a former insider on the subject, see Paul Starr, "What Happened to Health Care Reform," *The American Prospect*, Winter 1995. See also Paul Starr, "The Hillarycare Mythology," *The American Prospect*, September 2007.

75   *I later learned that more than 70 percent of people:* See the Henry J. Kaiser Family Foundation, The Uninsured: A Primer, October 2013; http://kff.org /report-section/the-uninsured-a-primer-2013-tables-and-data-notes.

4: INNER-CITY BLUES

79   *not the classic findings of an acute heart attack requiring immediate cardiac catheterization or clot-busting drugs:* The medical term for heart attack is myocardial infarction, or MI. One of the first steps in evaluating a patient with a suspected MI is to obtain an electrocardiogram (EKG). A waveform pattern known as ST-elevation MI, or STEMI, requires urgent restoration of blood flow. See Elliot Antman et al., ACC/AHA Guidelines for the Management of Patients with ST-Elevation Myocardial Infarction—Executive Summary, *Circulation* 2004; 110:588–636.

80   *watching TV medical dramas: ER*, the critically and commercially successful TV series, was at its peak during the mid- to late 1990s. The show was popular among medical students, especially those at Harvard, where the show's creator (Michael Crichton) and lead writer (Neal Baer) had attended. See Ellen Lerner Rothman, *White Coat* (New York: William Morrow and Company, 1999). *Chicago Hope*, created by prolific TV writer/producer David E. Kelley, also had a successful run during this period.

80   *Duke did not have a training program in this field:* Duke established an emergency medicine residency training program in 2002, two years after my graduation.

81   *Extreme emotional distress, such as in response to an earthquake:* On January 17, 1994, a major earthquake struck the Los Angeles area. On the day

of the earthquake, researchers noted a sharp increase in the number of sudden cardiac deaths. See Jonathan Leor, W. Kenneth Poole, and Robert Kloner, Sudden Cardiac Death Triggered by an Earthquake, *New England Journal of Medicine* 1996; 334:413–419.

81   *less dramatic but nonetheless mentally stressful scenarios could trigger cardiac events too:* For the classic article on the subject, see Alan Rozanski et al., Mental Stress and the Induction of Silent Myocardial Ischemia in Patients with Coronary Artery Disease, *New England Journal of Medicine* 1988; 318:1005–1012. See also James Blumenthal et al., Mental Stress-Induced Ischemia in the Laboratory and Ambulatory Ischemia During Daily Life, Association and Hemodynamic features, *Circulation* 1995; 92:2102–2108.

82   *rarely worked the way they did on TV medical dramas of the era:* See Susan Diem, John Lantos, and James Tulsky, Cardiopulmonary Resuscitation on Television; Miracles and Misinformation, *New England Journal of Medicine* 1996; 334:1578–1582.

82   *As physician Danielle Ofri writes:* See Danielle Ofri, *What Doctors Feel* (Boston: Beacon Press, 2013).

83   *Black women are more likely to die from heart disease:* Adjusting for age, black women are about 1.4 times more likely to die from heart attacks than white women. Nearly 22 percent of deaths from heart disease in black women occurred before age 65; only about 8 percent of such deaths occurred in white women under 65. See Michele Casper et al., Women and Heart Disease; an Atlas of Racial and Ethnic Disparities in Mortality, Centers for Disease Control and Prevention, 2000; http://stacks.cdc.gov/view/cdc/12169/. See also American Heart Association, African Americans and Cardiovascular Diseases, Statistical Fact Sheet 2013 Update; http://www.heart.org/idc/groups/heart-public/@wcm/@sop/@smd/documents/downloadable/ucm_319568.pdf.

83   *hypertension and diabetes are far more common:* Hypertension is about 40 percent more common among blacks as compared to whites. In 2010, the prevalence of diabetes for adult blacks was nearly twice as much as for white adults. See High Blood Pressure Facts, Centers for Disease Control and Prevention, 2014; http://www.cdc.gov/bloodpressure/facts.htm. See also

Minority Health, Black or African American Populations. Centers for Disease Control and Prevention, 2014; http://www.cdc.gov/minorityhealth/populations/REMP/black.html.

83   *black women are almost twice as likely as white women to be obese:* During 2006–2008, nearly 40 percent of black women were classified as obese in contrast to about 22 percent of white women. See Liping Pan et al., Differences in Prevalence of Obesity Among Black, White, Hispanic Adults, United States 2006–2008, *Morbidity and Mortality Weekly Report* 2009; 58 (27):740–744; http://www.cdc.gov/mmwr/preview/mmwrhtml/mm58 27a2.htm#tab1.

87   *Grady was caught in the vortex of political and economic forces:* For articles on the various troubles Grady experienced in the early 2000s, see "Portrait of an ER at the Breaking Point," *Newsweek,* May 7, 2007; Shaila Dewan and Kevin Sack, "A Safety-Net Hospital Falls into Financial Crisis," *New York Times,* January 8, 2008; Chris Megerian, "Night Falls on Grady," *The Emory Wheel,* December 6, 2007; and "Three Part Series: The Past, Present, and Future of Grady Memorial Hospital," *Creative Loafing Atlanta,* February 28, 2013, March 7, 2013, and March 14, 2013.

88   *problems were evident:* For example, A 2006 study ranked Grady near the bottom nationally in the treatment of heart failure and pneumonia. Hospital inspectors around this time reported broken medical equipment, sanitation issues, and poor recordkeeping that threatened the accreditation the hospital needed to participate in Medicare and Medicaid. In the emergency department, wait times routinely approached eight hours, sometimes longer. See the citations in the previous note for further details.

88   *between 3,000 and 3,500 trauma victims:* See Helen Kelley, Grady Hospital. Life and Death 24/7, *M.D. News, Metro Atlanta Edition* 5, no. 8 (August 2004).

89   *I estimated that about 20 percent of the doctors were black:* For an article examining the racial diversity within Emory University's Department of Emergency Medicine, see Sheryl Heron and Leon Haley, Diversity in Emergency Medicine—A Model Program, *Academic Emergency Medicine* 2001; 8: 192–195. The authors state that when Emory's program was started in 1975, all of the faculty and residents were white. By 2000, however, more

than one-third of the faculty was black, and more than 20 percent of the residents were black.

90   *For black male teens, homicide is the leading cause of death:* See Arialdi Minino, Mortality Among Teenagers Aged 12–19 Years: United States, 1999–2006. National Center for Health Statistics Data Brief, No. 37, May 2010.

90   *more than 90 percent of the time, young black homicide victims are killed by another black person:* See Erika Harrell, Black Victims of Violent Crime, Bureau of Justice Statistics, August 2007; http://www.bjs.gov/content/pub/pdf/bvvc.pdf.

91   *blacks make up more than 40 percent of inmates:* See Heather West, Prison Inmates at Midyear 2009—Statistical Tables, U.S. Department of Justice, June 2010; http://www.bjs.gov/content/pub/pdf/pim09st.pdf.

91   *talks often about his narrow escape from a life of crime:* See Sampson Davis, *Living and Dying in Brick City* (New York: Spiegel & Grau, 2013).

91   *Many black men face this dilemma:* See Wes Moore, *The Other West Moore* (New York: Spiegel & Grau, 2010); Ben Carson, *Gifted Hands* (Grand Rapids: Zondervan, 1990); and Otis Brawley, *How We Do Harm* (New York: St. Martin's Press, 2011).

92   *we could let down our guard:* The conversation that I had with Dr. Mason and Dr. Stephens is one of dozens I was part of in college, medical school, and law school. It underscores the tension between middle- and upper-class blacks and our poorer counterparts. This theme has been explored in the writings of several African American writers. See for example, Lawrence Otis Graham, *Member of the Club* (New York: Harper Collins, 1995); Sheryll Cashin, *The Failures of Integration* (New York: Public Affairs, 2004); and Eugene Robinson, *Disintegration* (New York: Doubleday, 2010).

92   *Ultimately, the value of Grady was such that it was deemed too important to fail:* For an insider's perspective on the process of saving Grady, see, Katherine Neuhausen, Awaking Advocacy: How Students Helped Save a Safety-Net Hospital in Georgia, *Health Affairs* 2013; 32 (6): 1161–1164.

93   *one white, one black, reminiscent of many buddy cop shows and movies:* This is a staple formula; see *Lethal Weapon, 48 Hrs., Beverly Hills Cop, Miami Vice,* and *Men in Black,* for example.

96   *Emergency departments are obligated by law to evaluate those who show up at their doors:* In 1986, Congress passed the Emergency Medical Treatment and Labor Act (EMTALA) in response to the prior practice where private hospitals would transfer poor, medically unstable patients to public hospitals. For further history on the origins of EMTALA, see David Ansell, *County: Life, Death and Politics at Chicago's Public Hospital* (Chicago: Academy Chicago Publishers, 2011).

96   *speculated that it is a way for the hospital to conduct a "wallet biopsy":* Arthur Kellerman quoted in "Portrait of an ER at the Breaking Point," *Newsweek*, May 7, 2007.

101   *Atlanta had one of the highest crime and murder rates:* Based on 1993 crime statistics, Atlanta was ranked by one publication in 1995 as the most dangerous city in America. Baltimore and Washington, D.C., were also near the top; see http://www.morganquitno.com/1st_safest.htm.

5: CONFRONTING HATE

106   *chart notations and abbreviations that had once looked like inscriptions from ancient times:* For example, a typical opening to a patient write-up might read: Mr. Jones is a 51-year-old male with a PMH of CAD s/p CABG x 3, CHF, IDDM, and CVA who presents with a two-day history of SOB. The translation is that Mr. Jones has a past medical history of coronary artery disease for which he has previously undergone cardiac bypass surgery with three grafts. He also has congestive heart failure, insulin-dependent diabetes mellitus, and cerebrovascular disease (prior stroke) and comes to the hospital with a two-day history of shortness of breath. This is a standard introduction. They are often far more complicated.

109   *not uncommon for patients to question the skills of interns and residents and ask to see the supervisor:* From both a legal and financial standpoint, the supervising physician, often referred to as an attending, is in fact the patient's "real doctor." However, in an academic hospital setting, the patient typically spends more time with the intern and resident doctors-in-training. Affluent patients, especially those requiring highly specialized

medical or surgical treatment, are more likely to request/demand the supervisor's direct involvement. For an interesting discussion on this subject, see Atul Gawande, *Complications* (New York: Henry Holt and Company, 2003).

112 *But that didn't mean things were easy:* There have been several excellent accounts of the struggles of internship year. Among the best nonfiction books covering the subject include Danielle Ofri, *Singular Intimacies* (Boston: Beacon Press, 2003); Robert Marion, *Intern Blues* (New York: William Morrow and Company, 1989); Sandeep Jauhar, *Intern* (New York: Farrar, Straus, and Giroux, 2008); and Fran Vertosick, *When the Air Hits Your Brain* (New York: W.W. Norton, 1996). The perils of internship training have also spawned widely read fictional accounts; see Robin Cook, *The Year of the Intern* (New York: Harcourt, 1972), and Samuel Shem, *The House of God* (New York: Richard Marek Publishers, 1978).

114 *black players make up more than 75 percent of NBA rosters:* See Richard Lapchick, The 2013 Racial and Gender Report Card: National Basketball Association, Executive Summary. According to their analysis, blacks made up 76.3 percent of NBA players in the year 2013; http://www.tidesport.org/RGRC/2013/2013_NBA_RGRC.pdf.

115 *encountered a family that didn't want her to treat their grandchild:* Women in Duke Medicine, An Oral History Exhibit, Dr. Jean Spaulding interview, October 3, 2006. Interview conducted by Jessica Roseberry.

115 *Nor were these stereotypes restricted to the South:* See Otis Brawley, *How We Do Harm* (New York: St. Martin's Press, 2011) and Pius Kamau, A Case of Mutual Distrust, *Journal of the American Medical Association* 1999; 282:410.

116 *detailed interviews of twenty-five African American physicians practicing in the New England states:* See Marcella Nunez-Smith et al., The Impact of Race on the Professional Lives of Physicians of African Descent, *Annals of Internal Medicine* 2007; 146: 45–51. For commentary on this article, see Joseph Betancourt and Andrea Reid, Black Physicians' Experience with Race: Should We Be Surprised? *Annals of Internal Medicine* 2007; 146: 68–69.

117 *I hadn't given thought to what other minority doctors might face:* Several Asian American physicians have explored this subject. For example, see Pauline

Chen, "When the Patient Is Racist," *New York Times*, July 25, 2013. See also Sachin Jain, The Racist Patient, *Annals of Internal Medicine* 2013; 158:623. For a particularly thoughtful essay looking at this issue from several minority perspectives, see Malathi Srinivasan, Today's Learning Point, *New England Journal of Medicine* 2001; 344:1474.

121 *Neurosurgeons Ben Carson and Keith Black described similar breakthroughs in their early years as doctors:* See Ben Carson, *The Big Picture* (Grand Rapids, Mich.: Zondervan, 1999), and Keith Black, *Brain Surgeon* (New York: Wellness Central, 2009).

122 *Patients with sickle-cell anemia have a reputation in the medical community for what is called drug-seeking behavior:* For two compassionate but realistic overviews on the subject see Samir Ballas, Ethical Issues in the Management of Sickle Cell Pain, *American Journal of Hematology* 2001; 68:127–132; and Pamela Pentin, Drug Seeking or Pain Crisis? Responsible Prescribing of Opioids in the Emergency Department, *Virtual Mentor* 2013; 15 (5):410–415; http://journalofethics.ama-assn.org/2013/05/ecas2-1305.html.

124 *Tuskegee syphilis study:* For a comprehensive, historical overview, see James H. Jones, *Bad Blood: The Tuskegee Syphilis Experiment* (New York: The Free Press, 1981).

124 *popular works have explored how the Tuskegee study was not an isolated incident:* For a detailed look into the history of how race has adversely affected the medical care of black Americans, see Harriet Washington, *Medical Apartheid: The Dark History of Medical Experimentation on Black Americans from Colonial Times to the Present* (New York: Anchor Books, 2006). For another gripping story that explores the historical intersection of race, poverty, and science, see Rebecca Skloot, *The Immortal Life of Henrietta Lacks* (New York: Crown Publishers, 2010).

124 *hone their skills on a disproportionately poor, black patient population:* Many of the top medical schools in the nation are located in cities with black populations that far exceed the national average of 13 percent. For example, Durham has a black population of about 39 percent; Boston (Harvard), 24 percent; Baltimore (Johns Hopkins), 64 percent; Philadelphia (University of Pennsylvania), 43 percent; St. Louis (Washington University in St. Louis), 49 percent; http://quickfacts.census.gov/qfd/states/. These

inner-city residents are more likely to present to emergency room and other acute-care settings where medical students and residents often work.

126 *Now it was my turn:* For excellent writing on the ways that doctors navigate death with patients and their surviving family members, see Abraham Verghese, *My Own Country* (New York: Simon and Schuster, 1994); Pauline Chen, *Final Exam* (New York: Albert A. Knopf, 2007); Jerome Groopman, *The Measure of Our Days* (New York: Viking Penguin, 1997); and Victoria Sweet, *God's Hotel* (New York: Riverhood Books, 2012). Danielle Ofri also poignantly explores end-of-life moments in her books (*Singular Intimacies, Incidental Findings,* and *How Doctors Feel*). Atul Gawande's most recent book, *Being Mortal*, deftly examines this subject.

6: WHEN DOCTORS DISCRIMINATE

129 *new national guidelines:* In July 2003 (when I began medical internship), the Accreditation Council for Graduate Medical Education (ACGME, for short) released sweeping guidelines restricting how much time interns and residents could work in the hospital. Among the most notable: a maximum 80-hour-per-week schedule averaged over four weeks; a maximum 30-hour duty shift; at least one day off per week averaged over a four-week period; and 10 hours of rest between shifts; http://www.acgme.org/acgmeweb /Portals/0/PFAssets/PublicationsPapers/dh_dutyhoursummary2003-04 .pdf.

129 *sparked in part by stories of tired doctors hurting patients:* For an overview of the Libby Zion case, largely credited with stimulating duty-hour reforms, see Barron Lerner, "A Case That Shook Medicine," *Washington Post,* November 28, 2006.

130 *wrote an editorial:* H. Jack Geiger, Race and Health Care—An American Dilemma? *New England Journal of Medicine* 1996; 335:815–816.

131 *a widely reported article that suggested that women and blacks with chest pain were less likely to be referred for the best cardiac care:* Kevin Schulman et al., The Effect of Race and Sex on Physicians' Recommendations for Cardiac

Catheterization, *New England Journal of Medicine* 1999: 340:618–626. This study was covered in the nation's top newspapers and was a feature on ABC's *Nightline.*

131   *though they later took a step back from the full claims of the study:* Five months later, the *New England Journal of Medicine* published a paper that reviewed Schulman's article and found that the reported gender and race disparities in cardiac evaluation, while not invalid, were overstated. See Lisa Schwartz et al., Misunderstandings About the Effects of Race and Sex on Physician's Referrals for Cardiac Catheterization, *New England Journal of Medicine* 1999: 341:279–283.

131   *Institute of Medicine added fuel to the discussion:* See Institute of Medicine, *Unequal Treatment: Confronting Racial and Ethnic Disparities in Health Care* (Washington, D.C.: The National Academies Press, 2002).

131   *a plethora of studies:* For example, studies found that black people were less likely to receive kidney transplants and knee replacements while being more likely to undergo C-sections and lower limb amputations. Ibid.

131   *John Edgar Wideman, in his 1984 family memoir:* John Edgar Wideman, *Brothers and Keepers* (New York: Holt, Rinehart and Winston, 1984).

131   *Henry Louis Gates Jr. writes in his childhood memoir:* Henry Louis Gates Jr., *Colored People* (New York: Vintage Books, 1994).

132   *Wes Moore recounts how his dad was taken to the emergency room:* Wes Moore, *The Other Wes Moore* (New York: Spiegel & Grau, 2010).

132   *acute epiglottitis:* The epiglottis is a small cartilage tissue in the throat that helps prevent food and liquid from entering the trachea, or windpipe. When infected, the epiglottis can swell and cause suffocation, as apparently happened to Moore's father.

132   *Various medical scholars and authors have provided historical context:* For a detailed exploration into the history of how race has adversely affected the care of black patients, see Harriet Washington, *Medical Apartheid: The Dark History of Medical Experimentation on Black Americans from Colonial Times to the Present* (New York: Anchor Books, 2006). See also John Hoberman, *Black & Blue* (Berkley: University of California Press, 2012). For a thoughtful look at how race can complicate the doctor-patient relationship, written from the perspective of a practicing physician, see David R. Levy,

White Doctors and Black Patients: Influence of Race on the Doctor-Patient Relationship, *Pediatrics* 1985; 75:639–643.

132 *when he described a black woman who had nine consecutive pelvic exams:* See David Satcher, Does Race Interfere with the Doctor-Patient Relationship? *Journal of the American Medical Association* 1973; 223 (13):1498–1499.

132 *occurred at Los Angeles County + USC Medical Center:* See Sonia Nazario, "Treating Doctors for Prejudice: Medical Schools Are Trying to Sensitize Students to Bedside Bias," *Chicago Sun-Times,* June 2, 1994.

133 *conservative medical writer Sally Satel would argue:* Dr. Satel, a psychiatrist and resident scholar at the American Enterprise Institute, has written extensively about the intersection of race and medicine and what she sees as a misguided effort by some to focus on health disparities in purely racial terms. See for example, Sally Satel and Jonathan Klick, "Biased Doctors? Don't Rush to Pull Out the Race Card," *National Review*, February 23, 2006. Satel argues that racial bias has a limited effect on health disparities and is a distraction from larger issues of class differences, which she states "makes a much greater contribution than race." Jonathan Glick and Sally Satel, "The Health Disparities Myth: Diagnosing the Treatment Gap," American Enterprise Institute for Public Policy Research, Washington, D.C. (2006). Satel also explores this subject in one of her books; see Sally Satel, *P.C., MD: How Political Correctness is Corrupting Medicine* (New York: Basic Books, 2000).

135 *I wondered if anyone else there had given any thought to this issue and shared any of my concerns:* For a discussion about the use of race in clinical cases, see Hamayun Nawaz and Allan Brett, Mentioning Race at the Beginning of Clinical Case Presentations: A Survey of US Medical Schools, *Medical Education* 2009; 43:1146–1154. The authors conclude: "we believe that the routine inclusion of race at the beginning of case presentations perpetuates incorrect assumptions about biological significance, promotes potentially faulty clinical reasoning, and reinforces socio-economic and cultural stereotyping." For an interesting, provocative, alternative viewpoint, see Sally Satel, "I Am a Racially Profiling Doctor," *New York Times Magazine.* May 5, 2002.

137 *difference between a public hospital where the doctors were paid on salary:* For a revealing and frequently cited article on how physician financial self-interest can influence medical care, see Atul Gawande, "The Cost Conundrum," *The New Yorker*, June 1, 2009. Cardiologist Sandeep Jauhar uses provocative examples from his clinical practice to illustrate these competing interests. See Sandeep Jauhar, *Doctored* (New York: Farrar, Straus and Giroux, 2014).

138 *Duke was one of the pioneers of the DASH diet:* Duke was among five national sites involved in the original mid-1990s study that investigated the role of dietary interventions in high blood pressure. During this timeframe, it was common to find recruitment pamphlets around the hospital and in local medical offices.

139 *The white coats revealed our hierarchy:* For a story about white coat-length hierarchy at Duke, see Calmetta Coleman, "Just Playing Doctor? Shorter Coats Make Young Residents Feel Naked," *Wall Street Journal*, February 2, 2000. For a similar discussion at several Boston-area hospitals, see Liz Kowalczyk, "Doctor, Nurse, or Student? Consult the White Coat," *Boston Globe*, April 10, 2007.

141 *various studies had demonstrated average reductions of 5 to 10 points (or more) with diet and exercise:* For a well-regarded article on the subject that came out in 2003 (my internship year), see Lawrence Appel et al., Effects of Comprehensive Lifestyle Modification on Blood Pressure Control, *Journal of the American Medical Association* 2003; 289 (16):2083–2093.

142 *Data from a subset of the DASH study suggested that black patients responded even better:* See Lawrence Appel et al., A Clinical Trial of the Effects of Dietary Patterns on Blood Pressure, *New England Journal of Medicine* 1997; 336:1117–1124, and Frank Sacks, Laura Svetkey et al., Effects on Blood Pressure of Reduced Dietary Sodium and the Dietary Approaches to Stop Hypertension (DASH) Diet, *New England Journal of Medicine* 2001; 344:3–10.

142 *studies that suggested that black people were less likely than whites to adhere to lifestyle changes:* See for example Jessie Satia, Joseph Galanko, and Anna Maria Siega-Riz, Eating at Fast Food Restaurants Is Associated with Dietary Intake, Demographic, Psychosocial and Behavioral Factors Among African-

Americans in North Carolina, *Public Health Nutrition* 2004; 7 (8):1089–1096.

145   *Several studies have explored the ways that people with mental illness receive worse medical care:* Most of the research in this area examines schizophrenia, bipolar disorder, and to a lesser extent, major depression, as these illnesses are more closely associated with adverse physical health problems. See Alex J. Mitchell et al., Quality of Medical Care for People with and without Comborbid Mental Illness and Substance Misuse, *British Journal of Psychiatry* 2009; 194:491–499 and Graham Thornicroft, Discrimination in Health Care Against People with Mental Illness, *International Journal of Psychiatry* 2007; 19 (2):113–122. For a personal, patient perspective on the issue, see Juliann Garey, "When Doctors Discriminate," *New York Times*, August 10, 2013.

146   *I had no reason to think of these doctors as racist in any classic sense:* Substantial attention has been paid in recent years to the possibility that unconscious (implicit) bias among health care professionals contributes to health disparities. See Alexander Green et al., Implicit Bias Among Physicians and Its Prediction of Thrombolysis Decisions for Black and White Patients, *Journal of General Internal Medicine* 2007; 22:1231–1238; and Adil Haider et al., Association of Unconscious Race and Social Class Bias with Vignette-Based Clinical Assessments by Medical Students, *Journal of the American Medical Association* 2011; 306 (9):942–951. For a broader discussion of these and related topics, see Lisa Cooper, A 41-Year-Old African American Man with Poorly Controlled Hypertension, *Journal of the American Medical Association* 2009; 301:1260–1272.

147   *supported by the Kaiser Family Foundation's 2002 national survey of physicians, published not long before our encounter with Gary:* National Survey of Physicians, Part 1: Doctors on Disparities in Medical Care. Washington, D.C.: 2002; http://kaiserfamilyfoundation.files.wordpress.com/2002/03/national-survey-of-physicians-part-1.pdf.

150   *He evidently saw me through a mental filter:* Pauline Chen briefly explores the potential pitfalls of cross-cultural doctor-patient interactions: "when I meet individuals whose race or ethnicity differ from mine," she writes, she "unconsciously taps into past experiences" and admits "it's difficult to

acknowledge that what I have tapped into may not always be fair." Pauline Chen, "Confronting the Racial Barriers Between Doctors and Patients," *New York Times*, November 14, 2008.

150   *Several authors have written about the negative stereotypes that many doctors associate with black patients:* For example, a 2000 study of nearly 200 physicians revealed that doctors reported negative opinions about black patients' intelligence, health behaviors, and ability to comply with treatments. See Michelle van Ryan and Jane Burke, The Effect of Patient Race and Socioeconomic Status on Physicians' Perceptions of Patients, *Social Science and Medicine* 2000; 50:813–828.

7: THE COLOR OF HIV/AIDS

154   *hearing lies was a daily part of my job:* For two recent perspectives about patient lying, see Sumathia Reddy, "I Don't Smoke, Doc, and Other Patient Lies," *Wall Street Journal*, February 18, 2013, and Daphne Miller, "Why Do My Patients Keep Secrets From Me? I Only Want to Help Them," *Washington Post*, March 14, 2010.

154   *Between 1995 and 1998, AIDS mortality in the United States dropped more than 60 percent:* From 1981 to 1995, the estimated annual number of deaths among persons with AIDS increased from 451 to 50,628. By 1998, that number had dropped from 50,628 down to 18,851. See HIV Surveillance—United States—1981–2008, *Morbidity and Mortality Weekly Report* 2011; 60 (21):689–693.

154   *reductions in death rates approaching 75 percent:* See Robert S. Levine et al., Black-White Mortality from HIV in the United States Before and After Introduction of Highly Active Antiretroviral Therapy in 1996, *American Journal of Public Health* 2007; 97 (10):1884–1892.

155   *black people accounted for a quarter of HIV cases during the first decade of the epidemic:* See HIV and AIDS—United States 1981–2000. *Morbidity and Mortality Weekly Report* 2001; 50 (21):430–434.

155   *In 1996, for the first time in the epidemic, more black people in America died of AIDS than whites:* See Update: Trends in AIDS Incidence, Deaths, and

Prevalence—United States, 1996, *Morbidity and Mortality Weekly Report* 1997; 46 (8):165–173.

155 *the color of HIV/AIDS in the United States continued to darken:* For a visual depiction of the statistical racial differences in HIV/AIDS, see HIV Surveillance by Race/Ethnicity, 2008–2011 data, National Center for HIV/AIDS, Viral Hepatitis, STD and TB Prevention, Division of HIV/AIDS Prevention. Available at http://www.cdc.gov/hiv/pdf/statistics_surveillance _raceEthnicity.pdf.

156 *that I started to fully appreciate the emotional weight of the diagnosis:* For excellent physician narratives that explore the emotional impact (on both doctor and patient) of delivering a HIV diagnosis, see Abraham Verghese, *My Own Country* (New York: Simon and Schuster, 1994); Jerome Groopman, *The Measure of Our Days* (New York: Viking Penguin, 1997); and Daniel Ofri, *Singular Intimacies* (Boston: Beacon Press, 2003).

157 *an indictment of one's characters or morals:* The controversial Pat Buchanan offered perhaps the most famous incendiary quote on the subject from the early years of the epidemic when he wrote in 1983: "The poor homosexuals— they have declared war upon nature, and now nature is exacting an awful retribution." For this quote and other provocative statements, see "Pat Buchanan's Greatest Hits," *Washington Post*, February 4, 1987.

163 *something I'd read and heard so much about:* The term *down-low* became popular in the media during the late 1990s and early 2000s, widely covered in print and television. See for example, Benoit Denizet-Lewis, "Double Lives on the Down Low," *New York Times Magazine*, August 3, 2003.

163 *AIDS first became known to the medical community:* For a comprehensive and engaging overview of the early history of the AIDS epidemic, see Randy Shilts, *And the Band Played On* (New York: St. Martin's Press, 1987).

163 *the Centers for Disease Control published a case report:* This is the first reported description in the medical literature describing HIV/AIDS. See Pneumocystis Pneumonia—Los Angeles, *Morbidity and Mortality Weekly Report* 1981; 30:250–252.

163 *article about forty-one gay men in New York and California:* See Lawrence Altman, "Rare Cancer Seen in 41 Homosexuals," *New York Times*, July 3, 1981.

164 *the case of Ryan White:* For a brief summary of his life, see Dirk Johnson, "Ryan White Dies of AIDS at 18; His Struggle Helped Pierce Myths," *New York Times*, April 9, 1990.

168 *the same way so many did back in the earliest days of HIV/AIDS:* For graphic accounts of some of the flagrant discrimination directed toward patients with AIDS in the 1980s, see Randy Shilts, *And the Band Played On*, and Abraham Verghese, *My Own Country*.

170 *the incidence of these AIDS-defining cancers has decreased greatly:* See Meredith Shiels, Cancer Burden in the HIV-Infected Population in the United States, *Journal of the National Cancer Institute* 2011; 103:753–762.

170 *Lung cancer is also more common in patients with HIV/AIDS:* See for example, Jacques Cadranel et al., Lung Cancer in HIV Infected Patients: Facts, Questions and Challenges, *Thorax* 2006; 61 (11):1000–1008, and Deepthi Mani et al., Lung Cancer in HIV Infection, *Clinical Lung Cancer* 2012; 13(1):6–13.

171 *documented the first two cases of AIDS in women in 1983:* See Epidemiologic Notes and Reports. Immunodeficiency Among Female Sexual Partners of Males with Acquired Immune Deficiency Syndrome (AIDS)—New York, *Morbidity and Mortality Weekly Report* 1983; 31 (52):697–698.

171 *most recent estimates place that number at more than 60 percent:* For this and other data about black women and HIV infection, see HIV Surveillance by Race/Ethnicity, 2008–2011 data, National Center for HIV/AIDS, Viral Hepatitis, STD and TB Prevention, Division of HIV/AIDS Prevention. Available at http://www.cdc.gov/hiv/pdf/statistics_surveillance_race Ethnicity.pdf. See also Women and HIV/AIDS in the United States, Henry J. Kaiser Family Foundation, March 6, 2014; http://kff.org/hivaids/fact-sheet/women-and-hivaids-in-the-united-states.

172 *higher rates of other sexually transmitted diseases:* The presence of other sexually transmitted infections increases the probability of both transmitting and acquiring HIV during sexual contact. For a brief summary, see http://www.cdc.gov/std/hiv/STDFact-STD-HIV.htm. Gonorrhea, chlamydia, and syphilis are all far more commonly seen in blacks than in whites, see, for example, http://www.cdc.gov/nchhstp/healthdisparities/African Americans.html.

174 *has spoken at length about his experiences as a gay Harvard medical student in the 1980s:* See Mark A. Schuster, On Being Gay in Medicine, *Academic Pediatrics* 2012; 12:75–78.

174 *Chen recounted a similar version of medical antigay bias:* See Pauline Chen, "Does Medicine Discourage Gay Doctors?" *New York Times,* April 26, 2012.

175 *There is some data to support this contention:* See Shelby Grad, "70% of African Americans Backed Prop. 8, Exit Poll Finds," *Los Angeles Times,* November 5, 2008, and Changing Attitudes on Gay Marriage, The Pew Research Center's Religion and Public Life Project, June 2013. For an editorial on the subject, see Bill Maxwell, "Homophobia: It's a Black Thing," *Tampa Bay Times,* June 17, 2011.

176 *a handful of gay black celebrities have spoken on the issue:* See, for example, Bill Carter, "Gay CNN Anchor Sees Risk in Book," *New York Times,* May 15, 2011, and Cavan Sieczkowski, "Lee Daniels, Gay 'Butler' Director, Says 'Black Men Can't Come Out,'" *Huffington Post,* August 20, 2013.

176 *blacks are the group least able to afford such attitudes:* For data on the higher rates of HIV/AIDS among gay and bisexual black men, see http://www.cdc .gov/hiv/risk/racialethnic/bmsm/facts/. For a narrative discussion on the subject, see Donald G. McNeil Jr., "Poor Black and Hispanic Men Are the Face of HIV," *New York Times,* December 5, 2013.

8: Matching

181 *following a serious suicide attempt:* One classic way (still taught today) of assessing the nature of a suicide attempt is to characterize it by the risk of death involved and the likelihood that someone can intervene to prevent the suicide. For example, a person who waits until their spouse is gone for the weekend before taking 100 sleeping pills and using a butcher knife to cut their wrist would generally be regarded as having made a high-risk, low-rescue attempt. In contrast, a person who takes a half-dozen aspirin tablets and uses a plastic knife to scratch their wrist directly in front of their spouse would be considered to have made a low-risk, high-rescue attempt. See

Avery Weisman and J. William Worden, Risk-Rescue Rating in Suicide Assessment, *Archives of General Psychiatry* 1972; 26 (6):553–560.

182 *modernized in requiring a bar-coded ID badge rather than a clunky key to come and go:* Psychiatric units where people can be brought and kept against their wishes (i.e., involuntarily) are, by nature, locked to keep patients from walking out. Several workrooms and treatment rooms on each unit are also locked. In the older psychiatric hospitals where I have worked (both public and private), different units within the hospital required different keys, resulting in my having to carry five or six extra keys. Many times, I would get the keys confused and waste countless minutes.

183 *Haldol was given in a dose of 5 milligrams, while Ativan was given in 2-milligram doses:* Haldol (haloperidol) is an antipsychotic medication used to treat the active psychotic symptoms of schizophrenia. Ativan (lorazepam) is a sedative medication commonly used to treat anxiety. The combination, particularly when injected, typically causes a rapid tranquilizing effect. A study done from my years in training declared this combination "the treatment of choice for acute psychotic agitation." See John Battaglia et al., Haloperiodol, Lorazepam, or Both for Psychotic Agitation? *American Journal of Emergency Medicine* 1997; 15 (4):335–340. A more recent review indicated potential side effects with this treatment approach and the need for further research into this field of study. See Melanie Powney et al., Haloperidol for Psychosis-Induced Aggression or Agitation, *The Cochrane database of systematic reviews* 2012; http://www.ncbi.nlm.nih.gov/pubmed /23152276.

187 *He even allowed Suzanne to observe him for "cheeking":* I'm not aware of data on this subject, but "cheeking" is a known occurrence in psychiatric hospitals and prisons. See, for example, Paul von Zielbauer, "Inmates Discarding Medicine Pose Problem," *New York Times*, October 27, 2003.

193 *Just 3 percent of all psychiatrists in America at the time were black:* See Jeanne Miranda et al., Mental Health in the Context of Health Disparities, *American Journal of Psychiatry* 2008, 165 (9):1102–1108. This article reported that while black people comprised about 13 percent of the U.S. population, they made up 3 percent of psychiatrists, 2 percent of psychologists, and 4 percent of social workers.

193 *Durham had a population more than 40 percent black:* In 2000, Durham's population was 43.5 percent black. In 2010, it was 41 percent black. See http://censusviewer.com/city/NC/Durham.

198 *By the mid-1970s, the proportion of black medical students had nearly tripled:* In the 1968–1969 academic year, 266 black students enrolled in U.S. medical schools, comprising 2.7 percent of national totals. By 1974–1975, that number had increased to 1,106 black students, or 7.5 percent of the total number. See Association of American Medical Colleges, Diversity in Medical Education: Facts and Figures 2012, *Diversity Policy and Programs,* Fall 2012; www.aamc.org/publications.

198 *The first main challenge to this new order: Regents of the University of California v. Bakke,* 438 U.S. 265, 1978. See note to page 23 for further background on this case.

198 *federal appeals court ruling that struck down race-based affirmative action programs: Hopwood v. Texas,* 78 F. 3d 932 (5th Cir. 1996). For a left-leaning slant on this decision and the similar University of California Regents ban on racial preferences, see Peter Applebome, "Affirmative Action Ban Changes a Law School," *New York Times,* July 2, 1997. For a right-leaning view, see Terence J. Pell, "Texas Must Choose Between a Court Order and a Clinton Edict," *Wall Street Journal,* April 2, 1997.

198 *They found that black doctors served black patients at six times the rate as other physicians:* See, for example, Miriam Komaromy et al., The Role of Black and Hispanic Physicians in Providing Health Care for Underserved Populations, *New England Journal of Medicine* 1996; 334:1305–1310. The authors explicitly discuss the political concerns of the era, noting: "These issues are particularly timely because affirmative-action programs were recently abolished in the California state university system and affirmative-action policies have become a prominent political issue."

199 *a related group of studies found that black patients tended to have more positive interactions with black physicians:* These studies found that black patients were more likely to rate black physicians as excellent and to describe feeling that their preventive care and other health needs had been met. Another study reported that same-race appointments were longer in duration and rated by black patients as more satisfying. See Somnath Saha et al.,

Patient-Physician Racial Concordance and the Perceived Quality and Use of Health Care, *Archives of Internal Medicine* 1999; 159:997–1004; Lisa Cooper et al., Patient-Centered Communication, Ratings of Care, and Concordance of Patient and Physician Race, *Annals of Internal Medicine* 2003; 139:907–915; and Lisa Cooper-Patrick et al., Race, Gender, and Partnership in the Patient-Physician Relationship, *Journal of the American Medical Association* 1999; 282:583–589.

199 *a position advocated by leading mainstream medical organizations:* For position statements from the American College of Physicians, Institute of Medicine, and Association of American Medical Colleges on affirmative action and the care of minority patients, see Racial and Ethnic Disparities in Health Care: A Position Paper of the American College of Physicians, *Annals of Internal Medicine* 2004; 141:226–232; Unequal Treatment: Confronting Racial and Ethnic Disparities in Health Care, Institute of Medicine, 2002; and Jordan Cohen, The Consequences of Premature Abandonment of Affirmative Action in Medical School Admissions, *Journal of the American Medical Association* 2003: 289 (9):1143–1149.

199 *Some of the research in this area has shown no additional benefits to black patients:* For example, a 2008 paper investigated the care of depressed patients in primary care settings and concluded that black physicians were no more likely than white physicians to discuss depression symptoms with black patients; see Bri Ghods et al., Patient-Physician Communication in the Primary Care Visits of African-Americans and Whites with Depression, *Journal of General Internal Medicine,* 2008; 23:600–606. Another study observed that black patient-doctor encounters did not result in improved rates of lifestyle counseling for obese patients; see Sara Bleich, Impact of Patient-Doctor Race Concordance on Rates of Weight-Related Counseling in Visits by Black and White Obese Individuals, *Obesity* (Silver Spring) 2012; 20:562–570. These authors speculated that in some instances, other factors, such as physician gender, patient socioeconomic status, and patient cultural beliefs and patterns, might have greater influence on the patient-doctor dynamic than race alone.

199 *while critics have argued that several influential studies were either methodologically flawed or overstated their conclusions:* For a broader critique of the

rationale that black doctors confer greater benefits to black patients, see Jonathan Glick and Sally Satel, *The Health Disparities Myth: Diagnosing the Treatment Gap* (Washington, D.C.: American Enterprise Institute for Public Policy Research, 2006).

199 *There have even been some reports that hint at the possibility that black doctors, for a variety of reasons, might deliver a lower quality of care:* In 2004, Peter Bach of the Memorial Sloan-Kettering Cancer Center looked at primary care visits by black and white Medicare beneficiaries. In exploring the well-established principle that black patients generally receive lower-quality health care than white patients, they found that black patients and white patients in their study were to a large extent treated by different physicians. Nearly a quarter of the black patients in the study saw black physicians, some of whom were part of the larger physician group that was less likely to be board certified and more likely to report facing difficulties getting their patients high-quality specialty referrals, high-quality diagnostic imaging, and nonemergency hospital admission. To be clear, Bach and colleagues do not in any way state or imply that black physicians might be delivering a lower quality of care (for whatever reason), nor was their study designed to evaluate this specific issue. See Peter Bach et al., Primary Care Physicians Who Treat Blacks and Whites, *New England Journal of Medicine* 2004; 351:575–584.

For a more direct look at some of the problems faced by graduates of historically black medical schools, see Andrew Julian and Jack Dolan, "Historically Black Medical Schools Struggle to Compete for Dollars, Students," *Hartford Courant,* June 30, 2003. This article reported that graduates of Howard and Meharry face substantially higher disciplinary actions by state medical boards than most other schools. Among the potential causes proffered: institutional financial problems that compromise the quality of education; difficulty attracting quality black students due to more aggressive recruitment from more prestigious, predominately white schools; a patient population that is much sicker and more difficult to treat; and possible racism of state disciplinary boards toward black doctors. For an article emphasizing that minority doctors are more likely to care for sicker patients, see Ernest Moy and Barbara Bartman, Physician Race and Care of Minority and Medically Indigent Patients, *Journal of the American Medical Association* 1995; 273:1515–1520.

199 *International medical graduates (IMGs) constitute about 25 percent of American doctors:* This is based on 2006 data. For a brief overview of recent trends with IMG physicians, see http://www.ama-assn.org/ama/pub/about-ama/our-people/member-groups-sections/international-medical-graduates/imgs-in-united-states.page?.

199 *In a 2005 essay:* See Alok Khorana, Concordance, *Health Affairs* March/April 2005; 24 (2) 511–515.

9: DOING THE RIGHT THING

207 *a mixture of schizophrenia and bipolar disorder in his case:* Schizophrenia is characterized by a variety of impairing symptoms such as delusional beliefs, auditory hallucinations (hearing voices), and distorted thought, speech, and behavior patterns. Bipolar disorder (also known as manic-depression) is characterized by distinct episodes of depression and mania (or hypomania), the latter involving periods of euphoria, excessive energy, less need for sleep, excessive risk-taking, and impaired judgment, among other symptoms. Individuals with schizoaffective disorder can exhibit features from both disorders.

207 *made him tired all the time and made his muscles too stiff:* Fatigue is a common side effect of many, if not most, antipsychotic medications. The older antipsychotics (called typical or first-generation) can cause muscle stiffness through their blockage of dopamine receptors, sometimes causing symptoms similar to what is seen in Parkinson's disease.

207 *The only problem was that it caused him to gain weight:* The newer antipsychotic medications (called atypical or second-generation) are, with a few exceptions, highly associated with weight gain.

210 *estimated that behavioral choices account for at least 900,000 deaths each year:* See J. Michael McGinnis et al., The Case for More Active Policy Attention to Health Promotion, *Health Affairs* March/April 2002; 21(2):78–93.

210 *A large body of research has shown the important role of culture and environment:* For a review article on the subject, see Nancy Adler and Katherine

Newman, Socioeconomic Disparities in Health: Pathways and Policies, *Health Affairs* 2002; 21(2):60–76.

210 *such factors have a direct effect on health disparities:* For detailed discussions on the ways that socioeconomic class and race intersect with respect to health, see Stephen Isaacs and Steven Schroeder, Class—The Ignored Determinant of the Nation's Health, *New England Journal of Medicine* 2004; 351:1137–1142; Ichiro Kawachi et al., Health Disparities by Race and Class: Why Both Matter, *Health Affairs* 2005; 24:343–352; and David Williams and Pamela Braboy Jackson, Social Sources of Racial Disparities in Health, *Health Affairs* March/April 2005; 24:325–334.

212 *There are many barriers:* For discussions on the various factors that discourage physician-based nutrition and exercise counseling, see Robert Kushner, Barriers to Providing Nutrition Counseling by Physicians: A Survey of Primary Care Practitioners, *Preventive Medicine* 1995; 24:546–552; Gary Foster et al., Primary Care Physicians' Attitudes About Obesity and Its Treatment, *Obesity Research* 2003; 11:1168–1177; and Jian Huang et al., Physician's Weight Loss Counseling in Two Public Hospital Primary Care Clinics, *Academic Medicine* 2004; 79:156–161.

212 *sense that nutrition talk is better left to dieticians:* In a 2003 survey of more than 600 primary care physicians, a little less than half reported feeling confident in their ability to prescribe a weight loss program for their patients. See Gary Foster et al., Primary Care Physicians' Attitudes About Obesity and Its Treatment.

212 *experience has made many doctors cynical about patient behavior and the likelihood for change:* For brief, thoughtful articles that explore this subject, see Sandeep Jauhar, "No Matter What, We Pay for Others' Bad Habits," *New York Times*, March 29, 2010; Pauline Chen, "Getting Patients to Take Charge of Their Health," *New York Times,* January 12, 2012; and Danielle Ofri, "When the Patient Is 'Noncompliant,'" *New York Times,* November 15, 2012.

213 *basics of secondary prevention:* Primary prevention involves protecting healthy people from developing a disease or suffering an injury, for example, receiving a vaccine or wearing a seat belt. Secondary prevention takes place

after an illness has occurred, such as taking daily aspirin following a heart attack or stroke. In Adrian's case, he had already experienced a mini-stroke, so the neurologists' recommendations were part of a secondary prevention strategy.

216   *black people, who are 50 percent more likely than whites to be obese:* For data on higher obesity rates among black people, especially among women, see Liping Pan et al., Differences in Prevalence of Obesity Among Black, White, and Hispanic Adults, United States 2006–2008, *Morbidity and Mortality Weekly Report* 2009; 58 (27):740–744; http://www.cdc.gov/mmwr /preview/mmwrhtml/mm5827a2.htm#tab1.

217   *Given the impact that physician advice can have on patient behavior:* For example, a 2011 study concluded that physician counseling on obesity was associated with greater efforts by patients to lose weight; see Robert Post et al., The Influence of Physician Acknowledgment of Patient's Weight Status on Patient Perceptions of Overweight and Obesity in the United States, *Archives of Internal Medicine* 2011; 171:316–321. A 2000 study found that physician advice was associated with greater efforts by patients to quit smoking and make positive changes in diet and physical activity, see Matthew Kreuter et al., How Does Physician Advice Influence Patient Behavior? Evidence for a Priming Effect, *Archives of Family Medicine* 2000; 9:426–433. An older study looking at cigarette smoking reached similar conclusions, see Erica Frank et al., Predictors of Physicians' Smoking Cessation Advice, *Journal of the American Medical Association* 1991; 266:3139–3144.

219   *Why was making a long-term healthy change so difficult?:* For perhaps the best overview and discussion of the individual, health system, and doctor-patient barriers to effective blood pressure control for African Americans, see Lisa Cooper, A 41-Year-Old African American Man with Poorly Controlled Hypertension, *Journal of the American Medical Association* 2009; 301 (12):1260–1272.

219   *Researchers have speculated that strong cultural influences . . . might make it more difficult for black patients to follow a healthy diet:* For a recent review on the subject, see Dawn Epstein et al., Determinates and Consequences of

Adherence to the Dietary Approaches to Stop Hypertension Diet in African-American and White Adults with High Blood Pressure: Results from the ENCORE Trial, *Journal of the Academy of Nutrition and Dietetics* 2012; 112:1763–1773.

220 *A 2012 study:* Ibid. For a personal perspective on the subject from a black physician, see Khaalisha Ajala, "How Soul Food Stymies African-Americans' Low Salt Efforts," ABC News medical unit, available at: http://abcnews.go.com/Health/soul-food-stymies-african-americans-low-salt-efforts/story?id=17265086&singlePage=true.

220 *surveys have indicated that black people are more accepting of—and in some cases indicate a preference for—heavier body types:* See for example, Rashida Dorsey et al., Racial/Ethnic Differences in Weight Perception, *Obesity* 2009; 17:790–795.

221 *The Meharry-Hopkins Cohort study explored our health dilemma on a larger scale:* See John Thomas et al., Cardiovascular Disease in African-American and White Physicians: The Meharry Cohort and Meharry-Hopkins Cohort Studies, *Journal of Health Care for the Poor and Underserved* 1997; 8:270–283.

10: BEYOND RACE

224 *the first black student to attend medical school at Duke:* For profiles of Delano Meriwether, see "Medical Miracle: Meriwether Beats All Odds on Track & in Life," (New York) *Daily News*, January 14, 2007; Sandy Treadwell, "Hey, I Can Beat Those Guys," *Sports Illustrated*, January 18, 1971; and Robert Boyle, "Champion of the Armchair Athletes," *Sports Illustrated*, February 22, 1971. Meriwether was on the cover of this issue.

229 *Some critics expressed reasonable concerns:* Many critiques of the Affordable Care Act (ACA) come across as overtly partisan. For authors who seem to take a balanced approach in weighing the pros and cons of the ACA, see Darshak Sanghavi, "Don't Celebrate Yet," *Slate*, June 28, 2012; Steven Brill, "Bitter Pill: Why Medical Bills Are Killing Us," *Time*, February 20, 2013;

Tina Cheng and Paul Wise, Promise and Perils of the Affordable Care Act for Children, *Journal of the American Medical Association* 2014; 311:1733–1734; and Mehroz Baig, "A Physician's Take on the Affordable Care Act, Interview with Dr. Victoria Sweet," *Huffington Post,* April 15, 2014; http://www.huffingtonpost.com/mehroz-baig/a-physicians-take-on-the-_b_5155995.html.

230 *North Carolina, like its neighboring Southern states, largely opposed Obamacare and rejected the law's provision:* Along with extending private insurance coverage to individuals through a variety of mechanisms, the Affordable Care Act relies on a large expansion of Medicaid, a joint federal-state program for the poor. In the 2012 U.S. Supreme Court decision, *National Federation of Independent Business v. Sebelius,* the court allowed individual states to decline the expansion of Medicaid. In what largely mirrors (although not perfectly) the red state–blue state divide in recent elections, the blue states have mostly chosen to opt-in to the Medicaid expansion while the red states have mostly elected to opt-out of the expansion. North Carolina, under the leadership of Governor Pat McCrory (R) and a Republican legislature, has shifted to the "red state" ledger since President Obama narrowly won the state in the 2008 election.

230 *Analysis from the Kaiser Family Foundation:* For data on Medicaid expansion, see The Coverage Gap: Uninsured Poor Adults in States That Do Not Expand Medicaid—Issue Brief 8505-02, Kaiser Family Foundation, April 2, 2014; http://kff.org/health-reform/issue-brief/the-coverage-gap-uninsured-poor-adults-in-states-that-do-not-expand-medicaid.

230 *While I agreed that having Medicaid was better than having no health insurance:* The effectiveness of Medicaid in improving health has yielded some interesting results. See Benjamin Sommers et al., Mortality and Access to Care Among Adults After State Medicaid Expansions, *New England Journal of Medicine* 2012; 367:1025–1034. This study found that state Medicaid expansions in New York, Maine, and Arizona were "significantly associated with reduced mortality as well as improved coverage, access to care, and self-reported health." Another study found that Medicaid recipients in Oregon showed no significant improvement in measured physical outcomes (blood pressure, cholesterol, glycated hemoglobin levels), but exhibited

lower rates of depression and reduced financial strain after receiving Medicaid. Katherine Baicker et al., The Oregon Experiment—Effects of Medicaid on Clinical Outcomes, *New England Journal of Medicine* 2013; 368:1713–1722. Further study in this area is needed. One future approach might involve comparing various health and financial parameters from a state that accepted Affordable Care Act Medicaid expansion with a similar state that declined the expansion.

236 *The problems take three forms:* For a journalistic-style overview of the multiple factors that are involved with health disparities, see Chelsea Conaboy, "Racial and Ethnic Disparities in Health—and How to Fix Them," *National Journal,* March 13, 2014. Using Philadelphia as the focus for the article, Conaboy concluded: "the main obstacle to good health is poverty." See also Peter Kilborn, "Nashville Clinic Offers Case Study of Chronic Gap in Black and White Health," *New York Times,* March 21, 1998. In an interview with black doctors treating black patients at Meharry Medical College, the doctors there felt that health disparities were "a socioeconomic thing," and that in order to reverse them "you have to reverse a whole way of being." For a narrative and historical look at the subject, see Fitzhugh Mullan, Still Closing the Gap, *Health Affairs* 2009; 28:1183–1188.

238 *And it is here that the Affordable Care Act:* For a book-length examination written in support of the Affordable Care Act, see Ezekiel Emanuel, *Reinventing American Health Care* (New York: Public Affairs, 2014). For a similar perspective written in shorter form, see the writings of Harvard surgeon and medical writer Atul Gawande: "Now What?" *The New Yorker,* April 5, 2010; "Something Wicked This Way Comes," *The New Yorker,* June 28, 2012; and "States of Health," *The New Yorker,* October 7, 2013.

Other medical writers, while supportive of the core feature of expanding health insurance coverage, have voiced skepticism about certain aspects of the Affordable Care Act. See for example, Darshak Sanghavi, "Bringing Down the House," *Slate,* June 23, 2009, and Darshak Sanghavi, "Grand Illusion," *Slate,* January 20, 2010. In both articles, Sanghavi articulates his doubts that an individual insurance mandate will be effective in extending affordable health care coverage to the uninsured. See also Jerome Groopman, "Health Care: Who Knows 'Best'?" *New York Review of Books,* February 11, 2010, and

Jerome Groopman and Pamela Hartzband, "Sorting Fact from Fiction on Health Care," *Wall Street Journal,* August 31, 2009. Groopman raises concerns about whether the health care law's early emphasis on expert-based guidelines and "best practices" might interfere with doctor-patient health care decision making.

238   *One side has taken a race-focused approach:* For articles on cultural competency, see Joseph Betancourt, Cultural Competence—Marginal or Mainstream Movement, *New England Journal of Medicine* 2004; 351:953–955, and Sunil Kripalani et al., A Prescription for Cultural Competence in Medical Education, *Journal of General Internal Medicine* 2006; 21:1116–1120. For a related paper that focuses on physician workforce aspects, see Fitzhugh Mullan et al., The Social Mission of Medical Education: Ranking the Schools, *Annals of Internal Medicine* 2010; 152:804–811. This article ranks the quality of schools based on the percentages of graduates who practice primary care, work in underserved health areas, and who are under-represented minorities.

238   *The other method is more race-neutral:* For writings that take a more race-neutral approach to improving the health of black patients, see Jonathan Glick and Sally Satel, *The Health Disparities Myth: Diagnosing the Treatment Gap* (Washington, D.C.: American Enterprise Institute for Public Policy Research, 2006), and David Mechanic, Policy Changes in Addressing Racial Disparities and Improving Population Health, *Health Affairs* 2005; 24:335–338. Mechanic asserts: "it is important to think carefully about interventions and not assume that initiatives directed at reducing such disparities bring the largest gains in advancing the health of black citizens. Increasingly, much of the policy discussion is focused on whether disparities are increasing or decreasing and less so on which interventions can bring the largest health gains for all." Finally, see Darshak Sanghavi, "Color Bind: How to Fix Racial Disparities in Medical Care," *Slate,* August 14, 2009. Sanghavi offers evidence to assert that "universal quality-improvement plans coupled with publicly reported measures are the best way to cut health disparities," and that "these kinds of race- and class-blind interventions are arguably the *only* ones proven to reduce disparities on a meaningful scale."

238   *On the individual level:* For an interesting take on the patient's perspective, see Sherrie Kaplan and Sheldon Greenfield, The Patient's Role in Reducing Disparities, *Annals of Internal Medicine* 2004; 141:222–223. The authors argue against doctor-patient race matching and cultural competence training as panaceas to remedy disparities, asserting that "focusing solely on physicians and the clinical setting is meeting only half the challenge." They propose formal "patient training programs" that teach minority patients to "make the most of those brief office visits" with physicians.

239   *Ongoing public and private efforts to encourage healthier lifestyles:* The most well-known recent campaign in this realm has been Michelle Obama's Let's Move! initiative. It launched in 2010 with the ambitious goal of solving the problem of childhood obesity within a generation. The program organizes its work around five pillars: giving kids a healthy start in life; empowering parents and caregivers to make healthy choices for kids; improving school food; ensuring access to healthy food; and promoting physical activity. It is not surprising that this campaign has been criticized by the political right, which has raised concerns about excessive government interference. But it also has critics on the left, who argue that it doesn't go far enough to address the role of income inequality in obesity and other health-related disparities.

239   *there are clear signs of progress:* For data on reductions in teen pregnancy, see National Vital Statistics Report, *Births: Final Data for 2010* 61, no. 1 (August 2012). For data highlighting a lower infant mortality rate among blacks and an increased life expectancy, see National Vital Statistics Report. *Deaths: Final Data for 2010* 61, no. 4 (May 2013). For information on the reduction in violent crime among black people since the mid-1990s, see Erika Harrell, "Black Victims of Violent Crime," Bureau of Justice Statistics, August 2007.

Selected Bibliography

Books on Medical Practice and Training

Ansell, David. *County*. Chicago: Academy Chicago Publishers, 2011.

Austin, Paul. *Something for the Pain*. New York: W.W. Norton, 2008.

Black, Keith. *Brain Surgeon*. New York: Wellness Central, 2009.

Brawley, Otis. *How We Do Harm*. New York: St. Martin's Press, 2011.

Carson, Ben. *Gifted Hands*. Grand Rapids: Zondervan, 1990.

———. *The Big Picture*. Grand Rapids: Zondervan, 1999.

Chen, Pauline. *Final Exam*. New York: Knopf, 2007.

Cook, Robin. *The Year of the Intern*. New York: Harcourt, 1972.

Davis, Sampson. *Living and Dying in Brick City*. New York: Spiegel & Grau, 2013.

Emanuel, Ezekiel. *Reinventing American Health Care*. New York: Public Affairs, 2014.

Gawande, Atul. *Complications*. New York: Henry Holt and Company, 2002.

———. *Better*. New York: Henry Holt and Company, 2007.

———. *Being Mortal*. New York: Henry Holt and Company, 2014.

Groopman, Jerome. *The Measure of our Days*. New York: Viking Penguin, 1997.

Jauhar, Sandeep. *Intern*. New York: Farrar, Strauss, and Giroux, 2008.

———. *Doctored*. New York: Farrar, Strauss, and Giroux, 2014.

Klass, Perri. *A Not Entirely Benign Procedure*. New York: Putnam, 1987.

Konner, Melvin. *Becoming a Doctor*. New York: Viking Adult, 1987.

Lerner, Barron. *The Good Doctor*. Boston: Beacon Press, 2014.

Marion, Robert. *Intern Blues*. New York: William Morrow and Company, 1989.

———. *Learning to Play God*. New York: Addison-Wesley, 1991.

Mukherjee, Siddhartha. *The Emperor of All Maladies*. New York: Scribner, 2010.

Mullan, Fitzhugh. *White Coat, Clenched Fist*. New York, Macmillan, 1976.

Nuland, Sherwin. *How We Die*. New York: Knopf, 1994.

Ofri, Danielle. *Singular Intimacies*. Boston: Beacon Press, 2003.

———. *Incidental Findings*. Boston: Beacon Press, 2005.

———. *What Doctors Feel*. Boston: Beacon Press, 2013.

Reilly, Brendan. *One Doctor*. New York: Atria Books, 2013.

Rothman, Ellen. *White Coat*. New York: William Morrow and Company, 1999.

Shem, Samuel. *House of God*. New York: Richard Marek Publishers, 1978.

Shilts, Randy. *And the Band Played On*. New York: St. Martin's Press, 1987.

Sweet, Victoria. *God's Hotel*. New York: Riverhead, 2012.

Verghese, Abraham. *My Own Country*. New York: Simon & Schuster, 1994.

Vertosick, Frank. *When the Air Hits Your Brain*. New York: W. W. Norton, 1996.

White, Augustus. *Seeing Patients*. Cambridge: Harvard University Press, 2011.

BOOKS ON RACIAL AND CLASS THEMES

Carter, Stephen L. *Reflections of an Affirmative Action Baby*. New York: Basic Books, 1991.

Cashin, Sheryll. *The Failures of Integration*. New York: Public Affairs, 2004.

———. *Place, Not Race*. Boston: Beacon Press, 2014.

Cosby, Bill, and Alvin Poussaint. *Come On People*. Nashville, Thomas Nelson, 2007.

Cose, Ellis. *The Rage of a Privileged Class*. New York: Harper Collins, 1993.

Gasman, Marybeth. *The Morehouse Mystique*. Baltimore: Johns Hopkins University Press, 2012.

Gates, Henry Louis, Jr. *Colored People*. New York: Knopf, 1994.

Golden, Daniel. *The Price of Admissions*. New York: Crown, 2006.

Graham, Lawrence Otis. *Member of the Club*. New York: Harper Collins, 1995.

Hoberman, John. *Black and Blue*. Berkley: University of California Press, 2012.

Hrabowski, Freeman, et al. *Beating the Odds*. New York: Oxford University Press, 1998.

Jones, James H. *Bad Blood*. New York: Free Press, 1981.

Kahlenberg, Richard. *The Remedy*. New York: Basic Books, 1996.

———, ed. *Affirmative Action for the Rich*. New York: The Century Foundation, 2010.

Kennedy, Randall. *Sellout*. New York: Pantheon, 2008.

———. *The Persistence of the Color Line*. New York: Pantheon, 2011.

McWhorter, John. *Losing the Race*. New York: Free Press, 2000.

———. *Winning the Race*. New York: Gotham Books, 2005.

Moore, Wes. *The Other Wes Moore*. New York: Spiegel & Grau, 2010.

Robinson, Eugene. *Disintegration*. New York: Doubleday, 2010.

Sander, Richard, and Stuart Taylor Jr. *Mismatch*. New York: Basic Books, 2012.

Satel, Sally. *PC, MD: How Political Correctness is Corrupting Medicine*. New York: Basic Books, 2000.

———. *The Health Disparities Myth*. Washington, D.C.: American Enterprise Institute, 2006.

Skloot, Rebecca. *The Immortal Life of Henrietta Lacks*. New York: Crown, 2010.

Steele, Shelby. *The Content of our Character*. New York: St. Martin's Press, 1990.

———. *A Dream Deferred*. New York: Harper Collins, 1998.

Suskind, Ron. *A Hope in the Unseen*. New York: Broadway Books, 1998.

Washington, Harriet. *Medical Apartheid*. New York: Anchor Books, 2007.

West, Cornel. *Race Matters*. Boston: Beacon Press, 1993.

Wideman, John Edgar. *Brothers and Keepers*. New York: Holt, Rinehart and Winston, 1984.

Williams, Juan. *Enough*. New York: Crown, 2006.

Acknowledgments

It's hard for me to believe that I've actually written a book, and I'd feel like a cheat if I left taking all of the credit. The first round of thanks goes to all of the patients and patient family members who have allowed me into their lives. I am a better person for having gotten to know each of you, however briefly, and I can only hope that I've returned some small part of this goodwill back into your lives.

On the writing front, Rebecca Gradinger has been all one can ask for in a literary agent. When she offered to represent me, I knew that I was in good hands. The same is true for my editor, Anna deVries, whose diligent efforts shaped this book into something much grander than I initially envisioned.

Several people were immensely helpful at the early stages of the writing process, including Tom Linden, Doris Iarovici, Peder Zane, Peggy Payne, and Paul Austin. Jane Harrigan deserves special mention in this regard; without her, I seriously doubt I would have ever gotten an agent or book contract. Longtime friends Christine Wilder, Kevin Woodson, and Jattu Senesie all provided valuable insights and edits.

My supervisors and colleagues at Duke University Medical Center and the Durham VA Medical Center have been wonderful in supporting my professional life as a psychiatrist. There are too many of you to name individually, but you know who you are. Special mention must go out to H. Keith Brodie, Dan Blazer II, Jean Spaulding, and Brenda Armstrong—all Duke mainstays—for their advice, encouragement, and support throughout my work on this book.

I'd be remiss without thanking the authors whose books on medicine and race I've cited in the bibliography. Each of you, in your own way, has been an inspiration for my efforts.

Finally, I have to end by giving thanks to my family. I'm a loner by nature and don't make friends easily, so you all have really been my foundation. Mom and Dad, I'll never be able to express how grateful I feel to have been born into your home. To my brother, Bryan, the example you've set as student, husband, and father is one that all young black men should have. And to Kerrie, my wife, you and our two boys are what make every day worth living.

About the Author

DAMON TWEEDY is a graduate of Duke Medical School and Yale Law School. He is an assistant professor of psychiatry at Duke University Medical Center and a staff physician at the Durham VA Medical Center. He has published articles about race and medicine in the *Journal of the American Medical Association* and the *Annals of Internal Medicine*. His columns and op-eds have appeared in *The New York Times*, the *Chicago Tribune*, the *Raleigh News & Observer*, and the *Atlanta Journal-Constitution*. He lives outside Raleigh-Durham, North Carolina, with his family.